DEATH, BURIAL, AND THE AFTERLIFE

DUBLIN DEATH STUDIES

DEATH, BURIAL, AND THE AFTERLIFE

DUBLIN DEATH STUDIES

Edited by Philip Cottrell & Wolfgang Marx

Carysfort Press

A Carysfort Press Book in association with Peter Lang
Death, Burial, and the Afterlife: Dublin Death Studies
Edited by Philip Cottrell & Wolfgang Marx

First published in Ireland in 2014 as a paperback original by
Carysfort Press, 58 Woodfield, Scholarstown Road
Dublin 16, Ireland

ISBN 978-1-78997-044-9
©2014 Copyright remains with the authors

Typeset by Carysfort Press

Cover design by eprint limited

Caution: All rights reserved. No part of this book may be printed or reproduced or utilized in any form or by any electronic, mechanical, or other means, now known or hereafter invented including photocopying and recording, or in any information storage or retrieval system without permission in writing from the publishers.

Dedicated to the Memory of

Pádraic Conway

Contents

Acknowledgements   xi

Illustrations, Tables, Musical Examples   xii

Introduction   1

1 | Empty Tombs and Apparitions: A Reflection on the Theological Significance of the Exhumation of the Remains of John Henry Newman.   17
       Pádraic Conway

2 | John Donne, Undone, Redone: the John Donne Monument Reconsidered.   33
       Philip Cottrell

3 | Stalin's Death and Afterlife.   65
       Judith Devlin

4 | The Mutilation and Non-Burial of the Dead in Homer's *Iliad*.   89
       Bridget Martin

5 | Identity and the Act of Dying: Sketching a Philosophical Perspective.   107
       Dan Farrelly

6 | 'emotional rather than cerebral'? Charles Villiers Stanford's *Requiem*.   121
       Wolfgang Marx

7 | Arrigo Boito and Giovanni Verga: the Body, Illness and Death in *Mastro-don Gesualdo*.   149
       Deirdre O'Grady

8 | Death, Medicine, Literature: Foucault in 1963.   167
       Douglas Smith

Contributors   183

Acknowledgements

The editors would like to express their sincere thanks to all contributors – particularly for their patience during the editing process. Special thanks are due to Bridget Martin for her support of the editorial process, as well as to Áine Kelly Conway for her help in preparing Pádraig Conway's essay. We are also extremely grateful to the members of the UCD research strand 'Death, Burial, and the Afterlife' as well as other participants in our symposia, public lectures and conferences whose interest and discursive contributions helped to develop the idea of this book and to shape its arguments and chapter structure. The UCD Seed Funding initiative contributed vital funding without which this project could not have been realised. Last, but not least, we thank Dan Farrelly, Eamonn Jordan, Lilian Chambers and everybody at Carysfort Press for the great enthusiasm and vigour which they brought to the project. They made the preparation of this volume a truly enjoyable experience.

Dublin, January 2014
Philip Cottrell & Wolfgang Marx

Illustrations

Fig. 1.1) Cardinal John Henry Newman (photographed by Herbert Barraud, 1887). Hulton Archive / Getty Images.

Fig. 1.2) Reliquary of Cardinal John Henry Newman. Shrine of the Blessed John Henry Newman at the Oratory of St Philip Neri, Edgbaston, Birmingham.

Fig. 2.1) Nicholas Stone, *Monument to John Donne*, 1631 / 2, London, St Paul's Cathedral. Conway Library, The Courtauld Institute of Art, London.

Fig. 2.2) Nicholas Stone, *Monument to John Donne*, 1631 / 2 (detail), London, St Paul's Cathedral. Conway Library, The Courtauld Institute of Art, London.

Fig. 2.3) Martin Droeshout, *Portrait of John Donne in his Winding Sheet* (after a lost original of 1631), engraved frontispiece to John Donne, *Deaths Duell*, London, 1632.

Fig. 2.4) Comparative photomontage reconstruction of the pose adopted by Donne in his winding sheet using a live model.

Fig. 2.5) Anon, *Monument to Bishop John Wakeman* (d.1549), Tewkesbury Abbey (the arrangement is not original – the *transi* figure originally occupied the chamber below. The *gisant* effigy is lost).

Fig. 2.6) Anon, *The Tomb of Sir Richard Herbert*, 1600 (detail of *gisant* and *transi*), St Nicholas, Montgomery, Wales.

Fig. 2.7) Melchiorr Salaboss, *The Cornwall Triptych*, 1588 (detail of *transi*), St Mary's, Burford, Shropshire.

Fig. 2.8) Wenceslaus Holler, *Tomb of Dean John Colet*, engraving from William Dugdale, *The History of St Paul's Cathedral in London* (London, 1658).

Fig. 2.9) Anon, *Infant Funerary Brass of Elyn Bray*, 1516 (rubbing), St. Mary's, Stoke d'Abernon, Surrey.

Fig. 2. 10) *The Turin Shroud* (detail), Cathedral, Turin. The Bridgeman Art Library / Getty Images.

Fig. 3.1) Joseph Stalin lying in state in the hall of Trade Union House, Moscow, 12th March 1953. Hulton Archive / Getty Images.

Fig. 3.2) The Bodies of Lenin and Stalin in the Kremlin Mausoleum.

Fig. 7.1) Arrigo Boito, photographed in 1885. Universal Images Group / Getty Images.

Fig. 7.2) Giovanni Verga, photographed in 1900. Mondadori / Getty Images.

Tables

4.1) Post-mortem mutilation in Homer's *Iliad* incorporating threats, allusions and actual occurrences.

6.1) Text distribution in the requiem settings by Verdi, Stanford and Dvořák.

Music Examples

6.1) Stanford, *Requiem*, Introit, begin

6.2) Verdi, *Missa da Requiem*, Introit, begin

6.3) Stanford, *Requiem*, Introit, opening 'Requiem aeternam' (soprano)

6.4) Stanford, *Requiem*, Kyrie, begin (soprano)

6.5) Stanford, *Requiem*, Gradual, begin (soprano)

6.6) Stanford, *Requiem*, Offertory, 'Quam olim Abrahae' theme

6.7) Stanford, *Requiem*, Sanctus, begin (altos)

6.8) Stanford, *Requiem*, Agnus Dei et Lux aeterna, begin

Introduction

Philip Cottrell & Wolfgang Marx

> Nor dread nor hope attend
> A dying animal;
> A man awaits his end
> Dreading and hoping all;
> Many times he died,
> Many times rose again.
> A great man in his pride
> Confronting murderous men
> Casts derision upon
> Supersession of breath;
> He knows death to the bone –
> Man has created death.[1]

'Man has created death.' This last line of William Butler Yeats's poem 'Death' sets a long train of thought in motion. Animals, Yeats points out, are not aware of death, so they can neither dread nor hope for it. Man, in turn, knows death 'to the bone', and therefore spends a lot of time contemplating it. Driven by fear or hope, some of us may get obsessed with it, anticipating death many times, yet survive all those imagined demises until the real end comes. So while all living matter – plants as much as animals – has to die, only human beings have at some stage become aware of this fact and can (or rather, cannot avoid) engaging with this knowledge. In this respect, man has indeed 'created' death as something that for all intents and purposes only exists for us because we are aware of it.

However, a case can also been made for the opposite proposition. In *Being and Time*, Martin Heidegger developed his concept of being as something not hovering in a metaphysical otherworld, but rather something thrown into our world, engaged with its conditions and its resulting problems and fears – chief among them the fact that our human existence is limited. This is why Heidegger re-defined being as 'being-toward-death' ('Sein zum Tode'), elaborating at a fundamental level on the old wisdom that the fact that we don't know how long our life will be makes each moment of it much more valuable to us. Thus, being is closely tied to time, and for Heidegger our existence is shaped by a constant state of anticipation; an awareness of, and worrying about, the finality of our current state of being and whatever may follow it: 'Being-toward-death is the anticipation of a potentiality-of-being of *that* whose kind of being is anticipation itself.'[2] Death fundamentally determines our existence, and our different responses to this fact are what makes us individual. 'Death does not just 'belong' in an undifferentiated way to one's own Da-sein [be-ing], but it *lays claim* to it as something individual.'[3] Ignoring death is no way forward and, of course, unsuccessful in the long run; engaging with it by way of active anticipation is the far better option: 'anticipation does not evade the impossibility of bypassing death [...] but *frees* itself *for* it.'[4] In this way it can be claimed that death is what determines or creates our being as we experience it: death creates man. Ultimately there is, of course, no 'right' or 'wrong' position in this debate; both concepts highlight different approaches towards the finality of life and yield different insights into how the interaction of life and death has shaped human thinking and behaviour.

The study of the interaction of life and death in the humanities and the sciences has followed these and many other leads. In fact, with the exception of love, no topic other than death has probably been the subject of consideration in a larger multitude of disciplines and been approached in so many different conceptual and methodological ways:

> Not only do people die in many different ways but perspectives on dying are like-wise various, representing a wide range of cultural, theoretical, philosophical, religious, literary and practical perspectives. Obvious though it may be, it is worth emphasizing that no one academic discipline, be it medicine or psychology or sociology or nursing studies, has a monopoly of insights into dying, with other studies adding merely footnotes. Dying is, par excellence, a topic for multidisciplinary treatment.[5]

These comments derive from an essay by Geoffrey Scarre on philosophical responses to dying. It was published in 2009 as part of a multidisciplinary anthology, *The Study of Dying*, edited by the sociologist and former director of the Centre for Death and Society (CDAS) at the University of Bath, Allan Kellehear. The book also includes essays which consider the theme of death and dying from a historical, art-historical, literary and cinematic point of view. As such, the project reflects a recent and developing trend in the expansion of 'death studies' beyond the realms of medicine and the social sciences towards other disciplines, particularly the humanities. This is also where the present book comes in.

Dublin Death Studies is intended as the first of a series of volumes which will showcase the work of scholars involved in the Death, Burial, and the Afterlife research strand at the College of Arts and Celtic Studies, University College Dublin. Founded in November 2007, the aims of this enterprise were threefold: firstly, to promote an Irish response to the flourishing international interest in death as a research theme across a variety of disciplines (it was therefore partly inspired by other research groups / organizations such as CDAS, and the European Danse Macabre Association which have a more focused interest in death as theme in artistic and literary culture); secondly, to bolster and extend the climate of interdisciplinarity which is characteristic of the humanities at UCD; thirdly, to foster a stimulating and mutually beneficial climate of discussion and discourse among colleagues and students who share an interest in death as a theme for study and research. To this end, several research colloquia and an extensive series of public lectures were organized over the course of three semesters between 2009 and 2010. These culminated in a one-day conference entitled *'Our Birth is Nothing but our Death Begun': the Role of Death, Burial and the Afterlife in Shaping Human Identity* on 25/26 September 2010. Speakers included not only scholars based at UCD but other leading international experts in death studies, from a variety of universities and institutions.

Most of the essays incorporated into the present volume were conceived as a direct result of these projects. They share an interest in investigating death as an individual, social and metaphorical phenomenon that may be exemplified by themes involving burial rituals, identity, and commemoration. The disciplines represented are as diverse as art history, classics, history, music, languages and literatures, and the approaches taken reflect various aspects of contemporary death studies. These include the fear of death, the role of death in shaping human identity, the 'taming' of death through ritual or aesthetic sublimation, and the utilization of death – particularly dead bodies – to manipulate social and political ends. The volume's reach is ambitious, covering matters of particular relevance to British and Irish history, to current international discourses in art history, philosophy and literary studies.

In Ireland the subject of death was never subject to the same sort of taboo status that, as many have argued, it attained in mainland Britain. It may therefore come as no surprise that an Irish university should form the context for a project designed to foster death as a discursive theme in the humanities. Here one should acknowledge how the country's traditional Catholicism and relative rurality have played their part in preserving an emphasis on the rituals of death and mourning (to the extent that these same rituals can seem rather alien to those not of an Irish background). Central to Philippe Ariès's influential, though somewhat controversial, notion of the familiar 'tamed death' of the Middle Ages was the close, even 'promiscuous' social coexistence of the living and the dead.[6] Due in part to the sustained religiosity of Irish society, a comparatively intimate connection persists between communities of the living and communities of the dead. Funeral rites, mourning rituals, and post-mortem masses are among those commonplace activities which keep the dead close. They continue to fulfil an essential aspect of everyday life, bolstering extended family ties, and facilitating a strong and expansive sense of community.

It is sometimes surprising for anyone not brought up in Ireland, just how often the discussion around the family dinner table turns to ancestry, to deceased friends, family members, the dead in general, and to those ill or dying. In this way death is not talked about in the abstract, but continually individualized, anecdotalized and catalogued (it is joked that the death notices of *The Irish Times* represent the country's most widely read newspaper column). It is one thing to think of death as something that happens to other people, and quite another to have a fair idea of who many of them are, and attend their removal and funeral even if they were not actually personal acquaintances. And so, funerals are regularly announced on local radio, and in conversation one often hears not only of the deaths of relatives, friends and acquaintances, but also of the deaths of *their* relatives, friends and acquaintances, and the obligation that is felt to pay last respects. In contrast, a typically British response to a funeral announcement might well be that it would be best to stay away, out of a belief that this is an intimate moment of grief for the immediate family, and not one in which the wider community should participate. Furthermore, the persistence, and prevalence, of Irish funerary rituals, and (despite the weakening position of the Catholic Church's institutional authority) the way in which faith in God and an afterlife retains its traditional importance, also seems to render the Irish experience of dying more familiar and knowable.

However, in all of this, there is also the realization that there is a clear difference between talking about the dead and talking about *death*. Amid staff and students at UCD the presence of the Death, Burial, and the Afterlife research strand has still provoked comment, surprise and curiosity. To adopt such an active interest in the theme of death, and to organize classes, lectures, and whole teaching modules around death's appearance in literature, music and the visual arts, is still seen by many as slightly strange, and even excessively morbid. Why should this be so? Death is the ultimate commonality – the one thing that unites us as human beings and something that is absolutely fundamental to the creative impulse. As Zygmunt Bauman has argued, death, or an awareness of the finitude of human experience, drives and defines culture – the mission of culture may be understood in terms of a need to establish a sense of meaning and permanency as a way of distracting from the inevitability of death and annihilation.[7] In this sense, death, not as a door leading to some sort of higher existence, but as a fundamental discontinuation of experience, also becomes the ultimate 'elephant in the room' of culture; to draw attention to its presence, is also to be reminded of its unsettling governance; to dwell too much on death, therefore, is sometimes seen as socially reprehensible, counterproductive and even psychologically unhealthy.

Early on in the life of the research strand, the academics involved were humorously dubbed 'the Death Squad' by one waggish colleague. This is typically expressive of the wry amusement which arises from what might be regarded as a perversely gloomy enterprise. This mordantly entertaining, if rather off-colour nickname also plays on the recurrent, irrational suspicion that anything / anyone overtly concerned with death may also be regarded as its potential agent or client – tempting fate or, in fact, tempting death. But equally, academics involved in the humanities seem increasingly drawn to death as a theme for study. The same is true for their students, at both undergraduate and postgraduate level, and for reasons that extend well beyond the sensationalist or puerile. This stems not so much from a wider concern with exploring the larger meta-narrative of culture and death in the manner of sociologists such as Bauman, but from an awareness of the richness of death as a theme manifest in the creative by-products of culture: in art, music, literature and folklore.

What may still seem rather strange is that, despite the inclusion of essays dealing with the Irish-born composer Charles Villiers Stanford and UCD's founding figure, Cardinal John Henry Newman, none of the topics covered in this volume consider the theme of death in an overtly Irish context. Nor was it the case that papers of an Irish dimension were especially prevalent in the colloquia and lecture series previously mentioned. But the relationship between death and Irishness has long since found its own outlet within the field of Irish cultural studies, in a lively postcolonialist discourse centred around issues of Irish nationhood and identity (this is certainly the case with themes involving Irish folklore, the response to national traumas such as the Potato Famine, or the political heroes who fell in the quest for Irish independence, and the Civil War). In a recently published study entitled *Death and Dying in Ireland, Britain and Europe* only two out of fourteen historical essays focus entirely on a non-Irish context.[8] By comparison, UCD's Death, Burial, and the Afterlife research strand has not proved to be the draw to academics engaged in Irish research themes that might have been envisaged. On the other hand, it shows that research undertaken in an Irish university focuses on areas and matters of importance far beyond the shores of this island, and that representatives of 'non-Irish' disciplines, such as classicists or modern language experts, have just as much to contribute to this discourse as those who engage most with Irish history, culture, art and folklore. In any case, this is one aspect of the strand's remit which could be actively developed in the future. There are also many more colleagues out there from a wide variety of fields studying issues centred on Death, Burial, and the Afterlife. Therefore, it is hoped that this volume will be the start of a series that showcases research from a plethora of disciplines and fosters an interdisciplinary cross-fertilization of ideas and methodologies.

Before embarking on a more detailed discussion of the subjects that are represented here, it must be acknowledged that in the process of compilation, the editors became all too acutely aware of the futility of approaching the subject of death from a fundamentally dispassionate and objective standpoint. In *Representations of Death* of 1999, Mary Bradbury writes that 'there is no such thing as academic distance when we come to study death'.[9] She then tells of having recently been asked to read a colleague's manuscript, and how she came across a passage in which the writer movingly described the death of his own wife – also an old university friend of Bradbury's. This was how Bradbury came to learn of the death of her friend, and the shock was such that she found herself gasping for breath: 'Suddenly the false veil of academic objectivity was torn away and I came face to face with all the pain and confusion that can be aroused by this most challenging of subjects'.[10] In a similar fashion, the editors were also distressed by the death, following a prolonged battle against cancer, of one of the contributors, Dr Pádraic Conway, Vice-President for University Relations at UCD, and Director of the UCD International Centre for Newman Studies. His death on the 5th of October 2012 took place less than a month after the submission of the final draft of his essay.

As a means of commemorating a popular and much respected colleague, it is appropriate that Dr Conway's essay should begin this volume. But there are other reasons for giving it such prominence, including the fact that it deals with the controversial burial and exhumation of UCD's founding father, its first rector Cardinal John Henry Newman. Newman died and was buried in 1890 in Rednal, Worcestershire, but in 2008 his mortal remains were disinterred. This prefaced the public display and sanctification of his relics, reburial at the Oratory Church, Birmingham, and eventual beatification by the Catholic Church. As Conway's essay highlights, what was unearthed – or rather what wasn't – offered more potential for scandal than substance: although certain burial items were retrieved, Newman's body had mysteriously vanished. The idea that it should have completely disintegrated is partly contradicted by a scientific study of the preserving properties of the local soil. The whiff of sensation was fanned by journalists who questioned whether Newman's contemporaries had buried him at all, or at least in the designated spot, as a result of suspicions over his sexuality. Newman had left clear instructions that he was to be buried alongside his late, intimate friend, Fr Ambrose St John. The elements certainly make for a good story (the suggestion of homosexuality makes the closet / coffin analogy almost too irresistible), and in 2011, some Catholic groups reacted with annoyance to the broadcast on BBC Radio Four of *Gerontius* – an award-winning play authored by Stephen Wyatt which examined the controversial relationship between Newman and Fr Ambrose.

Conway's essay addresses the problems of a sensationalist, overly dramatic, and reductive response to the nature of Newman and Ambrose's relationship, but it is also closely concerned with the Christological resonances of the episode's imagery – particularly the idea of the empty tomb. Conway discusses the way in which Newman's burial and quasi-exhumation amounts to an instructive sermon of sorts; its theme being how life, death and existence are not explicable wholly in terms of the material substance of the body. In discussing these issues, Conway draws on the writings of Seamus Heaney, the Nobel-Prize-winning Irish poet and insightful observer of social and cultural matters. Heaney's passing (and the worldwide public reaction to it) during the final preparative stages of this volume can again serve to remind us of the interdependent relationship between man and death.

This sets up an analogous relationship with the second chapter of this volume: Philip Cottrell's study of the death and commemoration of another clergyman, the seventeenth-century poet and preacher John Donne. In this case, as Cottrell argues, Donne took a far more active role in proceedings: his death was to some degree carefully stage-managed, and amounted to a sequence of acts in a wider *tableau vivant* (*mordant*?). The first act involved an actual sermon in which the dying Donne stepped into the pulpit in order to present his emaciated self as a personified *memento mori*. This living, speaking *transi* figure then underwent a gradual process of transmogrification into the idealized, ageless, and apparently near indestructible marble effigy which still commemorates Donne in St Paul's Cathedral, London. As far as Donne is concerned, it can safely be said that he was a man creating death – or at least his own afterlife – among the living. Both Cottrell and Conway also tackle the theme of Pauline preconceptions of the transformed and resurrected body within the context of Christian eschatology.

John Donne clearly was concerned not only with his afterlife in another world, but equally with how he would be remembered by the living after his passing. His activities during the final months of his life combined literary and artistic means to create an afterlife on earth that he himself had shaped as far as possible. In contrast, as the third essay in this volume makes clear, the memory of Joseph Stalin was shaped not by himself – indeed, despite his advancing age he seems to have had no premonition of his impending death, and rumours about his possible assassination after an initial stroke still abound. As Judith Devlin points out, the institutions of the Soviet state – led by members of the inner circle of communist rulers – engaged in a grand display of funerary theatrics that makes for an interesting comparison with the institutional forces brought to bear on the exhumation and public display of Newman's relics. Devlin's perceptive analysis of the management and display of Stalin's body illustrates how this most secular and unsaintly of men was subject to the type of sanctifying rituals more traditionally associated with holy figures, particularly latter-day saints such as Newman. Although one hesitates in drawing a too glib analogy between the workings of the Catholic Church and

Stalinist Russia, it is also clear how institutions of mass appeal and authority, in this case represented by Church and State, are keen to manipulate the display, burial and effigizing of their leaders to serve their own ends. However, in the way each episode depended on bestowing a starring role to the semi-sanctified body of the deceased, they also demonstrate the extremely precarious basis upon which the carapace of such public, quasi mystical funerary rites and rituals rest. It is here that the duality between the 'natural' and the 'political/social' body of the deceased is writ large, and it is the inevitable fragility of the one that often needs to be veiled, controlled, and forestalled in order to sustain the power and integrity of the other – in this context, Devlin herself draws attention to the influential theories of Ernst H. Kantorowicz, as expressed in *The King's Two Bodies* of 1957.[11]

It is clear that, with regard to Stalin's frail, natural body, a process of veiling began long before the dictator's death. Devlin draws attention to the way the Soviet press increasingly abandoned photographs of the ageing leader in favour of idealized painted imagery that portrayed him as a superhuman figure. This had inherent disadvantages when it came to the actual role that Stalin's unprepossessing 'pockmarked' body was expected to play as it lay in state for the edification of the thousands who filed past his bier. However, a miraculous sanctification of the natural body was to be effected by its perceived imperviousness to further corruptibility – as with Lenin before him, this was to be secured through artificial means as a result of embalming, and it was originally decided that both leaders would lie in state together in their glass-fronted mausoleum in the Kremlin. But when it became politically inexpedient to preserve a sense of Stalin's equality with Lenin, the body was removed and interred. In many ways, here it is again man who creates death, although in this case it was not the dying man himself but his successors who made the crucial decisions governing the commemorative measures and the display of the body.

Devlin notes how the panoply of Stalin's funerary rites, including the embalming of the body, was ultimately dependent on what had been previously accorded to the Tsars of Russia. Their claim to divine right to rule accorded their governance a mystical authority comparable to sainthood, a condition of which was the miraculous preservation of the body. This also underscores the importance and presence of relics within traditional Christian belief. Even where the mortal remains of a figure destined for sainthood – such as Newman – are no longer extant, any associated items then achieve their own venerable status. And so, the few grave items that were recovered from Newman's plot became foci of devotion and were placed in a ceremonial glazed container for a public viewership. In Newman's case, particular emphasis was given to a bloodstained scrap of material which seemed to take on a quasi-Eucharistic resonance. In one sense, however, having virtually no body at all may actually prove just as effective as having one miraculously intact where some divine mystery over its disappearance might be entertained, and such was the case with Newman. In effect, the outcome of Newman's (non)exhumation may also be judged a happy miracle: despite the effort taken to dig him up and rebury him in accordance with a higher, institutional desire to induct him into the company of saints, the reluctance of the earth to yield up his body meant that his last wishes were ultimately respected; he lies alongside Fr Ambrose still.

Here one is also drawn back to Donne, to his famous poem *The Relic* and to the sanctified imagery of the poet's plea to be buried with a bracelet of his lover's hair as a means of effecting a reunion at the graveside:

> When my grave is broke up again
> Some second guest to entertain,
> [...]
> And he that digs it, spies
> A bracelet of bright hair about the bone,
> Will he not let us alone,
> And think that there a loving couple lies,
> Who thought that this device might be some way
> To make their souls, at the last busy day,
> Meet at this grave, and make a little stay?
> [...]
> Then, he that digs us up, will bring
> Us, to the Bishop and the King,
> To make us relics; then,
> Thou shalt be a Mary Magdalen, and I
> A something else thereby;[12]

However, as a literary point of reference, it is to Homer to whom Conway turns in mulling over the intensity of the friendship between Newman and Father Ambrose. Conway drew attention to a passage from the *Iliad* where the ghost of Patroclus requests that his mortal remains should be buried alongside Achilles. This is an episode also discussed by Bridget Martin in the fourth essay in this volume as part of an elaboration of how the attitudes towards burial and the memory of the dead can take many different shapes in the *Iliad*. In describing the warriors' fear of posthumous mutilation at the hands of an enemy or by wild animals; she differentiates the degrees of humiliation involved (decapitation or dismemberment, removal of the armour, denial of a burial so that the corpse is left to be torn apart by predators). Being denied a proper burial resulted in the loss of honour among surviving comrades in battle – in itself a considerable concern for the ancient Greek warrior. Maintaining an image of physical beauty after death was crucial for him, yet this was impossible if the onset of decomposition was an object of public display, or if animals were allowed to dismember the bodies of the fallen. However, as Martin argues, an even more important reason to fear non-burial (including a lack of proper burial rites) was the belief that it would diminish the dead's social status in the Underworld; the resultant state of 'social liminality' is one in which the individual is neither fully alive nor completely dead. It is again Patroclus who urges Achilles to grant him a burial as otherwise the former cannot take his proper place in Hades. This presupposes an interesting concept: all things being well, the social status of this world is somehow replicated in the next one. Non-burial is repeatedly used as a threat before enemies engage in battle while a proper burial is the privilege of the victor. Agamemnon's fate after death serves as an example of how the lack of proper burial rites prevents a high-ranking warrior (and even a king) from fully leaving the world of the living in order to take up their 'rightful' place in the next world – while Agamemnon was Achilles's superior in the world of the living, the latter enjoys a far higher position and the admiration of his peers when Odysseus encounters him in the Underworld during his travels after the fall of Troy. In many ways, here man creates death, in that the treatment of the slain enemy will have a huge impact on the afterlife, both with regard to the memories retained by the living and the position they occupy in the Underworld.

The last text in this volume to focus on the individual's encounter with death deals with the work of Josef Pieper – a German philosopher who operated in the borderland between philosophy and Christian faith. Dan Farrelly's engagement with Pieper's thinking covers the fears and expectations arising from an anticipation of death, and the strategies which develop as a means of coping with them. Influenced by Thomistic thinking, Pieper set out to refute the claims of some modern scientists which hold that, today, believing in a creator has become a redundant activity. According to Pieper, this makes annihilation of the individuum after death a certainty – something most human beings cannot countenance. Creating a link back to the opening chapter of this volume, Farrelly cites Newman's *Dream of Gerontius* as an example of the existential fear man feels in the face of death, and the need to effect a way of overcoming or at least containing it. Pieper claims that, throughout all our lives, we experience many examples of an operative 'higher consciousness', whether we call it God or something else. On this basis, he develops his own variation of Pascal's wager: we can either choose to believe in God, thus acknowledging our status as creatures and the assurance of an afterlife that comes with it, or we don't, thus accepting death as the end of our existence (all of this, Farrelly acknowledges, is of course entirely based on Western ways of thinking – Eastern religious thinkers might reach different conclusions). Therefore, opting for God is the better choice – a choice, Pieper states, which we not only face at the moment of dying, but every day, thereby influencing the way in which we live our lives. This places Pieper close to Heidegger's view that the anticipation of death shapes our outlook on life, and consequently the 'death creates man' side of the equation. However, while Heidegger never mentions an afterlife and is only concerned with our time before death, according to Pieper it forms the crucial motivation for our choice. Yet, in some ways, his argument – like Heidegger's – focuses on life, rather than afterlife: both philosophers primarily try to advise on how to live, although the motivation behind Pieper's recommendation as to the choice presented is rooted in the afterlife while Heidegger never considers the option of life after death.

With Wolfgang Marx's subsequent chapter on Charles Villiers Stanford's *Requiem* we enter a different area of death studies: that of artistic sublimation and symbolic representation. These are specific functions of works of literature, art, or music which do not primarily address individuals' fears of death by, for example, trying to prepare for the experience of dying or increasing the chances of an afterlife. Rather, they address the living, and console those who have lost someone (rather than as a means of preparing them for their own death). Meanwhile, in the case of symbolic representations, the demise of a individual can assume an almost educative function in that it stands in for something much bigger, such as the death of a style or an epoch. Nicholas Stone's sculptural effigy of John Donne is, of course, a work of art in its own right, but its genesis was rather unusual in that it was the immediate result of its subject's engagement with his own imminent demise. Stanford's *Requiem* – the first full setting of the Latin mass of the dead by an Irish composer – was written in memory of Frederic Leighton, the most famous English painter of his day and a friend of the composer, yet it does not try to intercede on behalf of the departed in order to shorten his time in purgatory (the primary original function of the liturgical requiem mass); nor does it offer immediate consolation to grieving family or friends (a secondary function which the mass fulfils to this day). Stanford's composition marks an important step in the aestheticization of a death ritual: the transference of the requiem as a musical genre from the church to the concert hall where it addresses a paying audience rather than those immediately affected by a bereavement. In this specific case, the resulting work had to negotiate its position in a cultural war between Germanic and Italianate styles (represented at that time particularly by Brahms's *A German Requiem* and Verdi's *Missa da Requiem*) which clearly affected its reception. Stanford – so goes Marx's thesis – modelled his composition mainly on Antonín Dvořák's Requiem composition which represents an aesthetic contemplation of the relationship between life and death. While Stanford did not fully engage with the Czech's ingenious concept, he created a powerful dramatization of the text which, in itself, represents a *tour de force* through the fears and hopes related to death and the afterlife.

Literature can represent the symbolic function of death much better than the semantically far less conclusive medium of music. Deirdre O'Grady's assessment of Giovanni Verga's *Mastro-Don Gesualdo* of 1889 places the novel in the aesthetic context of the Italian *Scapigliatura* movement which had Arrigo Boito as one of its main standard bearers. Both writers mark their field's transition from Romanticism to Realism. O'Grady uses three of Boito's poems which, in their descriptions of a mummy, an anatomy lesson, and a sculpted torso, exemplify a new, almost 'scientific' realism. More importantly, however, while all three poems centre on the depiction of the human body as either a corpse or a sculpture, O'Grady reveals how they all use these depictions as symbols of more general issues: the mummification of thought, the analytical dissection of an art work, and the negative consequences of the passing of time. Boito, O'Grady argues, thus engages in 'poetic discourses on death, non-burial and immortality of the human form as a metaphor for art and its manipulation by critics'. Verga, conversely, focuses in his novel on the depiction of socio-political change during the period of the early *Risorgimento* – the movement which championed Italian reunification between the Napoleonic wars and the 1860s. When the Sicilian author describes the death of individuals, they always stand for much more: the decline of the Trao family as members of the minor nobility (in comparison to the Mottas as representatives of the new, rising middle classes) etc. But it is not only the death of humans that is imbued with symbolic valence here; the depiction of their decaying, 'dying' palaces perhaps constitutes an even more immediate and evocative picture. Both the realism in which death is depicted by Verga, and his way of using individual lives (and architecture) as symbols of social change are by no means unique or confined to Italy; Thomas Mann's *Buddenbrooks* would represent another example stemming from a different culture and country.

The final essay of this collection contemplates methodological approaches to death studies at a meta-level – including some pursued in the previous chapters. As a result, this provides the volume with a fitting conclusion. Douglas Smith investigates the changing attitudes towards death as represented in two seminal books by Michel Foucault, namely *Birth of the Clinic* and *Death and the Labyrinth* (both published in 1963). On the one hand, Foucault describes and analyses changes in thinking about death and the dead body in the late eighteenth century, when rational investigation based on scientific methods became prevalent for the first time. This approach, however, ultimately turned death from a deeply personal experience into an impersonal process of organ failure; almost a non-event described in terms of (and confined to) clinical study rather than individual concern. But, in addition to this more descriptive analysis, several meta-levels can be distinguished. In many ways, Foucault's methodology resembles the object of his study in that, for example, he provides autopsy-like analyses of past attitudes towards autopsies. And, as Smith points out, the two books mark a decisive shift in Foucault's thinking; away from an approach based on semiology and literary critique towards pathology and autopsy practices. Furthermore, a metaphorical use of the death category is also evident when Foucault talks of the death of literature and literature-based methods of analysis. Finally, Smith outlines another metaphorical role of death in relation to language when he describes Foucault's emerging view of language (rather than mortality) as a constituent component of the human condition, yet one that is based on the death of intrinsic meaning in words. Here it appears as if Foucault would side with neither Yeats nor Heidegger (if language rather than death is a fundamental component in creating man), but this is true only in the most immediate sense – death returns to its central role in shaping the human condition through its manifold metaphorical uses at meta-levels.

Bibliography

Ariès, Philippe, *Western Attitudes Toward Death: From the Middle Ages to the Present*, translated by Patricia M. Ranum (Baltimore: The Johns Hopkins Press, 1975).

Bauman, Zygmunt, *Mortality, Immortality and Other Life Strategies* (Stanford: Stanford University Press, 1992).

Bradbury, Mary, 'Dying and Philosophy,' in *Representations of Death. A Social and Psychological Perspective*, edited by Allan Kellehear (London and New York: Routledge, 1991).

Donne, John, *The Complete English Poems* (London: Penguin, 2004).

Elias, Norbert, The Collected Works of Norbert Elias: Vol. 6 The Loneliness of the Dying in Our Time and Humano Conditio: Observations of the Development of Humanity on the Fortieth Anniversary of the End of a War (8 May 1985), translated by Edmund Jephcott (Dublin: University College Dublin Press, 2010).

Heidegger, Martin, *Being and Time. A Translation of* Sein und Zeit, translated by Joan Stambaugh (Albany: State University of New York Press, 1996).

Kantorowicz, Ernst H., *The King's Two Bodies: A Study in Medieval Theology* (Princeton: Princeton University Press, 1957).

Kelly, James, and Mary Ann Lyons, eds., *Death and Dying in Ireland, Britain and Europe. Historical Perspectives* (Kildare: Irish Academic Press, 2013).

Scarre, Geoffrey, 'Dying and Philosophy,' in *The Study of Dying. From Autonomy to Transformation*, edited by Allan Kellehear (Cambridge: Cambridge University Press, 2009), 147-162.

Yeats, William Butler, 'Death,' in *W.B. Yeats. The Poems*. Everyman, edited by Daniel Albright (London: Dent, 1994).

---

[1] William Butler Yeats, 'Death,' in *W.B. Yeats. The Poems*. Everyman, ed. Daniel Albright (London: Dent, 1994), 284. The poem (dated 13 September 1927) was written in reaction to the assassination of Kevin O'Higgins on 10 July 1927 and first published in 1933 as part of the collection *The Winding Stair and other Poems*.

[2] Heidegger Martin, *Being and Time. A Translation of* Sein und Zeit, transl. Joan Stambaugh (Albany: State University of New York Press, 1996), 242.

[3] *Ibid.*, 243.

[4] *Ibid.*

[5] Geoffrey Scarre, 'Dying and Philosophy,' in *The Study of Dying. From Autonomy to Transformation*, ed. Allan Kellehear (Cambridge: Cambridge University Press, 2009), 147-162: 154.

[6] See Philippe Ariès, *Western Attitudes Toward Death: From the Middle Ages to the Present*, trans. Patricia M. Ranum (Baltimore: The Johns Hopkins Press, 1975), particularly 13-14 and 24. For a sceptical response to Ariès's argument for a serene acceptance of death that was common in pre-modern society see Norbert Elias, *The Collected Works of Norbert Elias: Vol. 6 The Loneliness of the Dying in Our Time and Humano Conditio: Observations of the Development of Humanity on the Fortieth Anniversary of the End of a War (8 May 1985)*, trans. Edmund Jephcott (Dublin: University College Dublin Press, 2010), 11.

[7] Zygmunt Bauman, *Mortality, Immortality and Other Life Strategies* (Stanford: Stanford University Press, 1992) – see in particular the comments expressed on pages 3-4.

[8] James, Kelly, Mary Ann Lyons (eds), *Death and Dying in Ireland, Britain and Europe. Historical Perspectives* (Kildare: Irish Academic Press, 2013).

[9] Mary Bradbury, 'Dying and Philosophy,' in *Representations of Death. A Social and Psychological Perspective*, ed. Allan Kellehear (London and New York: Routledge, 1991), XIX.

[10] *Ibid.*, XX.

[11] Ernst H. Kantorowicz, *The King's Two Bodies: A Study in Medieval Theology* (Princeton: Princeton University Press, 1957).

[12] John Donne, *The Complete English Poems* (London: Penguin, 2004), 75-76.

1 | Empty Tombs and Apparitions: a Reflection on the Theological Significance of the Exhumation of the Remains of John Henry Newman[1]

Pádraic Conway

To begin a consideration of the theological significance of the exhumation of the remains of John Henry Newman (fig. 1.1), one could do worse than reflect on the following passage from *The Sunday Times* of October 5, 2008:

> The grave of the Venerable John Henry Cardinal Newman (1801 – 1890) was excavated with the utmost care on Thursday 2 October 2008, Feast of the Guardian Angels. During the excavation the brass inscription plate which had been on the wooden coffin in which Cardinal Newman had rested was recovered from his grave. It reads (in English translation): 'The Most Eminent and Most Reverend John Henry Newman Cardinal Deacon of St George in Velabro Died 11 August 1890 RIP'. Brass, wooden and cloth artefacts from Cardinal Newman's coffin were found. However there were no remains of the body of John Henry Newman.

The sense of shock at this non-discovery was conveyed in their own distinct way by the scions of Lord Rothermere in a headline of the 4th of November 2008: 'Did prudish Victorians refuse to bury Britain's next saint alongside his male friend – because they feared he was gay?'. The 'male friend' in question was Newman's Oratory confrere, Fr Ambrose St John, who had pre-deceased him in 1875 and Newman had indeed made a very specific request to be buried in the same grave as Ambrose. Alan Bray's book *The Friend*, which was published in 2003, describes in overtly theological terms the friendship of Newman and Ambrose St

John.[2] The book's explicit intent was to find some universal component within the experiences of intimacy and friendship without becoming bound up in a discourse that insists on immediately and irrevocably defining persons as homosexual / not homosexual. In this, Bray's work draws heavily on the exemplarist theology of the 12th century Cistercian Aelred of Rievaulx and his *De Spirituali Amicitia* (Of Spiritual Friendship).[3]

Bray begins his consideration of Newman's friendships in Chapter 7 of his book with a quote from the *Iliad* where the ghost of Patroclus appears to Achilles and says, 'Ah suffer that my bones may rest with thine.'[4] Bray goes on to describe the setting at Rednal, near Birmingham, where – at least until his (sort of) exhumation in October 2008 and his (sort of) re-interment in the Oratory Church, Birmingham in November 2009 – Newman was buried in the same grave as Ambrose St John. Bray describes how, in a note of 23 July, 1876, just a year after Ambrose's death, Newman instructed that he be buried alongside his friend: 'I wish, with all my heart, to be buried in Fr Ambrose St John's grave – and I give this as my last, my imperative will.'[5] Such was his determination that his will be carried out that he returned twice to his 1876 note to strengthen it, adding in February 1881 the words: 'This I confirm and insist on' and, at a later indeterminate date, the phrase 'and command', the last word being underlined.[6] He further instructed that if a memorial tablet was to be put up in the Oratory at Birmingham, it should read: 'Joannes Henricus Newman, Ex Umbris et Imaginibus, In Veritatem [John Henry Newman, from shadows and images into truth]'.[7]

After pointing out that Newman and Ambrose are not the only ones to share a grave at Rednal, Bray goes on to suggest that the initial bond between them was forged with a particular intensity because of the historical circumstances in which they met. Their first encounter was at the consecration of Ampfield Church, in John Keble's parish in the spring of 1841. They were received into the Roman Catholic Church at almost exactly the same time: Ambrose on October 2 and Newman on October 9, 1845. Bray writes:

> It is difficult perhaps for us now to grasp how great a gulf Newman's reception into the Catholic Church created for him and how much it made an outcast of him in Victorian England. He would not meet John Keble again for almost twenty years and the same was true of many of his friends and companions: he would never see his sister Harriet again. These losses

created an enduring bond between Newman and St John which would never be broken.[8]

'Their bond was spiritual' Bray goes on to state in categoric terms. He describes Newman's account of a conversation with St John mere hours before he died in which he expressed the hope that he had never committed a mortal sin in the course of his priestly life. Bray acknowledges that one needs to be suspicious of hagiography, but he nonetheless sees this as a 'definitive' statement, given Newman's time and culture. 'Their love was not the less intense for being spiritual' he concludes, 'Perhaps it was more so'.[9]

It is a characteristic of Bray's work that he attends to material culture – in this case, primarily the graveyard at Rednal and Newman's still-preserved room in the Oratory – as much as he does to written sources.[10] He gives us a vivid description of the altar in Newman's room with pictures of his closest friends, whom he would remember at mass, on the wall beside it: as well as Ambrose, these include Frs Edward Caswall and Joseph Gordon, the last two of whom died before Newman and occupied the graves on either side of Ambrose St John. Gordon died as early as 1853 and Newman attributed his premature death to the efforts Gordon had made on his behalf during the Achilli libel case.[11] It is to Gordon that Newman's *The Dream of Gerontius* is dedicated.

Nonetheless, Bray argues that there was a distinct and pre-eminent quality to Newman's love for St John, one in which, he suggests, Newman was convinced that he had experienced something of the nature of friendship itself. Bray goes on to speak of Newman's wish to be buried with St John as having, in common with the similar stories he describes throughout his book, the context of 'a tenacious religious faith … in which kinship and friendship lay at the heart of religion's role'.[12] He goes on to argue that it was Newman's precise intention to express this centrality of friendship in insisting so imperatively that he be buried with his brother priest.

Classical scholar and theologian that he was, Newman could not have been unaware of Aelred's work or its central declaration: *Deus amicitia est* ('God is friendship'). Nor would he have been unaware of the transformation which it wrought on the reading of secular classical works such as the previously mentioned episode in the Iliad involving Patroclus and Achilles. The key for Bray lies in the text of his monument, cited in a letter sent by Pope John Paul II to Bishop Vincent Nichols of Birmingham in January 2001 to mark the bicentenary of Newman's birth: 'Ex umbris et imaginibus in veritatem' ('from shadows and images into truth').[13] For Newman, friendship was the dim reflection in this world of 'what will be our unending delight when one with God in the next'.[14] His burial with Ambrose St John was, Bray asserts, 'his last sermon'. Bray died in 2001, and did not live to see the publication of his own book, let alone Newman's exhumation. Whatever significance Newman may have placed on his corporeal disappearance, we might well wish to consider whether, *pace* Bray, it was the empty tomb of John Henry Newman that was in fact his last, great, Easter sermon.[15]

Newman's Last Sermon

One discovers another way of looking at the empty tomb of John Henry Newman in considering the following contemporary report of his funeral from the Birmingham Post:

> When the rites had been achieved, the crowd without the gates was suffered to enter by batches and see the grave; and then the coffin was covered with mould of a softer texture than the marly stratum in which the grave is cut. This was done in studious and affectionate fulfilment of a desire of Dr. Newman's which some may deem fanciful, but which sprang from his reverence for the letter of the Divine Word; which, as he conceived, enjoins us to facilitate rather than impede the operation of the law 'Dust thou art, and unto dust shalt thou return.'[16]

It is unusual in circumstances such as those of Newman's exhumation to find no bones whatsoever but to have a plate survive. Prof. John Hunter of Birmingham University's Department of Archaeology did draw attention at the time to the fact that there were no archaeologists present at the exhumation; it was carried out by workmen who might well have missed smaller items such as teeth, which tend to be among the most resilient elements. He also suggested that the acidity of the soil alone would not be sufficient to bring about full decomposition in little over 100 years.[17]

What comes through very strongly from the two principal strands of our reflection so far is how deliberate and purposeful Newman was in relation to his own death. He was insistent to an obsessive degree on where he would be buried and with whom; he laid down very precise details about how his coffin was to be treated. When we take into account his own theological predispositions and convictions, it seems almost too obvious to state that we cannot do justice to the phenomenon which is Newman's death and exhumation without bringing theological reflection to bear. This is not to take away from the barely begun work of the archaeologists. It is merely to suggest that even when we achieve a more satisfactory explanation of the material data, it will not be the last word.

Theological, Cultural and Poetic Views of Death

A lot started with an empty tomb – including contemporary tales of how disciples must have robbed the body from the sepulchre provided by Joseph of Arimathea. We will now go on to consider how Newman's own empty tomb can prompt us to reflect afresh on some of the central elements of death and resurrection in the Christian tradition.

The theologian Karl Rahner – someone who could never be accused of ducking the question of death – delivered his last lecture at a conference on February 11-12, 1984.[18] The conference was held in Freiburg in honour of his 80th birthday which took place on March 5th of that same year. The last section of Rahner's lecture was called 'What is to Come'. In it Rahner offered a personal reflection on death and eternal life, one given added poignancy by the fact that he died just six weeks later on March 30th. He is critical, though in very kindly terms, of talk of eternal life which makes it seem more like a continuation of what we are used to in this life. Such talk is 'clothed too much with realities with which we are familiar'. It does not do justice to what he calls the 'radical incomprehensibility' of it all. We cannot, he insists, downgrade the direct vision of God in eternal life 'to one pleasant activity alongside others'. If, on the other hand, we have the courage to accept, in a spirit of faith and hope, 'the immense terror that is death', we can experience it as filled with 'God's all-absorbing and all-giving love'. But it is, as always for Rahner, a case of 'both-and'; there is no escaping the terror for any of us.[19] There is never a resurrection without a cross.

In *Keeping Hope Alive*, the *magnum opus* of the Irish theologian Dermot Lane, the author begins his reflections on the permanence of death by citing Philip Larkin's poem *Aubade*.[20] David Lodge has called Larkin the bard of *timor mortis* (fear of death) and for the author of *Aubade*, death is a frighteningly imminent, if frequently obscured, event:

> ... just on the edge of vision
> A small unfocused blur [...],
> . . . .
> Most things may never happen; this one will.

Death, for Larkin, is:

> The sure extinction that we travel to
> And shall be lost in always. Not to be here,
> Not to be anywhere,
> And soon; nothing more terrible, nothing more true.[21]

Aubade is as much a riposte to a type of Modernist aesthetics which Larkin saw as complacently focused on epiphanies as it is to both religion and philosophy, each of which gets a belt in this great, bleak poem. However, as Seamus Heaney has pointed out, as Larkin aged, 'his vision got arrested into a fixed stare at the inexorability of his own extinction. Human wisdom seemed to him a matter of operating within our mortal limits and of quelling any false hope of ... outfacing the inevitable.'[22] Nowhere is the quelling executed more dramatically than in *Aubade*. In his reflections on the poem, Heaney describes 'the imagination's stalemate between the death-mask of nihilism and the fixed smile of a pre-booked place in paradise'.[23] None of us are spared the pressure of the void and the absurd; they are part of the intellectual air we breathe. Heaney cites the Polish poet and Nobel Prize winner Czeslaw Milosz as protesting against a whole strain of modern literature which has conceded victory to the void. Poetry must not make this concession, Milosz and Heaney assert.

Larkin's *Aubade* was first published in the *Times Literary Supplement* in December 1977, and was referred to in office correspondence as 'Christmas without the baby'.[24] Indeed, Heaney remarks that it would be hard to think of a poem more opposed to the life-enhancing symbolism of the Christ child in the Christmas crib. For Heaney, it is 'the definitive post-Christian English poem, one that abolishes the soul's pretension to immortality and denies the Deity's personal concern'.[25] Heaney again cites Milosz who criticizes the way in which Larkin has endowed death with the supreme authority of law and universal necessity while the human person is reduced to nothing, to a bundle of perceptions or an interchangeable statistical unit. But poetry, Milosz protests, has always been on the side of life and its fulness. And faith in life everlasting has always been larger, deeper than religious creeds which expressed only one of its forms. In his own critique of *Aubade,* Heaney goes back to poetry's mythical origins, and notes, not with approbation, that the poem does not make the Orphic effort to haul life back up the slope against all the odds. *Aubade* in fact reneges on what Yeats called the spiritual intellect's great work. Heaney nails his own colours to the mast most compellingly and unreservedly when he asserts 'the goal of life on earth, and of poetry as a vital factor in the achievement of that goal, is what Yeats called in "Under Ben Bulben" the "profane perfection of mankind"'. In explicit condemnation of the world-view offered by Larkin, Heaney states that 'it is essential that the vision of reality which poetry offers be transformative, more than just a printout of the given circumstances of its time and place'. The poets, in the act of writing outstrip such conditions, even as they observe them. For human beings to bring about the most radiant conditions for themselves to inhabit, the creative writer 'transfigures' current conditions; this is what Heaney calls 'the redress of poetry'.[26]

Commenting on our *tempora* and *mores*, Lane observes how in the past people were more shy about mentioning sex but spoke freely about death; today one could say that the reverse is the case.[27] Our experience of death has been transformed radically by both the Marxist critique of 'pie in the sky' and advances in technology which have brought us to the point where universal annihilation has become a distinct, humanly-enabled possibility. Lane quotes Louis Evely who states: 'In wishing to live without dying, one dies without having lived.'[28] But the variety and ingenuity of our attempts to deny death are striking. Some forms of classical dualism took the view that it was 'only the body' which died, the soul remaining immune from decline, decay and decomposition. Karl Rahner, betraying the influence of Heidegger, is scathing of such approaches which would have 'the so-called soul viewing the fate of its former partner unaffected and undismayed as from above'.[29]

In an article, published in *Commonweal* in July 1993, Daniel Callahan critiques the ultimately flawed efforts of science, therapy and the law to help us deal with death:

> We hate death, I believe, because it means the end of that life which has given us what we have, and what we can become. We no less hate death because it is the final, the crowning reminder once and for all that we are finite bounded creatures. We see death at the end of the road in our lives, but it is forever foreshadowed in living our daily lives. We cannot have everything we want in life. We cannot have our dreams live on forever, even if we can achieve them for a time. We cannot stop things from going wrong, however much we dedicate ourselves to control. Could we bear death better if life were perfect? Probably not. The pain of separation from life would be all the greater. It is our human condition that is the problem, of which death is the great token. But only the token.[30]

Lane too is critical of both psychological and naturalistic approaches which over-emphasize the continuity of death, making of it something more like the final meeting in a project-planning process rather than the radical discontinuity which it in fact is.[31] For both Lane and Rahner, it is only when we face honestly this radical discontinuity that we can speak authentically of hope, even of God. The experience of death brings us up against the limits of life; it raises in the deepest and most personal sense the question of salvation, the question of God. Because it is only when we can find no resources within ourselves, when we are confronted with radical self-insufficiency – in more poetic terms, when 'self knows that self is not enough' – that real hope, hope focused on something beyond the self, arises.[32]

Bodily Resurrection

Dermot Lane rightly states that we will fail to understand correctly in theological terms the life, death and resurrection of Jesus if we do not accord to eschatology its proper place at the centre of theology.[33] This applies equally to any theological reflection on the exhumation and empty tomb of John Henry Newman. Long marginalized as the study of the 'four last things' – death, judgement, heaven and hell – eschatology is, in fact, 'a powerful reminder that all theological claims are subject to the qualifications and reservations that come from the promise of an open eschatological future'.[34] A properly configured theology, on these terms, sees the life, death and resurrection of Jesus as a single event that constitutes the eschatological turning point of history. In the life of Jesus and particularly in the death and resurrection, the *Eschaton* is experienced by the disciples as having dawned.

It is important to note the unity of life, death and resurrection in the foregoing. It is a tendency unfortunately reinforced by the Christian liturgical calendar and the poverty of much of its catechetic and homiletic explication, to see the resurrection as something that happened 'a few days after' the crucifixion. Lane is crystal clear that the phrase 'on the third day in accordance with the scriptures' is to be read in strictly theological – not chronological – terms. The secondary clause, 'in accordance with the scriptures' refers back to texts as diverse as Hosea 6:1ff:

> Come, and let us return unto the LORD: for he hath torn, and he will heal us; he hath smitten, and he will bind us up. After two days will he revive us: in the third day he will raise us up, and we shall live in his sight.[35]

The term refers, in a technical and not a chronological sense, to the day of deliverance and the dawning of salvation. It is 'on the third day' that Abraham is delivered from sacrificing Isaac (Gen 22:4), that

Joshua leads the Israelites into the Promised Land (Josh 3:2) and that Yahweh appears on Mount Sinai (Ex. 19:11). Similarly, the pericopae relating to the empty tomb and post-resurrection appearances of Jesus are designed to convey that, after Calvary, the disciples had a new experience of Jesus, distinct and different from the pre-Calvary experience. It is this new, eschatological presence of Christ that animates the disciples and their subsequent preaching and ministry. In relation to this new eschatological or risen presence, the intent behind the resurrection pericopae is to demonstrate that the resurrection is neither a resuscitation nor a return to what was the case before. Neither is it a purely subjective experience within the hearts and minds and spirits of the disciples. It is God's eschatologically transformative action on the life and death of Jesus within history.

Lane is insistent that the language of the resurrection can only be 'metaphorical, symbolic and analogical.' [36] It is in fact excessive literalism that is the most serious barrier to proper understanding of the resurrection pericopae. This same literalism raised its head in autumn 2008 in much of the reportage on Newman's exhumation. What is being argued here is that the experience of this latter-day empty tomb, whatever the archaeologists may ultimately determine, has an intrinsic theological significance in that it compels us to reflect on our own presuppositions, many of them tacit and unspoken, about life, death and resurrection, especially about bodily resurrection and in what it might consist. But for now, let us turn briefly to St Paul.

The Pauline Context

For Paul, a being without a body is, literally, unthinkable. His anthropology and consequently his view of the body is more Hebrew than Greek, broadly understood.[37] Classical Greek anthropology, such as we find in the *Phaedo*, sees the soul as a higher form of being than the body, one which will survive death. The intellectual hegemony of the classical Greek tradition, reinforced in modernity by the Cartesian *cogito*, means that words like 'soul' and 'spirit' come to us with what Gadamer termed a *wirkungsgeschichtliches Bewusstsein* (historically effected consciousness) that means it is near impossible for us not to absorb some of their dualist connotations.[38]

Paul's kerygmatic theology of the resurrection is set out in the fifteenth chapter of his first letter to the Corinthians, with its core in 1 Cor. 15:3-5:

> ³For I handed on to you as of first importance what I in turn had received: that Christ died for our sins in accordance with the scriptures, ⁴and that he was buried, and that he was raised on the third day in accordance with the scriptures, ⁵and that he appeared to Cephas, then to the twelve.

Because the Corinthians believed that only part of a man died, so they believed that only part of a man survived. Paul is very critical of this. In 1 Cor. 15:44, he speaks of the *soma pneumatikon*, the spiritual body that is raised. For Paul, *soma* or body is not to be taken as identical to *sarx* or flesh; it is *sarx* that decomposes after death. *Soma* is the necessary vehicle of relationality, to one's self, the other, the cosmos and to God. As the mode of the self's being present to others, *soma* is the whole person in relationship; it is the possibility and the reality of relationship, including the relationship to the transcendent. Soma is the expression of the person from birth through glorification. The *soma pneumatikon*, the spiritual body in 1 Cor. 15:44 is not then a body constructed from some miraculous spiritual substance; it is the totality of the human person that is finally in the dimension of God – spiritual refers to the dimension in which the body is and is relating, not to the stuff of which it is made. This is the truest meaning of the corporeality of the resurrection.

Paul is scathing of the literalists: 'But someone will say, "How are the dead raised? And with what kind of body do they come?" You fool!' (1 Cor 15:35f.). He uses imagery from horticulture to describe the transformation from *soma psychicon* to *soma pneumatikon* – and it is important to remember that, for Paul in a pre-scientific age, the transformation from seed to flowering plant is due to a direct divine intervention. The relationship between *soma psychicon* and *soma pneumatikon,* between earthly and risen body is identical to that between seed and full-grown plant: 'And you do not sow the body which is to be, but a bare grain' (1 Cor 15:37) – there can be no *soma pneumatikon* without the death of *soma psychicon*: because death is the last enemy to be destroyed (1 Cor 15:26).

Conclusion

At a Mass for the Feast of All Saints in November 2008 at the Birmingham Oratory 'all eyes were drawn, again and again, to the glass and gilded-wood casket, the size of a very small doll's house'.[39] This ornate box contained the earthly remains of John Henry Newman (fig. 1.2). It was set on a velvet-covered catafalque to the side of the sanctuary. The remains were few: some hair, soil from Newman's grave, a fragment of bloodstained linen and a small wooden crucifix. It is part of the process of canonization in the Roman Catholic Church that relics of the saint are available for public veneration. The remnants at the Birmingham Oratory express a minimalist rendering of this fact.

The sermon at the mass was preached by Fr Paul Chavasse, Provost of the Birmingham Oratory and then the chief postulator of Newman's cause. He did not evade the issues on the minds of many in the specially invited congregation. This, he said, was 'a rather unusual event ... some would say, odd'. The 'proper thing to do' was normally to leave a person's remains in their last resting place. But these, he went on, are special circumstances: 'In the Church of Christ there has been since the earliest days the desire to have the protection of saints, and this expresses itself in the seeking for the assurance given by their abiding physical presence'. And yet, as he acknowledged, the remains within that little casket were 'sparse' and, besides, people might think it 'premature or presumptuous' to treat them as saintly relics since Newman had still not been raised to the altar. He was equally frank about the emotions felt when the grave yielded little or nothing. 'There was a feeling of peace, peace of mind', he said, 'that after all Cardinal Newman's fondest wishes had actually been fulfilled.'[40]

As one sat in the Oratory at Birmingham that November, Rilke's ninth Duino Elegy came to mind:

> *Here* is the time for the *sayable, here* is its homeland.
> Speak and bear witness. More than ever
> the Things that we might experience are vanishing, for
> what crowds them out and replaces them is an imageless act.[41]

To attempt to escape from the imageless act, the '*Tun ohne Bild*', that is death is nothing more or less than to attempt to escape from being human. In many and varied ways in the past, religion has been misused as an attempted means of such an escape. I hope that, if it has achieved nothing else, this essay has demonstrated how the iconic absence that was John Henry Newman's empty tomb serves to interrogate any such death and life-denying option.

Bibliography

Bray, Alan, *The Friend* (Chicago: University of Chicago Press, 2003).
Callahan, Daniel, 'Cramming for your finals: Make death a part of life,' in *Commonweal* Vol. 120/13 (July 16, 1993), 11-15.
Conway, Pádraic, 'Rahner and Newman: Men of Letters,' in *Studies in Theology Society and Culture 3: Karl Rahner: Theologian for the Twenty-First Century*, eds. Pádraic Conway and Fáinche Ryan (Bern: Peter Lang, 2010).
Cornwell, John, 'An Absence Yet A Presence,' *The Tablet*, 8 November 2008, 8.
Cornwell, John, *Newman's Unquiet Grave: The Reluctant Saint* (London / New York: Continuum, 2010).
Dunn, James D. G., ed., *The Cambridge Companion to St Paul* (Cambridge: Cambridge University Press, 2003).
Evely, Louis, *In the Face of Death* (New York: The Seabury Press, 1979).
Gadamer, Hans-Georg, *Truth and Method* (London and New York: Continuum, 2004).
Heaney, Seamus, 'Joy or Night: Last Things in the Poetry of W.B. Yeats and Philip Larkin,' in Seamus Heaney, *The Redress of Poetry: Oxford Lectures* (London: Faber and Faber, 1995), 146-163.
Kennelly, Brendan, *Familiar Strangers: New & Selected Poems 1960-2004* (Northumberland: Bloodaxe Books Ltd, 2004).
Ker, Ian, *John Henry Newman: A Biography* (Oxford: Oxford University Press, 1990). Lane, Dermot A., *Keeping Hope Alive: Stirrings in Christian Theology* (Dublin: Gill and Macmillan, 1996).
Lodge, David, *Deaf Sentence* (London: Penguin, 2008).
McGrath, Francis J., ed., *The Letters and Diaries of John Henry Newman, Vol. XXXII: Supplement* (Oxford: Oxford University Press, 2008).
Lane, Dermot A., *Keeping Hope Alive: Stirrings in Christian Theology* (Dublin: Gill and Macmillan, 1996).
Mitchell, Stephen, ed. and trans., *The Selected Poetry of Rainer Maria Rilke* (New York: Vintage, 1984).
Newman, John Henry, Lectures on the Present Position of Catholics in England: Addressed to the Brothers of the Oratory (London: Burns and Lambert, 1851).
Rahner, Karl, 'Ideas for a Theology of Death,' *Theological Investigations* 13 (London: Darton, Longman and Todd, 1975), 169-186.
Rahner, Karl, 'Experiences of a Catholic Theologian,' in *Theological Studies*, 61 (2000), 3-15.

---

[1] Edited posthumously by Philip Cottrell and Wolfgang Marx.
[2] Alan Bray, *The Friend* (Chicago: University of Chicago Press, 2003).
[3] Newman would have been well aware that Aelred's work is itself a commentary on Cicero's *De Amicitia*.
[4] Bray, *The Friend*, 289.
[5] *Ibid.*, 291.
[6] *Ibid.*, 291.
[7] *Ibid.*, 291.
[8] *Ibid.*, 292.
[9] *Ibid.*, 293.
[10] *Ibid.*, 294-5 and 299 -300.
[11] Giacinto Achilli was a former Dominican priest who had been sentenced to imprisonment by the Roman Inquisition for sexual assault and immorality.

He had subsequently become a Protestant and fled Italy to avoid imprisonment. In 1850, he came to England at the invitation of the Evangelical Alliance and went on a lecture tour, denouncing the corruptions of Rome. Newman in turn denounced Achilli in the fifth of his series of *Lectures on Catholicism in England,* later published in book form as *Lectures on the Present Position of Catholics in England: Addressed to the Brothers of the Oratory* (London: Burns and Lambert, 1851). The Achilli affair is best summarised in Ian Ker, *John Henry Newman: A Biography* (Oxford: Oxford University Press, 1990), 372-75.

[12] Bray, *The Friend,* 297.

[13] Letter of the Holy Father John Paul II on the Occasion of the 2nd Centenary of the Birth of Cardinal John Henry Newman, http://www.vatican.va/holy_father/john_paul_ii/letters/2001/documents/hf_jp-ii_let_20010227_john-henry-newman_en.html, accessed September 3, 2012.

[14] Bray, *The Friend,* 304.

[15] For a similar iteration of Bray's analysis of the relationship between Newman and Ambrose St John within the context of the theology of Karl Rahner see Pádraic Conway, 'Rahner and Newman: Men of Letters,' in *Studies in Theology Society and Culture 3: Karl Rahner: Theologian for the Twenty-First Century,* eds Pádraic Conway and Fáinche Ryan (Bern: Peter Lang, 2010), 61-76.

[16] Reproduced in Francis J. McGrath, ed., *The Letters and Diaries of John Henry Newman, Vol. XXXII: Supplement* (Oxford: Oxford University Press, 2008), 654.

[17] See http://news.bbc.co.uk/2/hi/uk_news/england/7672099.stm, accessed 4 September, 2012.

[18] Karl Rahner, 'Experiences of a Catholic Theologian,' in *Theological Studies,* 61 (2000), 3-15.

[19] *Ibid.,* 14.

[20] Dermot A. Lane, *Keeping Hope Alive: Stirrings in Christian Theology* (Dublin: Gill and Macmillan, 1996), 43.

[21] *Times Literary Supplement,* 3952, (23 December, 1977), 1491. The reference to Larkin as 'bard of '*timor mortis*' derives from David Lodge, *Deaf Sentence* (London: Penguin, 2008), 306.

[22] Seamus Heaney, 'Joy or Night: Last Things in the Poetry of W.B. Yeats and Philip Larkin,' in Seamus Heaney, *The Redress of Poetry: Oxford Lectures* (London: Faber and Faber, 1995), 146-163: 147.

[23] *Ibid.,* 153.

[24] See Mick Imlah's introduction to Larkin's poem on the magazine's website, 19 December 2007 [http://www.the-tls.co.uk/tls/reviews/other_categories/article757904.ece] accessed 29 January 2013.

[25] Heaney, 'Joy or Night,' 155.

[26] See *Ibid.,* 159.

[27] Lane, *Keeping Hope Alive,* 45.

[28] Louis Evely, *In the Face of Death* (New York: The Seabury Press, 1979), 1.

[29] Karl Rahner, 'Ideas for a Theology of Death,' in *Theological Investigations* 13 (London: Darton, Longman and Todd, 1975), 169-186: 179.

[30] Daniel Callahan, 'Cramming for your finals: Make death a part of life,' in *Commonweal* Vol. 120/13 (July 16, 1993), 11-15: 15.

31 Lane, *Keeping Hope Alive*, 51ff.
32 Brendan Kennelly, *Familiar Strangers: New & Selected Poems 1960-2004* (Northumberland: Bloodaxe Books Ltd, 2004), 425.
33 For this and much of the following reflection, Lane, *Keeping Hope Alive*, in particular: 1-41.
34 Lane, *Keeping Hope Alive*, 2.
35 Biblical references, unless otherwise stated, are to the *New Revised Standard Version*, 1989.
36 Lane, *Keeping Hope Alive*, 101.
37 A useful summary of the thinking of Paul on the resurrected body may be found in Alan F. Segal, 'Pauls Jewish Presuppositions,' in *The Cambridge Companion to St Paul*, ed. James D. G. Dunn (Cambridge: Cambridge University Press, 2003), 159.
38 See Hans-Georg Gadamer, *Truth and Method* (London / New York: Continuum, 2004), 335.
39 John Cornwell, 'An Absence Yet A Presence,' *The Tablet*, 8 November 2008, 8. Cornwell went on to treat the issues associated with Newman's grave more extensively in his *Newman's Unquiet Grave: The Reluctant Saint* (London and New York: Continuum, 2010).
40 See Cornwell, 'An Absence,' 8 for the following citations from Chavasse's homily.
41 Stephen Mitchell, ed. and trans., *The Selected Poetry of Rainer Maria Rilke* (New York: Vintage, 1984), 201, with German text in parallel on page 200.

Fig. 1.1) Cardinal John Henry Newman (photographed by Herbert Barraud, 1887). Hulton Archive / Getty Images.

Fig. 1.2) Reliquary of Cardinal John Henry Newman. Shrine of the Blessed John Henry Newman at the Oratory of St Philip Neri, Edgbaston, Birmingham.

2 | John Donne, Undone, Redone: the John Donne Monument Reconsidered[1]

Philip Cottrell

Nicholas Stone's effigy of John Donne (1572-1631) in St. Paul's Cathedral, London (figs. 2.1 and 2.2) is a strange and elegant example of seventeenth-century English tomb sculpture. Although upright, Donne appears enveloped in a body-hugging burial shroud gathered into two frilly ruffs at the head and feet. Only the face, with its shuttered eyelids, raffish beard, and benign, half-smiling expression, manages to breach this unsettling cocoon. The clean, moist appearance of the drapery and the softly-nuanced modelling of the features testify to Stone's position as the finest sculptor of the English Baroque.[2] But as the figure totters out of its niche, precariously balanced on the lip of a classical funerary urn, it inevitably recalls the outlandish attitudes of the busking 'living statues' which are now a mainstay of the busy high street – a not so glib analogy given that the dying Donne seems to have personally modelled for the monument, clad in his own winding sheet and standing on an urn-shaped box.

Surprisingly, only three writers – all Donne scholars – Nigel Foxell, Helen Gardner and, more recently, R.S. Peterson, have given serious, prolonged thought to the statue's appearance and development. [3] Peterson in particular has compiled an impressively thorough analysis of the monument's later history, and intends to publish more at the time of writing. With this in mind, the following essay merely wishes to offer some thoughts on the broader art-historical context of the statue, as a preface to further research. Its relationship to *transi* tomb iconography and the intimate role played by art in the deathbed rituals of the period are of particular interest; I wish to highlight the way in which Donne's modelling for the monument, and the lost preparatory sketch that resulted, deserve more rigorous attention for the way in which they reflect a fascinating relationship between 'art' and the 'art of dying' in early modern Europe.

Standing and Sitting: Donne's Last Days

Donne died on the 31st March 1631, and the statue was installed within eighteen months of this. At his death, Donne was the Dean of St. Paul's, and his effigy is the only monumental figure to have survived, more-or-less intact, from the Norman cathedral which perished in the Great Fire of 1666. It is hard to credit the old story that the statue simply slid off its pedestal during the conflagration and torpedoed its way into the safety of the crypt. But amid a multitude of reclining tomb effigies, the statue's unusual, upright, lozenge-like shape probably facilitated its rescue. Peterson has demonstrated that it remained propped up in the crypt of Wren's church until its 'resurrection' (the word is well chosen) in 1873 when it was reinstalled south of the choir, in a place roughly analogous to that which it once occupied.[4] In his *Lives* of 1658, Donne's earliest biographer, Izaak Walton, gave a remarkable account of the statue's genesis:

> [Donne] sent for a Carver to make for him in wood the figure of an Urn, giving him directions for the compass and height of it; and to bring with it a board, of the just height of his body.

The passage continues in parenthesis, as if Walton is quoting from an authoritative, though unidentified source:

> These being got, then without delay a choice Painter was got to be in readiness to draw his picture, which was taken as followeth.—Several charcoal fires being first made in his large study, he brought with him into that place his winding-sheet in his hand, and having put off all his clothes, had this sheet put on him, and so tied with knots at his head and feet, and his hands so placed as dead bodies are usually fitted, to be shrouded and put into their coffin, or grave. Upon this urn he thus stood, with his eyes shut, and with so much of the sheet turned aside as might show his lean, pale and death-like face, which was purposely turned towards the East, from whence he expected the second coming of his and our Saviour Jesus.

Walton then appears to continue in his own words:

> In this posture he was drawn at his just height; and when the picture was fully finished, he caused it to be set by his bedside, where it continued and became his hourly object till his death,

and was then given to his dearest friend and executor Dr. Henry King, then chief Residentiary of St. Paul's, who caused him to be thus carved in one entire piece of white marble, as it now stands in that Church.[5]

Although the identity of the painter and the original sketch are lost, Martin Droeshout engraved the upper part of the original design as a frontispiece to the text of Donne's last sermon, published under the title of *Deaths Duell* in 1632 (fig.2.3).[6]

Helen Gardner is particularly notable for her sceptical response to Walton's story. She accepted that Donne had sanctioned the image, but was it feasible that a middle-aged dying man could stand, feet together, on a raised pedestal for long enough to model for a preparatory drawing? Surely the artist would require only a likeness of the face; perhaps Donne had actually been sketched *post-mortem* on his deathbed? Gardner also suggested that, in keeping with tradition, the statue was originally designed to be a recumbent *gisant*. Following observations made by the nineteenth-century sculptor Hamo Thorneycroft, she highlighted the ambiguous way drapery falls around the figure.[7] However, Stone's drapery is deliberately stylized in places, as is particularly apparent in the terminating ruffs, although the lower one may be a later repair.[8] Stone is also known to have employed more than one assistant on the work, so perhaps some confusion arose?[9]

It would be better to apply standards of verisimilitude to Droeshout's obviously less idealized likeness. An admittedly ad-hoc recreation of the pose using a living stand-in (fig. 2.4) endorses some of the effects observable in the engraving. As is appropriate to a standing figure, in Droeshout's image the topknot falls forward and is relatively flat, the shoulders are dropped, and the drapery is characterized by its vertical folds, which seem drawn tightly downwards to some point around, or below, the midriff (which is where Donne's hands are clasped in Stone's statue, and this also probably explains why the topknot has been pulled forward and downwards). Although the engraving is only half-length, one also notes that Donne appears not actually 'wound' into this winding sheet: a central seam of material suggests an arrangement designed to help the sitter to ease himself in *and* out of this macabre pupa. The slightly elevated viewpoint is more problematic since Donne was supposedly standing on a box, and some of the questions raised by Gardner and Peterson with regard to the evolution of the statue certainly deserve further analysis. However, I wish to restrict myself to re-examining the 'logic' of Walton's account, which is actually more plausible than Gardner would allow. Walton's sense of evidence seems to have been no less reliable than what might be expected of any conscientious biographer of the period. But if that is not saying much, one should also stress that Walton knew Donne reasonably well in later life, and was present at his bedside at some point during those final days, as a letter from Donne's executor Henry King seems to corroborate.[10] Walton's testimony actually squares rather well with what we know of Donne's background, activity as an art patron, and general philosophy. Certainly, Donne was not a man ever intent on taking death (literally) lying down. As early as 1608 he famously wrote to his friend Henry Goodyer that:

> I would not that death should take me asleep. I would not have him meerly seize me, and onely declare me to be dead, but win me, and overcome me. When I must shipwrack, I would do it in a Sea, where mine impotency might have some excuse; not in a sullen weedy lake, where I could not have so much as exercise for my swimming.[11]

In fact, Donne could be remarkably active *in extremis* as is apparent when, in 1623, he fell dangerously ill and was forcibly confined to bed. He was determined to keep a contemplative diary of the experience which was published the following year as *Devotions on Emergent Occasions*.[12] Probably conceived as a potential epitaph, it reveals Donne's increasingly determined wish to make something communicative and exhibitive out of his death.[13] By the time of the onset of the cancer that eventually killed him, he wrote in a letter that 'it hath been my desire and God may be pleased to grant it, that I might die in the Pulpit'.[14] It was an ambition he almost achieved when, on the 25th of February 1631, only a month from the grave, he preached a sermon in front of the court at Whitehall. He was shockingly emaciated, and Walton states that the sermon, which took death as its theme, was 'prophetically chosen' and that Donne 'presented himself not to preach mortification by a living voice: *but, mortality by a decayed body and a dying face* .... Donne had preach't his own Funeral Sermon' [my italics].[15] Walton's account then has Donne confined to the deanery until his death at the end of March, and it was during this period that he posed for a painter in his shroud. In fact, Donne actually attended an assembly of the Cathedral Governors a day after his sermon – a typical example of Walton's unreliability according to Gardner.[16] However, this also shows how, even when at death's door, Donne could draw on reserves of energy that were deeper than one might ordinarily suppose. His determined wish to model in his shroud in the manner Walton describes remains a real possibility. It was also appropriate that the posthumous publication of the sermon under the title of *Deaths Duell* should bear Droeshout's image of the wasted author in his shroud.

According to Walton, the issue of a funerary monument was urged upon Donne by Simeon Fox – his personal friend and doctor, (a bad sign if ever there was one).[17] Perhaps this should be seen from a palliative point of view, and from Fox's need to both exploit and quell his patient's restlessness, and to lend his dying days a consolatory sense of focus. The latter impulse may also be placed within the wider context of the period's fondness for contemplative rituals designed to prepare the individual for death. Surely Fox was also aware of Donne's predilection for effigizing himself in various affected guises and attitudes, a fact also acknowledged by Walton.[18] Of the numerous portraits Donne commissioned of himself, at least one, the 'Lothian Portrait' in the National Portrait Gallery, London, was present at the deanery when he died (see also below).[19] Fox now granted Donne the license he craved to briefly abandon the sickbed, and pose in his winding sheet for the unnamed 'painter of choice'. But even when he returned to bed, taking the resulting sketch with him, it seems that Donne remained active; busily putting his papers in order, including the text of *Deaths Duell* – this project being now intimately conjoined with the monument.[20]

Donne and the 'Art of Dying'

It is necessary to highlight the iconographic implications of the upright posture of Donne's funerary effigy as its shrouded appearance obviously presupposes a recumbent attitude in the sepulchre. Here one should consider the following passage from Donne's *Devotions*:

> Wee attribute but one priveledge, and advantage to Mans body, above other moving creatures, that he is not as others, grovelling, but of an erect, of an upright form ... A sicke bed is a grave; and all that the patient saies there is but a varying of his owne *Epitaph* ... I must practise my lying in the *grave* by lying still, and not practise my *Resurrection*, by rising any more.[21]

Perhaps in *standing* for this last portrait in his shroud, he was indeed practising his own resurrection (Walton has Donne facing east in the direction of the Second Coming), and one should acknowledge how a preoccupation with bodily resurrection runs as a rich vein throughout Donne's writings. His whole career was also defined by a wonderful resurrection of sorts: his first incarnation, inevitably associated with the affected, amorous melancholic of the Lothian

Portrait, encompasses his early life as a poetical dandy, man-about-town, and ambitious secretary to Samuel Egerton, Lord Keeper of England. The London of his early years was a heady Eden (rendered all the more piquant as his Catholic upbringing had threatened to prohibit such an existence) while Egerton's young niece, Anne More, represented Eve and the apple all rolled into one: their secret marriage of December 1601 provoked a famous scandal.[22] The long years of social limbo which resulted, and the struggle to regain patronage and financial security prompted the witty contemporary epigram, 'John Donne, Anne Donne, undone'.[23] His eventual rehabilitation was characterized by a remarkable transformation in 1615 into an Anglican clergyman, and rapid rise through the ranks thereafter. Yet, as James Winny asserts, the fear of erasure continued to haunt him:

> the portraits 'in several habits and in several postures' known to Walton represented Donne's lifelong attempt to externalize himself as a living reality, and to break away from the conviction that he was at best a creature 'not absolutely dead' ... the only image which he could willingly leave to posterity was the corpse-like figure within the knotted shroud which still perpetuates him ...[24]

It is important to wed this analysis of Donne's fondness for portraits of himself to his equally persistent obsession with the body's regeneration on the Day of Judgement. As John Carey observed, this was premised on a persistent fascination with the sub-atomic breakdown of the body in death. Donne declares the following in a sermon of 1627:

> One humour of our dead body produces worms, and those worms suck and exhaust all other humour, and then all dies, and all dries, and molders into dust and that dust is blowen into the River, and that puddled water tumbled into the sea, and that ebs and flows in infinite revolutions, and still, still God knows in what *Cabinet* every *seed-Pearle lies*, in what part of the world every grain of every mans dust lies ....[25]

Similarly, his last sermon refers to,

> this *death* after *death*, nay this death after burial, this *dissolution* after *dissolution*, this *death* of *corruption* and *putrifaction*, of *vermiculation* and *incineration*, of *dissolution* and *dispersion* in and *from* the grave ... my *mouth* shall be *filled* with *dust*, and the *worme* shall *feed*, and *feed sweetly* upon me.[26]

This obsession with putrefaction was not all that unusual for its day. It is a repetitive theme of not only the sermons, but also the painting and sculpture of the period to which Donne as a poet, clergyman, and connoisseur of the arts was especially attuned. It should also be remembered that, according to Walton, the sketch of Donne in his shroud was not immediately dispatched to Nicholas Stone, but remained propped up in front of Donne's bed where it 'became his hourly object till his death'.[27] Many scholars have ignored the significance of this lost sketch, which was not merely a by-product of the statue's development. Its contribution to a wider menu of preparative activity attendant on Donne's death deserves greater scrutiny. Its function should be related to the way in which the first 150 years of English Protestantism witnessed a burgeoning vogue for contemplative death rituals which retained a need for images of one sort or another and which stressed the importance of display; we read, for example, of men and women ordering their own funeral shrouds or sleeping next to their coffins, and *memento mori* images were often close at hand. These morbid pantomimes fashioned a new post-Catholic concept of *viaticum*, replacing the highly formalized deathbed theatrics that had prevailed hitherto.[28]

The use of such props is related to the evolving tradition of the *ars moriendi*: printed manuals for those who wished to fulfil the expectations of a pious, manageable death. Their format, which usually encompassed an almanac of the dying man's final experiences against the backdrop of a cosmic battle for his soul probably influenced Donne in his *Devotions* of 1624. They frequently contained illustrations that played an important role as aids to devotion.[29] The contemplation of edifying images helped to prepare the individual for death and dispel sinful thoughts, although the use of devotional art for this purpose was obviously more germane to Catholic culture: for example, on his deathbed Carlo Borromeo found solace in a particularly moving painting of the *Agony in the Garden*; Gianlorenzo Bernini painted a sobering canvas, the *Blood of the Redeemer*, in readiness for it to be hung in front of his deathbed, and also had it mass-produced as a print for the edification of other expiring devotees.[30] In the context of Protestant England, it is arguable that the sketch of Donne in his shroud reflects the way in which new idiosyncratic *memento mori* images replaced the Popish crucifixes and madonnas previously present at the bedsides of the dying.

As an exemplative tool of display for a wider public, art could also alleviate the detrimental impression of a 'bad death': when the courtier

Kenelm Digby – whose social circle intersected with Donne's – awoke one morning in May 1633 to find that his wife (the notorious beauty Venetia Stanley) had accidentally died from the youth-giving 'viper wine' he had administered to her the night before, one of the first people he sent for was Van Dyck. The painter arrived within 48 hours, before Venetia could be carved up in an autopsy ordered by the King. Van Dyck painted her propped up in bed, head in hand, with a serene, smiling expression (the painting survives in Dulwich Picture Gallery, London). Painter and patron even conspired to rub some blood back into the corpse's cheeks in order to make a better portrait; mindful of Gardner's unwarranted scepticism as to the practical need for Donne to model in his shroud, this at least stresses the serious thought given to painting 'dal naturale' – and the attention to detail attendant on such sittings; the need for the model's participation, and the portrait's perceived importance as a record of reality.[31]

The influence of an earlier Germanic vogue for deathbed portraits is worth mentioning here, as exemplified by a lost portrait of Erasmus of Rotterdam in death. Only a day elapsed between Erasmus's death and burial in Basel in July 1536, but his scholarly disciples still found time to draft in an artist to sketch his corpse for posterity (the sketch for the lost painting is preserved in the Öffentliche Kunstsammlung, Basel).[32] This foreshadows the role played by members of Donne's circle, particularly Simeon Fox and Henry King, as 'keepers of the flame': one suggested a commemorative marble effigy, while the other saw through its execution, even if the actual design concept was Donne's. Walton consulted King prior to expanding on his account of Donne's death in the 1658 edition of his *Lives* (the first to contain an account of the statue's genesis); it is therefore possible that it is King's eyewitness account that Walton quoted in the extract reproduced at the beginning of this essay.

It could be argued that Kenelm Digby was eager to convey the impression of his wife's smiling acquiescence to death as a means of fulfilling the contemporary requirements of an exemplative 'good death': the dread of sudden death – *mors improvisa* – prompted the need for a quasi-clairvoyant anticipation of death's arrival.[33] Similarly, the lengths to which Donne went in modelling in his shroud ought to be seen in the context of an elaborate panoply of activity designed to stress his prolonged precognition of death. One should also recall how, according to Walton, after the sketch was finished, on his sickbed Donne began to methodically put his worldly affairs in order. And then, with death finally imminent, he adopted a pose in bed that anticipated

Stone's effigy (albeit recumbent) and which was appropriate to how his body would be arranged in the grave.[34]

If Donne wished to micromanage both his death and the design of his monument, this also became a symptom of his need to control, and even 'overtake', death. Arguably, he employed a variety of strategies intended to siphon off some of death's dramatic power for his own purposes. But in preaching his own funeral sermon, and in modelling in his shroud, these creative dress rehearsals for death and resurrection could also become a performative and instructive act of faith. As far as presenting himself in his shroud is concerned, his 'audience' would ultimately extend far beyond the painter employed, or even those closest to him. The resulting monument created a didactic image of contemplation solemnized as a 'sermon in stone' and intended for widespread consumption. Equally, Donne's final appearance in the pulpit, his modelling for the monument, and the use of the sketch as the basis for an engraved frontispiece to *Deaths Duell* are all intelligible as one multifaceted, edifying epitaph. In this context, I wish to acknowledge R. C. Bald's instructive analysis:

> In considering the final weeks of Donne's life the reader must remember that the seventeenth century, unlike the twentieth, made no attempt to turn away its face from the facts of death ... Life, men thought then, was a preparation for death, and it behoved each one to be ready to meet it ... Walton's account of Donne's last days ... may seem extravagant, even macabre ... but it was in the tradition of his own age and evoked much admiration. Donne's lifelong talent for the dramatic gesture and the still vital force of his own personality enabled him to make of his own death a kind of new ritual expressing the doctrines of his religion.[35]

'Painters have presented to us with some horrour the *sceleton*': Donne's Monument in the Context of *Transi* Imagery

Donne's interest in imagery deliberately designed to facilitate a contemplation of death is evidenced by a painting of 'the skeleton' which is mentioned in his will of the 13th December, 1630.[36] In fact, numerous pictures are listed, and it is generally clear that Donne had a keen and educated appreciation for art: the deanery was decorated with high-quality devotional images, including a *Madonna and Child and St John* by Titian which subsequently passed through the hands of such prominent seventeenth-century art collectors as Charles I and Rogier de

Liancourt (a gentleman of Louis XIII's bedchamber); John Evelyn endorsed it as a 'very rare' example of its type.37 Donne's writings also betray a sophisticated knowledge of contemporary art theory, and it is not at all improbable that he wished to become actively and intimately involved with the fashioning of his final effigy in the manner Walton described.38

Donne's monument is also intelligible as a critique of the iconography of the traditional 'transi' tombs familiar to many parish churches. Frequently 'double decker' affairs, these portrayed recumbent, shrouded effigies of the deceased as they would appear mouldering in the grave below a representation of the same individual as in life. Many examples, such as that of John Wakeman (d.1549) (fig. 2.5 – only the *transi* itself survives, and in an incorrect position), have shrouds prominently knotted at the head and feet, although the material is drawn back to reveal the decaying, worm-addled corpse within.39 *Transis* appear quite late into the English renaissance: in 1600 a *transi* figure, which Donne almost certainly knew well, was incorporated into the Herbert Tomb at Montgomery Church on the Shropshire / Welsh border (fig. 2.6). It lies below the *gisant* effigies of Sir Richard Herbert and the wife who survived him, Donne's close friend, Magdalene Herbert. As an intimate of the family, Donne stayed at Montgomery in April 1613. Perhaps his journey took in Burford, which is still on the main route from the south-east.40 Its church contains a painted funerary triptych of 1588 portraying Richard Cornwall and his family. The predella bears a life-sized, shrouded *transi* that is remarkable for the way it anticipates Droeshout's engraving of the lost sketch of Donne in his shroud (fig. 2.7).41

Transi imagery has been understood in terms of a traditional belief in purgatory, and its function as an exhortation to the saying of post-mortem masses – a means of easing the torments of the dead which were frequently equated with the body's earthly corruption.42 However, with the evaporation of purgatory, a Protestant emphasis on bodily resurrection was introduced into areas of eschatological contemplation once occupied by a formalized belief in the continuous interaction between the living and the dead. Anglican orthodoxy dictated that the souls of the saved went straight to heaven, awaiting a reunification with their bodies at the Last Judgement. But there was still some confusion on this point, and Donne's obsession with bodily resurrection exemplifies a means of circumventing the void – spiritual, chronological and spatial – which threatened to interpose itself between the moment of death and Christ's second coming. One should also take into account Donne's personal fear of disconnection from the body social and the body politic. For a man of his Catholic upbringing, one might suppose that any inkling of a senseless (albeit temporary) 'nothing' after death would have 'out-purgatoried' purgatory. Therefore, his own monument naturally gave imaginative focus to the miraculous moment of resurrection and reintegration.

With the development of later seventeenth-century tomb formats, the traditional *transi* gave way to a new genre of 'resurrection monuments'. These represented the deceased as they would joyfully reappear in their winding sheets at Christ's return – active, and upright. Gardner was keen to separate this type from the intentions behind Donne's statue, but standing shroud effigies such as those to Henry Slingsby at Knaresborough (1633) and John Dutton at Sherbourne (1656-7), Gloucestershire, were directly and demonstrably inspired by the St Paul's monument. And it may be that Donne was himself influenced by earlier prototypical examples such as the wall monument to Susan Calmady (d.1617) in Tamerton Foliot, Devon which may antedate Donne's statue by more than a decade.[43] Gardner refuted Bald's assertion that the St. Paul's monument portrayed Donne's sleepy, somnambulant emergence from the grave (nearly all resurrection figures appear fully awake). This is problematic, yet such symbolism was appropriate to a Pauline sleep / death analogy common to the period and one frequently apparent in Donne's own writings.[44] On the other hand, the closed eyes may be direct evidence of an introspective concentration appropriate to the model's wish to enact his own resurrection, or it might well be even a response to what Gardner was keen to stress: the discomfort that the sickening Donne would have endured in maintaining an upright pose in modelling for his statue.

It is also possible that the practical advantages of these new upright resurrection figures had a direct bearing on Donne's plans for his monument. In 1560 an Elizabethan edict had saved tombs from iconoclastic destruction, and the instincts that lay behind ecclesiastic decoration, whether pious or commemorative, were now increasingly transferred into such monuments.[45] Upright resurrection figures allowed for a creative use of narrower, vertical wall spaces as churches became overcrowded with monuments. Gardner argued that it was the Cathedral authorities who probably realized that Donne's memorial could be transformed into an upright statue for an awkward vertical space between the entrance to the south aisle of the choir and the southeast pier of the central tower of St. Paul's (the location is recorded in a plan included in Dugdale's *History of St Paul's Cathedral* of

1658).[46] The next tomb along the south aisle of the choir was the grandiose monument to the former dean John Colet (the appearance of which is preserved in an engraving of 1658, fig. 2.8). This lost tomb incorporated a recumbent *transi* below a scallopshell-shaped niche that framed a bust of the deceased. Colet died in 1519, but the tomb was of a later design and refurbished as late as 1618.[47] At least one other dean of St Paul's, Donne's predecessor, Valentine Carey, was memorialized in this part of the church, and a position alongside Colet also made sense given that the latter had been a sympathetic colleague of Donne's famous ancestor, Thomas More (More's sister, Elizabeth, was Donne's great, great-grandmother).[48] At the same time, however, it is important to remember that Donne himself probably wished to avoid a grandiose canopy tomb in the manner of Colet's monument. In his will, Donne expressed the wish to be buried modestly, and Walton reveals that Fox anonymously donated 100 marks for the completion of the statue.[49] It is certainly possible, therefore, that Donne himself conceived of an economical, yet memorable design that was perfect for its location, as well as an appropriately innovative iconography. In some ways, Donne's monument constitutes an economical conflation of the symbolism of Colet's tomb as both the earthly and heavenly fate of the body were now to be reflected in one figure. Judith Hurtig has argued that Colet's tomb itself demonstrates a shift of Protestant emphasis in its portrayal of its *transi*: this seems not to have been in the form of a rotting cadaver, but a smooth, pristine skeleton. It thus functioned more generally as a symbol of death rather than as an outmoded emblem of bodily putrefaction:

> Colet does not appear to have been concerned with the suffering of his soul in purgatory, for which the *transi* had been such a powerful physical symbol. Rather the combination of the inscription which includes the line, 'Die to the world that you might live for God,' and the bust scallop shell, an old symbol of immortality, underscores [a] change in emphasis.[50]

Notwithstanding his frequent referencing of the imagery of putrefaction in his writings, it is therefore natural that Donne should naturally wish to intercept and reshape *transi* iconography when it came to his own tomb. His writings express reservations as to how much of the harrowing reality of death art could impress upon the viewer. Perhaps he had his own painting of the 'skeleton' in mind, when he declared that,

> Painters have presented to us with some horrour the *sceleton* ... but the state of a body, in the dissolution of the grave, no pencil can present to us. Between that excrementall jelly that thy body is made of at first, and the jelly which thy body dissolves to at last, there is not so noysome, so putrid a thing in nature.⁵¹

This closely echoes Thomas More's earlier attitude to the similarly-themed *Danse Macabre* mural once installed in the cemetery of the Old St. Paul's:

> we were never so greatly moved by the beholding of the dance of death pictured in Paul's, as we shall feel ourself stirred and altered, by the feeling of that imagination in our hearts.⁵²

A passion for art did not in any way undermine Donne's subscription to what was a standard conceit of the period: the triumph of word over image. To some extent, Donne's sermons occasionally engage in a quasi ekphrastic rivalry with *transi* tomb imagery. He could not even resist the challenge when he preached the funeral sermon of his close friend Magdalene Herbert in June 1627; one can only speculate as to what comfort the mourners might have drawn from his observation that, though dead, the deceased was still 'out and about':

> [T]hat *body* upon which you tread now, That *body* which now, whilst I speake, is mouldring, and crumbling into lesse, and lesse dust, and so hath some *motion*, though no *life*.

But, as Neil Rhodes has observed, Donne dwelt on the morbid details of putrefaction only as a means of stressing the miraculous nature of the body's eventual recomposition. The sermon continues:

> That *body* at last shall have her last expectation satisfied, and dwell *bodily*, with that *Righteousness*, in these *new Heavens* and *new Earth*, for *ever* and *ever*, and *infinite* and *super-infinite evers*.⁵³

Was Donne's own monument therefore intended as a polemical counterpoint to the traditional expectations of *transi* imagery (naturally implied by the presence of the shroud)?⁵⁴ The statue was not to show 'John Donne, undone', but 'John Donne, undone, *redone*', that is, *remade* on the Day of Judgement, and newly emergent from the grave. The shroud and the funerary urn unite medieval and classical emblemata, but both operate beyond their roles as generic symbols of death. They supply a nuanced context to the upright figure, and the narrative of its resurrection. The urn is particularly appropriate here: a new feature of English tomb imagery, it references cremation and

Donne's emphasis on the particular disintegration of the body as a prelude to its stupendous reconstitution.⁵⁵ As for the shroud, whereas the loose winding sheets of *transi* effigies deliberately disengorge their desiccated contents, here the drapery of Donne's effigy shrink-wraps the body like a second skin. Only the head emerges from a vulvic aperture in this chysalids. This imagery seems appropriate given the following passage in Donne's last sermon which plays on the traditional motto of NASCENTES MORIMUR:

> in our mothers *wombe* wee are *dead so*, as that wee do *not know* wee *live* ... In the *wombe* wee have eyes *and see not, ears and heare not* ... the death of the wombe, is an entrance, a delivering over to another death, the manifold deathes of this world .... Wee have a *winding sheet* in our Mothers wombe, which growes with us from our conception, and wee come into the world, wound up in that *winding sheet,* for wee come to seek a grave...'⁵⁶

To some extent, the closed eyelids and muffled ears of Donne's statue further evoke a uterine emergence from a senseless state of pre-nascense. An intermingling of the imagery of infancy and death also reminds us that the funerary art of the period yielded one other influential template for Donne's statue – the upright funerary brasses which showed swaddled infants ready for burial (fig. 2.9). Poignant reflections of the high infant mortality rate of the period, their general similarity to the swaddled nature of Donne's upright statue is striking.⁵⁷

Mindful of the popular belief that the resurrected were reconstituted in an ideal form at the age of 33, one also notes that Stone's effigy deliberately departs from the ageing, emaciated likeness of the original sketch as reflected in Droeshout's engraving. Was this at Stone's inclination or Donne's instruction?⁵⁸ If we accept Walton's account, it is at least clear that an accurate likeness mattered greatly to Donne, as did his need to play an active, participatory role in its production. Here the notion of Donne's desire to 'imprint' himself comes into play, and it is tempting to connect his statue's posture, and the way the drapery closely adheres to the body, to the Turin shroud (fig. 2.10), which Donne discusses in a sermon of Easter 1630, and which he may even have encountered firsthand on a visit to Italy years before. He observed how the shroud had clung to the figure within, and imprinted the exact dimension of Christ's body with the 'glue' or 'gumme' of his blood.⁵⁹ The cryptic inscription that accompanied Droeshout's engraving as part of the frontispiece to *Deaths Duell* strengthens the significance of this famous relic to Donne. It reads: CORPORIS HAEC ANIMAE SIT

SYNDON, SYNDON JESU, AMEN'. Gardner argued that it was almost certainly composed by Donne himself, and may be translated as: 'May the shroud of the body be the shroud of the soul: the shroud of Jesus'.[60]

Finally, given Winny's earlier comments regarding the need to refashion himself in effigy, it is arguable that as Donne felt himself fading from existence, the notion of recreating himself in a more durable form – a marble statue – became irresistible. His wish to physically integrate himself into the processes of its creation by modelling in his shroud, was crucial to a desire to transfer something of himself into a surrogate. If nothing else, Donne's resurrection in effigy was a counterbalance to his bodily dissolution. This was an incremental process initiated by what resembles a primitive piece of performance art which involved modelling for a painter in his shroud. This resulted in the life-sized sketch – a simulacrum which Donne had propped up in front of his own bed till his death. As with the Turin Shroud, the sketch became a mirrored imprint that reassured him of his continued presence in the world just as he was passing out of it. And here one thinks of the 'out of body' experiences of those who have been brought back from the brink of death. Could this phenomenon symptomize consciousness's emergency response to the moment at which the threat of the annihilation of the ego is at its most acute and irrevocable? Then we come to the final stage in this process of imprinting, the statue itself, which still anticipates Donne's resurrection from the sepulchre. With a poetical irony that Donne would surely have appreciated, in 1666 the marble effigy was itself resurrected from the smouldering embers of fiery tribulation, and eventually installed in its present position as a powerful testament to the visuality of Donne's sense of self.

Bibliography

Bald, Robert Cecil, 'Historical Doubts Respecting Walton's *Life of Donne,*' *Essays in English Literature from the Renaissance to the Victorian Age,* eds. Millar MacLure and Frank William Watt (Toronto: University of Toronto Press, 1964), 69-84.

Bald, Robert Cecil, *John Donne – A Life* (Oxford: Oxford University Press: 1970).

Beaty, Nancy Lee, *The Craft of Dying – A Study in the Literary Tradition of the 'Ars Moriendi' in England* (New Haven and London: Yale University Press, 1970).

Bevan, Jonquil, '*Hebdomeda Mortium:* The Structure of Donne's Last Sermon,' *The Review of English Studies,* New Series, 45, no. 178 (May, 1994), 185-203.

Boase, Thomas Sherrer Ross, *Death in the Middle Ages: Mortality, Judgement and Remembrance* (New York: McGraw Hill, 1972).

Carey, John, *John Donne: Life, Mind and Art* (London: Faber and Faber, 1981).

Cohen, Kathleen, *Metamorphosis of a Death Symbol* (Berkeley / Los Angeles: University of California Press, 1973).

Cooper, Tarnya, *Searching for Shakespeare*, exh. cat. National Portrait Gallery, London, 2 March to 29 May 2006 (New Haven and London: Yale University Press, 2006).

Coster, Will, 'Tokens of Innocence: Infant Baptism, Death and Burial in Early Modern England,' in *The Place of the Dead – Death and Remembrance in Late Medieval and Early Modern Europe*, eds. Bruce Gordon and Peter Marshall (Cambridge: Cambridge University Press, 2000), 266-287.

Brejon de Lavergnée, Arnauld, *L'inventaire Le Brun de 1683 – La Collection des tableaux de Louis XIV* (Paris: Editions de la Réunion des Musées Nationaux, 1987).

Donne, John, *The Divine Poems*, ed. Helen Gardner (Oxford: Clarendon Press, 1952).

Donne, John, *Devotions Upon Emergent Occasions Together with Death's Duel* (Ann Arbor: University of Michigan Press, 1959).

Donne, John, *The Sermons of John Donne*, eds. Evelyn Simpson and George Reuben Potter (University of California Press, 1953-62).

Duffy, Eamon, *The Stripping of the Altars: Traditional Religion in England c. 1400-1580* (New Haven and London: Yale University Press, 1992).

Evelyn, John, *The Diary of John Evelyn*, ed. Esmund Samuel De Beer, II (Oxford, 1955).

Flynn, Dennis, *John Donne and the Ancient Catholic Nobility* (Bloomington: Indiana University Press, 1995).

Foxell, Nigel, *A Sermon in Stone: John Donne and His Monument in St Paul's Cathedral* (London: Menard Press, 1978).

Gardner, Helen, 'Dean Donne's Monument in St. Pauls,' in *Evidence in Literary Scholarship*, eds. R. Wellek and A. Ribeiro, (Oxford: Clarendon Press, 1979), 29-44.

Gosse, Edmund, *The Life and Letters of John Donne* (London: William Heineman, 1899).

Gittings, Clare, 'Venetia's Death and Kenlem's Mourning,' in *Death Passion and Politics – Van Dyck's Portraits of Venetia Stanley and George Digby*, exh. cat. Dulwich Picture Gallery, London, 1995 (London: Dulwich Picture Gallery, 1995).

Gittings, Clare and Peter Jupp, *Death in England – An Illustrated History* (Manchester: Manchester University Press) 1999.

Houlbrooke, Ralph, *Death, Religion, and the Family in England, 1480-1750* (Oxford: Oxford University Press, 1998).

Howarth, David, *Images of Rule – Art and Politics in the English Renaissance, 1485-1649* (London: Macmillan, 1997).

Hurley, Ann Hollinshead, *John Donne's Poetry and Early Modern Visual Culture* (Selinsgrove: Susquehanna University Press, 2005).

Hurtig, Judith W., 'Seventeenth-Century Shroud Tombs: Classical Revival and Anglican Context,' *Art Bulletin*, 64, no. 2 (June 1982), 217-228.

Hussey, Christopher, 'Burford, Shropshire,' *Country Life*, (December 26, 1947), 1310-1313.

Keynes, Geoffrey, *A Bibliography of Dr. John Donne*, 4th ed. (Oxford: Clarendon Press, 1973).

Keynes, Geoffrey, A Bibliography of Henry King D.D. Bishop of Chichester (London: Douglas Cleverdon, 1977).

Langdon, Helen, *Caravaggio – A Life* (London: Pimlico, 1998).

Irving Lavin, 'Bernini's Death,' *Art Bulletin*, 54, no.2 (June, 1972), 158-186.
Levy-Navarro, Elena, 'John Donne's Fear of Rumours in the *Devotions Upon Emergent Occasions* and the Death of John King,' *Notes and Queries* (December, 2000), 481 -3.
Llewellyn, Nigel, *Funeral Monuments in Post Reformation England* (Cambridge: Cambridge University Press, 2000).
Milgate, Wesley, 'Dr. Donne's Art Gallery,' *Notes and Queries*, 194 (July, 1949), 318-9.
Müller, Christian, 'A Drawing of Erasmus on his Deathbed Attributed to Hans Baldung Grien,' *The Burlington Magazine*, 132, no. 1044 (March, 1990), 187-194.
Novarr, David, *The Making of Walton's Lives* (Ithaca, New York: Cornell University Press, 1958).
Peterson, Richard Scot, 'New Evidence on Donne's Monument: I,' *John Donne Journal*, 20 (2001), 1-51.
Pevsner, Nikolaus, *The Buildings of England – South Devon* (London: Penguin Books, 1951).
Semler, Liam E., *The English Mannerist Poets and the Visual Arts* (Madison and London: Fairleigh Dickinson University Press, 1998).
Stone, Lawrence, *Sculpture in Britain: the Middle Ages* (London: Penguin Books, 1972).
Trapp, Joseph Burney, 'Colet, John (1467-1519),' in *Oxford Dictionary of National Biography* (Oxford: Oxford, University Press), Sept 2004; online edn., Jan 2008 [http://www.oxforddnb.com/view/article/5898], accessed 30 March 2010.
Walton, Izaak, 'The Life and Death of Dr. Donne,' in *LXXX Sermons Preached by that Learned and Reverend Divine John Donne* (London: 1640).
Walton, Izaak, *The Lives of Dr. John Donne, Sir Henry Wotton, Richard Hooker, George Herbert, and Dr. Robert Sanderson*, ed. T. Zouch (New York: A. S. Barnes and Co., 1854).
Wenley, Robert M.E., 'The Lothian Picture Collection: History and Context,' M. Litt thesis, University of St Andrews, 1990.
Whinney, Margaret, *Sculpture in Britain 1530-1830* (London: Penguin Books, 1971).
Wilson, K. J., 'More and Holbein: The Imagination of Death,' *Sixteenth Century Journal*, 7, no. 1 (April 1976), 51-8.
Winny, James, *A Preface to Donne* (London: Longman, 1970).

---

[1] I wish to gratefully acknowledge funding awarded by the *Irish Research Council for the Humanities and Social Sciences*, and express my sincere thanks to Peter McCulloch, Wolfgang Marx, Ciarán Woods, Richard S. Peterson, Simon Carter, Jason Ellis, David Gill, Teresa Heady, Lionel Marchant, Paula Murphy, Susan Owens, Martin Stancliffe, Robert Wenley and Jo Wisdom.

[2] For Stone's career see Margaret Whinney, *Sculpture in Britain 1530-1830* (London: Penguin Books, 1971), 24- 31.

[3] Nigel Foxell, *A Sermon in Stone: John Donne and His Monument in St Paul's Cathedral* (London: Menard Press, 1978); Helen Gardner, 'Dean Donne's Monument in St. Pauls,' in *Evidence in Literary Scholarship*, eds. R. Wellek and A. Ribeiro (Oxford: Clarendon Press, 1979), 29-44; Richard Scot Peterson, 'New Evidence on Donne's Monument: I,' *John Donne Journal*, 20

(2001), 1-51. The implications of the statue's accompanying epitaph have been discussed in particular by Foxell.

[4] The niche and decorative surround are a modern restoration. See Peterson, 'New Evidence,' 8 and 19-20.

[5] Reprinted in Izaak Walton, *The Lives of Dr. John Donne, Sir Henry Wotton, Richard Hooker, George Herbert, and Dr. Robert Sanderson*, ed. T. Zouch (New York: A. S. Barnes and Co.,1854), 110. The account does not appear in the first version of Walton's biography of Donne: Izaak Walton, 'The Life and Death of Dr. Donne,' in *LXXX Sermons Preached by that Learned and Reverend Divine John Donne* (London: 1640).

[6] Perhaps Martin Droeshout the Younger (1601- after 1639), but his actual identity remains a vexed issue. See Tarnya Cooper, *Searching for Shakespeare*, exh. cat. National Portrait Gallery, London, 2 March to 29 May 2006 (New Haven and London: Yale University Press), 48-50. See Gardner, 'Dean Donne's Monument,' 34 and Geoffrey Keynes, in *A Bibliography of Dr. John Donne*, 4th ed. (Oxford: Clarendon Press, 1973), 50-54. If King, future Bishop of Chichester, had retained ownership of the original sketch, it possibly perished when parliamentary forces sacked Chichester in 1643. See Geoffrey Keynes, *A Bibliography of Henry King D.D. Bishop of Chichester* (London: Douglas Cleverdon, 1977), xvi.

[7] See Gardner, 'Dean Donne's Monument,' 32, 35 -6, and 41-4.

[8] See Peterson, 'New Evidence', 11 and Foxell, *A Sermon*, 3.

[9] See Peterson, 'New Evidence,' 2-4, and Robert Cecil Bald, *John Donne – A Life* (Oxford: Oxford University Press: 1970), 533. In support of her thesis, Gardner ('Dean Donne's Monument', 40-1), noted that the figure is flat at the back below the head and shoulders, but she notes how an assistant keeper at the Victoria and Albert Museum, London stressed that the general positioning of the head and shoulders was far better suited to a vertical wall niche.

[10] See David Novarr, *The Making of Walton's Lives* (Ithaca, New York: Cornell University Press, 1958), 25-6. For another re-assessment, which also criticises Gardner's scepticism, see Jonquil Bevan, '*Hebdomeda Mortium:* The Structure of Donne's Last Sermon,' *The Review of English Studies*, New Series, 45, no. 178 (May, 1994), 185-203: 189.

[11] Quoted in Edmund Gosse, *The Life and Letters of John Donne* (London: William Heineman, 1899), I, 191.

[12] See Bald, *John Donne*, 450-1.

[13] Conscious of the rumours of the 1621 deathbed conversion to Catholicism of John King, Bishop of London (Henry's King's father, and the man who ordained Donne), Elena Levy Navarro argues that the *Devotions* were conceived as a means of preventing a similar slur on himself. Here one also recalls Donne's Catholic background; could the preparative activities that were finally attendant on his death in 1631 be understood in a similar context? See Elena Levy-Navarro, 'John Donne's Fear of Rumours in the *Devotions Upon Emergent Occasions* and the *Death of John King*,' *Notes and Queries* (December, 2000), 481 -3.

[14] Quoted in Gosse, *Life and Letters*, II, 268.

[15] Walton, *Lives*, 107-8.

[16] Gardner,'Dean Donne's Monument,' 30 -1.

[17] Walton, *Lives*, 109-110.

[18] *Ibid.*, 111.

[19] Bequeathed by Donne to Robert Kerr, Lord Ancram, perhaps as much on account of its tenebrist style as its subject matter. A precocious advocate of Rembrandt and Jan Lievens, Kerr imported their pictures into England by the time of Donne's death. See Robert M.E. Wenley, 'The Lothian Picture Collection: History and Context,' M. Litt thesis, University of St Andrews, 1990, 14 -24. On Donne's position as a connoisseur and collector see also Ann Hollinshead Hurley, *John Donne's Poetry and Early Modern Visual Culture* (Selinsgrove: Susquehanna University Press, 2005), 160-203, and Wesley Milgate, 'Dr. Donne's Art Gallery,' *Notes and Queries*, 194 (July, 1949), 318-9.

[20] See Novarr, *Walton's Lives*, 25-6.

[21] John Donne, *Devotions Upon Emergent Occasions Together with Death's Duel* (Ann Arbor: University of Michigan Press, 1959), 17-18.

[22] See Bald, *John Donne*, 130-7.

[23] Perhaps attributable to Donne himself – see Robert Cecil Bald, 'Historical Doubts Respecting Walton's *Life of Donne*,' in *Essays in English Literature from the Renaissance to the Victorian Age,* eds. Millar MacLure and Frank William Watt (Toronto: University of Toronto Press, 1964), 69-84: 76.

[24] James Winny, *A Preface to Donne* (London: Longman, *1970*), 46.

[25] Sermon of 19 November 1627 – see John Donne, *The Sermons of John Donne,* eds. Evelyn Simpson and George Reuben Potter (University of California Press, 1953-62), II, 98. See also John Carey, *John Donne: Life, Mind and Art* (London: Faber and Faber, 1981), 220.

[26] Donne, *Sermons*, X, 238.

[27] Walton, *Lives*, 110.

[28] On this subject see Ralph Houlbrooke, *Death, Religion, and the Family in England, 1480-1750* (Oxford: Oxford University Press, 1998), 57-59.

[29] See Nancy Lee Beaty, *The Craft of Dying – A Study in the Literary Tradition of the 'Ars Moriendi' in England* (New Haven and London: Yale University Press, 1970) and Eamon Duffy, *The Stripping of the Altars: Traditional Religion in England c. 1400-1580* (New Haven and London: Yale University Press, 1992), 313 – 7. The block books were the antecedents of more sophisticated English texts such as William Perkins's *A Salve for a Sicke Man* (dedicated to Donne's patroness the Countess of Bedford) of 1595 and Christopher Sutton's *Disce Mori* of 1600.

[30] See Helen Langdon, *Caravaggio – A Life* (London: Pimlico, 1998), 23, and Irving Lavin, 'Bernini's Death,' *Art Bulletin*, 54, no.2 (June, 1972), 158-186.

[31] See Clare Gittings, 'Venetia's Death and Kenlem's Mourning,' in *Death Passion and Politics – Van Dyck's Portraits of Venetia Stanley and George Digby*, exh. cat. Dulwich Picture Gallery, London, 1995 (London: Dulwich Picture Gallery, 1995), 54-68.

[32] See Christian Müller, 'A Drawing of Erasmus on his Deathbed Attributed to Hand Baldung Grien,' *The Burlington Magazine,* 132, no. 1044 (March, 1990), 187-194.

[33] On this see Duffy, *Stripping of the Altars*, 310.

[34] Walton, *Lives*, 113.

[35] See Bald, *John Donne*, 527-8.

[36] For Donne's will see Bald, *John Donne*, 523-5 and 563-7.

[37] See John Evelyn, *The Diary of John Evelyn*, ed. Esmund Samuel De Beer, II (Oxford, 1955), 114 and Arnauld Brejon de Lavergnée, *L'inventaire Le Brun*

38. *de 1683 – La Collection des tableaux de Louis XIV* (Paris: Editions de la Réunion des Musées Nationaux, 1987), 136-7.
38. See Liam E. Semler, *The English Mannerist Poets and the Visual Arts* (Madison and London: Fairleigh Dickinson University Press, 1998), 46-55.
39. On the *transi* tomb see Lawrence Stone, *Sculpture in Britain: the Middle Ages* (London: Penguin Books, 1972), 213-14.
40. See Bald, *John Donne*, 270.
41. See Christopher Hussey, 'Burford, Shropshire,' *Country Life*, (December 26, 1947), 1310-1313.
42. On this topic see Clare Gittings and Peter Jupp, *Death in England – An Illustrated History* (Manchester: Manchester University Press) 1999, 34.
43. Gardner, 'Dean Donne's Monument,' 37-40. One notes that Dutton was the brother in law of Donne's executor, Henry King. In 1653 an agent involved with a tomb for the Verney family was instructed to 'see Dr Dunns and other Tombes of Westminster or elsewhere before you speake with the Workmen'. See Nigel Llewellyn, *Funeral Monuments in Post Reformation England* (Cambridge: Cambridge University Press, 2000), 166-7 and 393, n. 74. On the Calmady monument see Nikolaus Pevsner, *The Buildings of England – South Devon* (London: Penguin Books, 1951), 274.
44. See Judith W. Hurtig, 'Seventeenth-Century Shroud Tombs: Classical Revival and Anglican Context,' *Art Bulletin*, 64, no. 2 (June 1982), 217-228. 222. However, Carey, *John Donne*, 198-201, argues that the idea of death as sleep held little attraction for Donne.
45. See Thomas Sherrer Ross Boase, *Death in the Middle Ages: Mortality, Judgement and Remembrance* (New York: McGraw Hill, 1972, 73.
46. See Gardner, 'Dean Donne's Monument,' 44. With recourse to Dugdale's plan, Peterson, 'New Evidence,' 25, affirmed that the statue would have faced south, along with its fellow wall tombs in that area of the church. However, thanks to ambiguities in Dugdale's labelling of the monuments, one cannot completely dismiss Bald's suggestion that if Donne's monument was squeezed into the pier itself it may well have faced east, as was appropriate to its iconography. See Bald, *John Donne*, 536. On this point, and the relevance of the inscription which accompanies the monument, see Foxell, *A Sermon*, pp.6-7. The inscription reads: JOHANNES DONNE SAC: THEOL: PROFESS: POST / VARIA STVDIA QUIBUS AB ANNIS TENERRIMIS / FIDELITER NEC INFELICITER INCVBIT INSTINCTV / ET IMPVLSV SPIR: SCTI MONI- / TV ET HORTATV / REGIS IACOBI ORDINES SACROS AMPLEXVS ANNO / SVO IESV 1614 ET SVÆ ÆTAT 42 DECANATV / HVIVS ECCLESae INDVTVS 27O NOVEMB: 1621 / EXVTVS MORTE VLTIMO DIE MARTII AO 1631. / HIC LICET IN OCCIDVO CINERE ASPICIT EVM / CVIVS NOMEN EST ORIENS. ['John Donne. Professor of Sacred Theology. After various studies to which from his early years he applied himself faithfully, and not unsuccessfully, by the power and inspiration of the holy spirit and on the advice and persuasion of King James he embraced holy orders in the year 1614 and in the 42nd year of his life. He was invested with the deanship of this church 27 November 1621. He was divested of it by death on the last day of March August 1631. He lies in fallen dust. He looks toward Him whose name is the Rising' – the translation is as in Peterson, 'New Evidence,' 21-22]. There were no hard and fast rules with regard to the orientation of similar resurrection monuments; many face east, or at least their figures are orientated in that direction and towards the altar,

but some of the most prominent examples, such as the Slingsby and Dutton monuments do not.

47 See Joseph Burney Trapp, 'Colet, John (1467-1519),' *Oxford Dictionary of National Biography* (Oxford: Oxford, University Press), Sept 2004; online edn., Jan 2008 [http://www.oxforddnb.com/view/article/5898], accessed 30 March 2010.

48 On Donne's antecedence see Dennis Flynn, *John Donne and the Ancient Catholic Nobility* (Bloomington: Indiana University Press 1995), particularly 20-35.

49 One notes Stone's account book records items of Donne's plate as part payment. See Gardner, 'Dean Donne's Monument,' 32 and Bald, *John Donne*, 533.

50 Hurtig, 'Seventeenth-Century Shroud,' 219-20.

51 From a sermon of Easter 1620 – see Donne, *Sermons*, III, 105.

52 Quoted in K. J. Wilson, 'More and Holbein: The Imagination of Death,' *Sixteenth Century Journal*, 7, no. 1 (April 1976), 51-8, 55.

53 Donne, *Sermons*, VIII, 92. For Rhodes's comments see John Donne, *Selected Prose*, ed. by Neil Rhodes (London: Penguin Books, 1987), 25.

54 With regard to a wider transformation of the *transi* into a symbol of anticipated bodily resurrection see Kathleen Cohen, *Metamorphosis of a Death Symbol* (Berkeley / Los Angeles: University of California Press, 1973), and also Hurtig, 'Seventeenth-Century Shroud,' 218-9.

55 Such an analysis is bolstered by the more emphatic resurrection iconography apparent in Stone's earlier funerary monument to the Duke of Buckingham in Portsmouth Cathedral of c.1628-30. The structure consists of a monumental urn out of which a phoenix rises amidst flames. The monument is capped by trumpet blowing angels of the apocalypse – see David Howarth, *Images of Rule – Art and Politics in the English Renaissance, 1485-1649* (London: Macmillan, 1997), 178-9. One also notes that in common with the funerary monuments of French royalty, Buckingham's heart was placed in the urn and this may have ramifications for the Donne monument. In 1723, Richard Gough visited the statue as it lay propped up in the crypt of St Paul's, and separated from its urn. Gough refers to 'Dr Donne's whole figure: the urn flat at top, and never open...'. This is curious and possibly suggests that the urn, which still bears the marks of fire damage, is actually hollow with some sort of stopper that allows it to bear the weight of the statue itself. Gough's comments are quoted in Peterson, 'New Evidence,' 12.

56 Donne, *Sermons*, X, 232.

57 See Will Coster, 'Tokens of Innocence: Infant Baptism, Death and Burial in Early Modern England,' in *The Place of the Dead – Death and Remembrance in Late Medieval and Early Modern Europe*, eds. Bruce Gordon and Peter Marshall (Cambridge: Cambridge University Press, 2000), 266-287.

58 But see Carey, *John Donne*, 225, for Donne's attitude to the transformed body, and also Houlbrooke, *Death, Religion*, 30-1.

59 See Donne, *Sermons*, IX, 197.

60 For Donne's possible visit to Turin see Bald, *John Donne*, 150. See also John Donne, *The Divine Poems*, ed. Helen Gardner (Oxford: Clarendon Press, 1952), 51 and Keynes, *A Bibliography...Donne*, 53.

Fig. 2.1) Nicholas Stone, *Monument to John Donne*, 1631 / 2, London, St Paul's Cathedral. Conway Library, The Courtauld Institute of Art, London.

Fig. 2.2) Nicholas Stone, *Monument to John Donne*, 1631 / 2 (detail), London, St Paul's Cathedral. Conway Library, The Courtauld Institute of Art, London.

Fig. 2.3) Martin Droeshout, *Portrait of John Donne in his Winding Sheet* (after a lost original of 1631), engraved frontispiece to John Donne, *Deaths Duell*, London, 1632).

Fig. 2.4) Comparative photomontage reconstruction of the pose adopted by Donne in his winding sheet using a live model.

Fig. 2.5) Anon, *Monument to Bishop John Wakeman* (d.1549), Tewkesbury Abbey (the arrangement is not original – the *transi* figure originally occupied the chamber below. The *gisant* effigy is lost).

Fig. 2.6) Anon, *The Tomb of Sir Richard Herbert*, 1600 (detail of *gisant* and *transi*), St Nicholas, Montgomery, Wales.

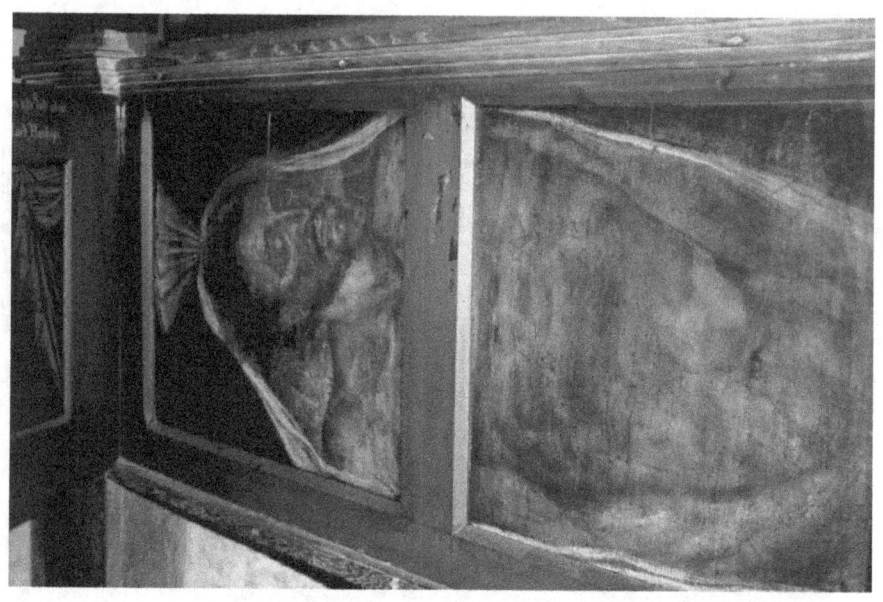

Fig. 2.7) Melchiorr Salaboss, *The Cornwall Triptych*, 1588 (detail of *transi*), St Mary's, Burford, Shropshire.

Fig. 2.8) Wenceslaus Holler, *Tomb of Dean John Colet*, engraving from William Dugdale, *The History of St Paul's Cathedral in London* (London, 1658).

Fig. 2.9) Anon., *Infant Funerary Brass of Elyn Bray*, 1516 (rubbing), St Mary's, Stoke d'Abernon, Surrey.

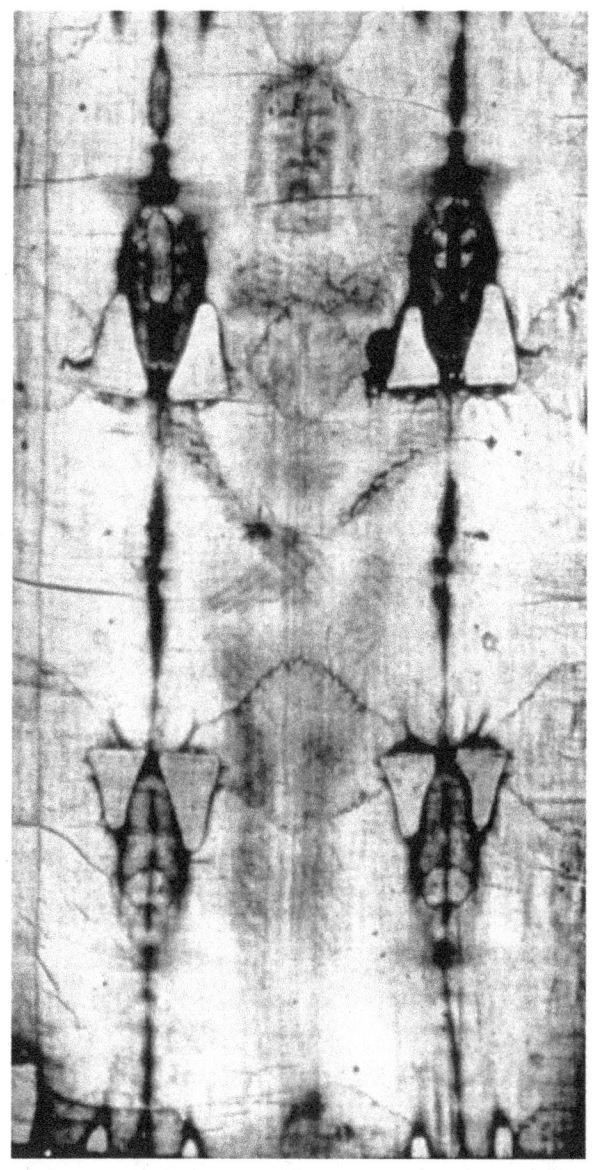

Fig. 2.10) *The Turin Shroud* (detail), Cathedral, Turin.
The Bridgeman Art Library / Getty Images.

3 | Stalin's Death and Afterlife

Judith Devlin

This chapter explores the place of death within the political and symbolic codes of Soviet power. Examining the ceremonies which marked the death of Stalin, it argues that the leader's demise was presented to the public in a manner that owed a significant debt to tradition. Stalin's expiry prompted a public performance of the myth of the benevolent leader, and of Soviet power, which in several respects rehearsed what Richard Wortman has called the 'scenarios of power' staged under the last Tsars. A theatrical representation of public grief and love, Stalin's funeral and post-mortem display in Lenin's mausoleum may have been played, as Weber suggests, primarily for the benefit of the ruling elite. However, it was a narrative in which the 'masses' not only acted out their part, but one in which they also seemed, to some extent, even to have believed. They also proved able on occasion to manipulate it for their own ends, in a manner that recalls popular appeals to the myth of the Tsar in the nineteenth century and earlier.[1] This suggests that the symbolic system exploited by the political powers in Russia changed less radically than might be expected, given the abrupt transition from Tsarist to Soviet rule.

The *Vozhd*'s Death

Stalin died on 5 March 1953 and was buried on 9 March. The circumstances of his death continue to cause controversy, not least because of the refusal to open the archives fully. He fell ill with a stroke on 1 March, and some historians continue to contend that, with his erstwhile secret police chief Beria's connivance, he may have been poisoned to prevent him moving against some of his colleagues in the

Politburo. In any event there was a delay of ten to twelve hours in summoning medical aid.[2] By universal agreement, the announcement of his death on 6 March caused consternation. His daughter, Svetlana Alliluyeva, recalled that many of his old colleagues (if not Beria), so long under his spell and at his side, wept but that they all 'realized that a deliverance of some kind was under way ... It was a release for me and for everyone else from a burden that had been weighing on the hearts and minds of us all.'[3] This relief had not yet spread to the wider public. The writer Ilya Ehrenburg recalled: 'I began to wonder: what will become of us now. But I could not think ... I was numb.'[4] Less sophisticated people were also at a loss. Natalya Dmitrievna Kukina, as a twelve year-old schoolgirl, recalls everyone in her school weeping, as did their old neighbour in their communal flat and her mother, although her father had been arrested before the war. The poet Yevgeny Yevtushenko explained:

> A sort of general paralysis came over the country. Trained to believe that Stalin was taking care of everyone, people were lost and bewildered without him. The whole of Russia wept. So did I. We wept sincerely with grief and perhaps also with fear for the future.[5]

The whole country plunged into official mourning. In schools, workplaces and factories, children and workers were assembled to be told the news; the press showed appropriate images of weeping and devout multitudes grouped around radios and loudspeakers in attitudes of reverent attention. For four days public mourning continued: public buildings and streets were decorated with symbols of grief. Commemorative meetings were held in institutions around the country: Yevtushenko remembered the poet and editor Alexander Tvardovsky sobbing as he read his poetry to similarly afflicted writers gathered to pay tribute to the dead leader; similarly, the film-maker Alexander Dovzhenko wept at the cinematographers' meeting.[6] The literary intelligentsia were kept busy producing entire numbers of journals, papers and magazines devoted exclusively to celebrating the life and achievements of the dead *vozhd'* (as the leader was called), illustrating the people's boundless grief and recapitulating the rites of the Stalin cult as they vowed to continue his work. Only in the camps was the news greeted with effusions of joy.[7]

These reactions may be explained in part by the prevalence of the Stalin myth. By the time of his death, Stalin was the object of an extravagant cult, which had reached its climax on his seventieth birthday, when the Academy of Sciences hailed him as the greatest genius of all times and as a scientist of outstanding significance. The chorus of adulation was joined by every institution in the country, down to Buryat-Mongolian primary schools and godforsaken collective farms, which sent their presents, pledges, expressions of eternal devotion and votes of gratitude for his fatherly love and care for them to the *vozhd'*. He was represented not only as an omniscient leader and epic hero but as an abstract figurehead. After the war, the real Stalin was rarely on view (and indeed he spent months resting in the south); absent in person, his idealized or implied presence was inescapable, with his image being reproduced everywhere, even in the most improbable locations, as the edition of *Ogonëk* produced for his birthday in 1949 illustrates. Stalin had ceased to be presented as a real man (after the war, *Pravda* preferred to reproduce paintings of him rather than publishing his photograph) and instead was presented as an almost superhuman figure. In fine art, he was depicted in regal settings, elevated above the admiring human horde at the top of staircases, in glittering gilded apartments under chandeliers, or benignly coming down to earth to greet the base multitudes. The cult rehearsed variations of the Stalinist fairy-tale in which – rather than the frog turning into a prince, or the miller's youngest son marrying the princess after undergoing a number of ordeals – heroes and heroines travel to the palace in the Kremlin to receive their rewards and join the governing class. Alexandrov's film *Bright Path* (1940) portrays a provincial record-breaking proletarian Cinderella whose dreams are fulfilled when she turns into a Soviet deputy and flies (magically!) to Moscow where, in the apotheosis, she is glimpsed mounting the staircase in the Kremlin (at whose summit, the viewer understands, she will meet Stalin).[8]

The analogy with the Tsar, who in the Winter Palace had his throne room at the top of the famous Jordan staircase, was surely not fortuitous, nor was the iconographic tradition whereby Stalin appeared bathed in a halo of light, like that which traditionally signified sanctity. Indeed, several of the cult's traditions (which were to recur in the public reaction to his death) recall elements of the mythology of the later Romanovs: loyal tributes and expressions of gratitude to the ruler; the idea of the Tsar as holy or as the little father. Stalin was not only the 'best friend' of little children but 'the beloved leader, father and friend' of adults too. Stalin had thus inherited, or attempted to claim, some of the charisma of the Tsars.

In many ways, the cult of Stalin – by dint of its emphasis on Stalin as an exceptional individual, creator and lynchpin of the regime – created problems for his successors. Monarchs might claim to be invested with divinely-sanctioned authority, while the dynastic principle solved the problem of succession and regime continuity. This obviously did not apply to the Soviet Union. Furthermore, Stalin's heirs were not only engaged in cut-throat competition to succeed him, they also did not want to continue what many of his younger colleagues felt to be outdated and counter-productive policies. Hence, while they did not want to perpetuate the myth, and the authority it conferred on his policies and manner of ruling, they could not afford to explode it either.

The situation was not without its analogies with Lenin's passing almost thirty years earlier. Lenin's death in January 1924 had come at a time of sharp infighting and policy debate within the Party's leadership and there were fears – present also in 1953 – about the regime's capacity to survive its founding father. The solution on that occasion had been to proclaim Lenin's immortality and, after an elaborate and carefully choreographed demonstration of national mourning at his funeral, to display his embalmed body on Red Square from July 1924. Lenin was turned into a secular saint, whose preserved body reflected his incorruptibility (the physical sign of sanctity in Orthodox tradition) and became the object of a ritual pilgrimage.[9] By 1940, sixteen million people were reported to have visited him in his Mausoleum, where he remained a symbol of the regime's integrity and legitimacy, a vital ingredient of its founding mythology.[10]

Funeral

It seemed initially that Stalin would be slotted into a similar position: safely interred, he could gradually be invested with whatever significance his heirs deemed appropriate. However, the leaders were inhibited both by the analogy with Lenin and the cult of Stalin. Stalin was too significant to be buried like any mere mortal. If the Lenin cult had provided the pretext and model for the Stalin cult, now Stalin – the 'Lenin of today', as Henri Barbusse had called him in 1935 – could not simply be consigned to the earth or be given less dignified treatment that that accorded to Lenin. The Stalin cult also made him a no less important figure in the regime's mythology, which it was not possible to shatter or reinvent overnight (even if anyone had felt secure enough to advance such an idea). Hence, the heirs had to organize suitably portentous obsequies. The funeral was thus to provide a staged and ritualized spectacle of public grief, which was intended both to reassure the populace and to reaffirm the regime's continuity, resilience and legitimacy. Given these functions, Stalin's obsequies could never have been other than a formal and conservative state ritual.

There was, by this time, a pattern to state funerals. Early Bolshevik funeral protocol, as Catherine Merridale has observed, aped pre-revolutionary upper middle-class ritual in all but its religious dimensions; the lying-in of the body, the honour guard, the vast wreaths and hierarchical corteges were typical of both. The priest's homily and religious service were replaced – in the Red funeral – by the singing of revolutionary hymns and stirring revolutionary declamations at the graveside.[11] Lenin's funeral, a more formal and carefully choreographed event than that of a mere revolutionary comrade, was to provide the model for Stalin's own funeral. We might identify its key features (emphasized in the documentary footage used by the film director Dziga Vertov in his *Three Songs of Lenin*) as those which would also be incorporated into Stalin's obsequies.[12] These included the lying-in-state (in the House of Columns in central Moscow, where Stalin was also laid out – fig. 3.1) while thousands of citizens came to pay their respects. Between his death on 21 January and funeral on 29 January, Lenin was visited by almost half a million people, while Stalin was also the object of a veritable pilgrimage. The central element was the funeral procession: in both instances, the coffin was carried by the heirs and colleagues in the Presidium (as the Politburo was then called), with the family behind them, high officials of Party and state and military men prominently represented in the cortege. The precedence of State over family, public persona over private individual, was thus unequivocally asserted in the protocol. Both funerals were accompanied by an artillery salute, factory sirens, five minutes' silence and (inevitably) funeral orations.[13]

Integral to the exercise too was the production of a vast literature (particularly voluminous and relentless in Lenin's case) praising the deceased, mourning meetings at schools and workplaces and commemorative gestures and rituals. As with Lenin, after Stalin's death, dozens of factories, farms and villages were named in his honour, while the Polish government proposed renaming Katowice as Stalinogrod.[14] Many of these features were characteristic not merely of the Party's public culture of death but also of Tsarist funeral ritual.

Stalin died at his dacha at Kuntsevo but, unlike Lenin, his body was not brought in ceremony to Moscow. It had to undergo the autopsy conventional for Tsars and *vozhdi* and preliminary embalming before being brought to the House of Columns on 6 March, where, amid heaps of flowers and wreaths, under dimmed and black-draped chandeliers and clad in its generalissimo's uniform, it lay in state for three days. An orchestra and the country's greatest musicians (including a hungry Sviatoslav Richter) provided an incessant musical accompaniment. Thousands of Muscovites and provincials poured into the centre of the city to pay their last respects, sobbing and weeping in an apparently spontaneous demonstration of grief. The throng was so intense and the crowd-control measures so inept (despite the presence of approximately 19,000 troops) that hundreds were crushed to death on the day before the funeral, although no hint of this appeared in the press coverage.[15] Despite this setback, the funeral itself went ahead as planned on 9 March, with delegations from the Soviet republics and provinces, from the Peoples' Democracies and the diplomatic corps, as well as 12,000 workers marshalled on Red Square to signify the world proletariat's prostration. By nine in the morning, these representatives of the whole nation and the world communist movement had gathered. At ten, the funeral procession began with the removal of the tributes, orders and medals Stalin had been awarded: these were so numerous, that it took half an hour to clear the way for the cortege. The coffin, on a gun-carriage, was preceded by the most important wreaths and followed by members of the Presidium, Central Committee, heads of fraternal parties and governments and finally by Stalin's surviving children. The order of precedence on Red Square retained this hierarchy, indicating that this was a state funeral whose significance was primarily political and in which the interests of the regime superseded those of the family. The funeral meeting on Red Square was relatively brief, lasting a little under an hour, with eulogies delivered by Malenkov, Beria and Molotov (indicating who was now in charge) and finishing just before midday. As the coffin was lowered into the mausoleum, an artillery salute from twenty-four guns was fired. Five minutes' silence was observed before the national anthem was intoned and the ceremonies concluded with a military parade and fly-past, signalling the might and recalling the victories of the Soviet state.[16] Stalin might be dead, but he had created a superpower whose ambition to endure was not to be underestimated.

The mourning ritual was staged not solely for the benefit of Moscow and the world press. Soviet papers and popular journals were filled with pictures of vast crowds of mourners and commemorative meetings were organized in all the major Soviet cities (with workers being ordered to attend). The funeral was accompanied by a carefully-prepared radio broadcast, designed to bring the proceedings to the whole country.[17] Just as Lenin's funeral had been filmed for a wider audience, so Stalin's obsequies were also the subject of a documentary film, *Farewell to the Leader*, supposedly a film of record, although edited to convey the official interpretation of events. Starting with a view of the hallowed Spassky Tower in the Kremlin, Red Square and the Mausoleum, it showed grieving Muscovites learning the news of Stalin's death. The crowds are then depicted paying their respects to the *vozhd'* in a Hall of Columns that, with its black draperies, dim light, heaps of flowers, palms and wreaths, has taken on the appearance of a baroque church. To the tragic tones of Tchaikovsky's Sixth Symphony, we finally glimpse Stalin in his coffin, guarded by Malenkov, Beria and, beside him, Stalin's children Vasily and Svetlana and then the other leaders. A representative selection of the imagined nation (the *narod*) is shown, united in grief despite their diversity: a simple working woman, a labourer, youthful communists, an old woman, children, delegates and dignitaries file past the bier, clasping handkerchiefs. Outside, we see more long queues of mourners (but no sign of the actual chaos). The common people are simply dressed; most are Russian or Slavic in appearance and here we may note a difference between this and footage of Lenin's funeral rites. Lenin was shown being mourned by a cross-section of Soviet citizens, including peasants in their sheepskin coats and exotic Orientals. In the interim, socialism was meant to have been achieved and the country to have become 'cultured': it was no longer appropriate to show too evident a poverty or a too backward peasantry. Equally, in the post-war Soviet Union, the Russians were elevated above other nationalities who, in the film, are shown participating in the funeral at a remove (listening to radio broadcasts).

Among the mourners are delegates from foreign communist parties and brother socialist countries, who have come to pay homage to Stalin, underlining their subordinate position of discipleship by carrying tributes of flowers and wreaths. They come, we are told, to express their grief (*skorb*) and fidelity to the friendship of the peoples. At this point, the film is unambiguously a demonstration of the power and reach of the Soviet Union, a point emphasized when an African and Indian are shown among the mourners. For three days and nights, according to the voiceover, this 'living river' of grief flowed through the hall. Thousands of wreaths are seen lining the route of the funeral procession, from the Hall to the adjacent Red Square, where enormous crowds of soldiers, delegates and workers hear the leaders deliver their eulogies. The 'whole country', we are told, is associated with these rites and collective farmers, workers and national minorities are shown listening attentively to loudspeakers relaying the radio broadcast. At the end of the mourning meeting, the leaders are shown carrying Stalin into the mausoleum. Midday strikes in the Kremlin tower, the turning point of the day: trains, all bearing Stalin's portrait, whistle, workers in factories, crowds in the streets all stand in silence.

Following the national anthem, the mood changes: the leaders atop the Mausoleum take the salute of the military parade to the sound of triumphant military music; flags flutter again atop their masts, order and life continue as workers swear an 'oath' to Stalin to continue to fulfil his will and carry out the Party's policies (in a clear imitation of Stalin's supposed 'oath' to Lenin, a hyperbolic ritual of the Stalin myth). Then, to the strains of Tchaikovsky, we see busy factories puffing productive smoke, the red banner of Lenin and Stalin flying.[18] The future, we understand, remains bright: the king has died but the state lives on. The film thus presented the funeral as a dramatic enactment of national mourning, might and recovery. From it were excised scenes which showed the poverty and indifference of dispirited people, scenes of slipshod or improvised ceremonial, where the workers looked bored or ragged.[19] Only attitudes which conveyed the desired interpretation were retained.

The most obvious omission from these stereotyped accounts of the last rites for Stalin was any allusion to the tragedy (mentioned above) which had occurred on the eve of the funeral. The authorities had put in place rigid crowd control measures, which had been approved at the highest level and which therefore precluded any improvisation or spontaneous amendment. When it was announced that public viewing of the body would close at two a.m. before the funeral, a stampede ensued. No-one had taken into account the huge numbers of people who had gathered in the squares and narrow street leading down to the House of Columns, where Stalin lay in state. The number of victims is still unknown but it was potentially a disaster for the new leadership. Dmitri Shepilov (later an enemy of Khrushchev, who headed the funeral commission) asserts that in Moscow people began to repeat 'Khodynka! Khodynka!', in reference to a similar tragedy which marred the coronation of Nicholas II in 1896 and which were seen as an evil omen.[20] Unlike the Tsars, however, the Party leaders were able to minimize the impact of the tragedy by ignoring it, emphasizing instead the pomp and ceremony of Stalin's funeral and the positive messages it conveyed: the greatness of the state, the unity of Party and people. In this, Stalin the man had been obscured: instead, he had come to symbolize the Russian and Soviet state and the great power it had become.

Obviously, Stalin's funeral was modelled on that of Lenin, but the similarities between it and Tsarist ceremonial are striking. Until Peter the Great, Tsars' funerals were modest affairs, primarily religious in emphasis and attended mainly by clergy, court and family. Only with Peter did they become part of an elaborate state ceremony, more secular than religious in significance. Borrowing from French and Swedish military and royal precedents, Peter introduced the lying-in-state, the tributes and decorations (wreaths and symbols), honour guards and elaborate processions, and the attendance – in visiting the body and following the funeral cortege – of representatives of the state (court, government, army, representatives of institutions, estates, provinces and cities of the empire). He also added the artillery salute and the public eulogy, largely secular in content, glorifying the Tsar's achievements and claiming that his spirit lived on in his reforms. Lest onlookers should fail to grasp the significance of what they saw, he was careful to introduce accompanying propaganda, describing and interpreting events.[21] If Peter's ceremonial was largely forgotten in the eighteenth century (too many murdered monarchs and coups) it was revived for the last three Tsars who died in the nineteenth century. On each occasion, the ritual was subtly adjusted to make new points about the nature of Russian state power and identity and, in a century of increasing literacy and political activism, accompanied by a large official literature of mourning and hagiography. A recurring theme was that of the ruler's supernatural virtue. Count S. S. Uvarov, Nicholas I's President of the Academy of Sciences and Minister of Education, borrowed from Peter I's eulogy to observe of Alexander I that 'it seemed that he was not subject to the general laws of Nature' – just as Zinoviev was to remark of Lenin. Alexander II was presented as (and to an extent became) a popular martyr, while the virtues of self-sacrificing devotion to, and ceaseless work on behalf of, the people were attributed to Nicholas I and Alexander III (as they were later to Stalin).[22]

The resemblances between Tsarist and Soviet ceremonial are most obvious in the case of Alexander III, who died in the Crimea in Livadia but was transported to Moscow to be displayed to a mourning nation in the Kremlin before his ceremonial funeral service and burial in Saint Petersburg. The press represented the whole people, young and old, rich and poor, humble labourers alongside imperial family paying their respects to the dead Tsar, in a simulacrum of universal devotion and grief in which the entire nation and state were present in the person of their symbolic representatives. This formula was to be copied in the rituals for both Lenin and Stalin. Verses by an officious poet, one Apollon Kolkhin, represented the *narod* grieving for Alexander as follows:

> They trudged from everywhere
> The children of national grief
> Like a solid wall, near the walls [of the Kremlin]
> They stood for whole days ...
> The Russian people poured
> Into the fortress like a powerful wave,
> There was rich and poor
> Equal before that giant,
> Who rested ... as if alive.[23]

The similarity between this and the images and commentary in *Farewell to the Vozhd'*, and even the metaphors employed in the script, are evident. Like Lenin and Stalin, Alexander is not only visited by the symbolic nation but he is also represented as being not entirely dead.

Nor do the similarities end there. Alexander III was embalmed (not wholly successfully) before going on display, although by the time the corpse reached St Petersburg it was beginning to decompose (a difficulty which was kept secret). Merridale argues that this was to emphasize the saintly status of the Tsar (the anointed one of God), whose body was thereby shown to be incorruptible, like an Orthodox saint.[24] It is ironic then that this process was applied also to the two self-conscious atheists who founded and formed the Soviet state, Lenin and Stalin. Even if their ceremonies excluded formal religious rites, the elements of veneration and ritual they included, and the language and metaphors of the commentary on Stalin's death and funeral, owed more to religious tradition and understanding of death than they did to Marxism.

The Bolsheviks adopted more of late Tsarist political culture and ritual than they would have cared to acknowledge. Indeed, the conceit of the Tsar's eternal life, invoked in relation to Alexander III, was consciously exploited by propagandists at the time of Lenin's death. Leonid Sosnovsky wrote: 'When Ilyich died, we still had Lenin.' It was in this context that Mayakovsky wrote his famous poem proclaiming Lenin's immortality and that slogans and posters began to proclaim that 'Lenin is always with us' and that 'Lenin lived, Lenin lives, Lenin will live.'[25] Stalin's immortality was also proclaimed in the flood of mourning propaganda that accompanied his death. The volume *Stalin in our Hearts* (1953) contains titles such as 'Eternally with Us', 'No, He

Did not Die' and 'The Immortality of the Leader', all rehearsing his immortality.[26] The officious scribbler Nikolai Gribachev consoled himself with the thought that:

> ... The great genius
> Did not expire -
> Stalin again
> From eternal immortality
> Will teach
> And direct us ...
> Stalin died –
> Stalin is eternally with us
> Stalin is life,
> And there is no end to life[27]

Thus for the Tsars and Soviets alike, the funeral became a symbolic ritual, in which State and nation were at one in paying tribute to a figure of exceptional virtue and virtual immortality, whose deeds would live on in his achievements and in his inspired people.

Stalin, like Lenin, lived on not merely as a rhetorical device but also as a physical presence at the heart of the Soviet state. Whereas the decision to embalm Lenin was taken almost two months after his death (it was hoped at first to preserve him by refrigeration), the Presidium resolved immediately after Stalin's death both on the usual autopsy and to embalm him, also commissioning the sculptor Manizer to take a death mask. Later the same day (on 6 March) they decided to place Stalin's embalmed body in a sarcophagus alongside Lenin in the mausoleum (fig. 3.2) and announced that a Pantheon should be built to the 'eternal glory of the great personages of the Soviet land', which they subsequently decided to erect south of Moscow State University.[28] According to a report to Khrushchev, the embalming process began the day after the funeral and was completed by 15 March.[29] Constructing the sarcophagus, however, was a staggeringly complicated operation. It could not be completed before July, not only because of the rare and valuable materials required but also because of its technical complexity, which necessitated the involvement of several ministries (including Finance, Transport, Machine-Building, Electric Industry, Defence) as well as a plethora of other actors and institutions, a research institute and a group of architects. This was no ordinary sarcophagus but a highly specialized quasi-refrigeration unit, given the need to keep the body in a rarefied atmosphere to prevent it from decaying.[30] In line with these instructions, Stalin was embalmed after the funeral and placed beside Lenin in a glass catafalque, looking smaller and more pock-marked than his official images had led people to believe (see fig. 3.1).³¹ As the medieval historian Kantorowicz observed, the ruler had more than one body: the physical one which died and the symbolic one, which represented the state and its divinely sanctioned authority.³²

Stalin's Afterlife

Stalin's afterlife was to be more problematic than Lenin's. The Party carefully monitored popular reaction to his death and funeral, reporting on meetings, resolutions and the observance of the rituals of public mourning and interpreting the mass conformity they observed as a sign of public devotion to the regime in the first instance and to the dead leader in the second. The leaders were reassured that local officials had the situation under control and the people were reacting in the 'right' way: all institutions and factories, public transport and cars were reported to have ground to a halt at noon on 9 March, while people bared their heads and stood, allegedly with tears in their eyes, for a minute's silence. Three long-distance trains stopped at Voskresensk (a town whose name coincidentally recalled the resurrection of Christ) and about a thousand passengers alighted to pay their respects to the dead leader. Crowds were cited as having listened attentively to the radio broadcast of the funeral. Efforts were made to choreograph the correct responses. The speech of the engineer Vinogradova at a mourning meeting at the enormous Hammer and Sickle factory in Moscow was relayed with complacency. 'Stalin died,' she declared, 'but eternal is his great enterprise (*delo*), it will live eternally' and she concluded by declaiming Gribachev's lines: 'Stalin died, but he is eternally with us, Stalin is life and there is no end to life.'³³ Such reports (in this instance by the Party boss of Moscow to his superiors) might gratify the authorities who received them but what do they tell us about people's actual feelings?

Even in retrospect, the editor of *Pravda* at the time, Dmitri Shepilov, was impressed by the public's apparent grief and stressed its authenticity. 'At memorial ceremonies, speakers poured out their grief – not because they were told to do so, but from the heart,' he opined.

> At *Pravda*, we received a torrent of telegrams, letters and articles about Stalin. They came from leading public figures, writers, scholars, workers and peasants, grown-ups and children, from all the republics of the Soviet Union and from abroad. My telephone rang incessantly; the callers all wanted their articles and tributes published without fail. What was this

– hypocrisy, humbug? No! With Stalin dead, there was no further need for pretense.

People were not to know that everything was about to change, but Shepilov took all the tributes at face value, citing, for example, Alexander Fadeev (the powerful Secretary of the Soviet Writers' Union), who hailed Stalin as 'the greatest humanitarian the world has ever known'. Many letters were, Shepilov believed,

> of an astonishing depth and sincerity. The words seemed soaked in drops of blood from hearts convulsed with unquenchable sorrow.

This bathos was not untypical of Stalinist writing for public consumption, where sentimentality, hypocrisy and self-deception were close bedfellows. Shepilov claimed that the public grieved for Stalin because he 'embodied' victory in the war and the growing prosperity (!) after it – triumphs in whose light the crimes of the Terror faded.[34] While one can readily accept that *Pravda*'s correspondence was enormous, its inspiration might more plausibly be ascribed to the public culture of the time than to personal grief. Members of the Stalinist elite, such as Fadeev, had long been trained in the right words and rituals: they knew what was expected of them and understood that it could imperil their position and even their safety to breach the established norms of conduct. The Party had made enormous efforts to instil these norms into the 'masses' too, through formal schooling, political and social instruction in youth organizations and the workplace, through publications and the mass media. Constant instruction in and exhortation about polite behaviour (*kul'turnost'*), right feeling, good taste and conduct was inextricably infused with political indoctrination and less exalted Soviet citizens imbibed these ideals or at least understood how to behave and speak in certain situations.

Many testimonies attest, however, to the ambiguity of the public reaction. The physicist Andrei Sakharov remembered that people 'worried about a general collapse, internecine strife, another wave of mass repressions.' He explained the confusion caused by the dictator's death:

> People roamed the streets, distraught and confused, with funeral music constantly sounding in the background. I too got carried away at the time. In a letter to Klava, obviously intended for her eyes only, I wrote: 'I am under the influence of a great man's death. I am thinking of his humanity.'

> ... I can't fully explain it – after all I knew quite enough about the horrible crimes that had been committed [...] to pass judgement on those responsible. But I hadn't put the whole picture together and in any case there was still a lot I didn't know. Somewhere in the back of my mind the idea existed, instilled by propaganda, that suffering is inevitable during great historic upheavals: 'when you chop wood the chips fly.' I was also affected by the general mourning ...35

Evgeniya Ginzburg recalled the hysterical weeping of the women victims of Stalinism in Kolyma but noted tartly that they

> were capable of switching at once to a more sober discussion of the implications of Stalin's death quite abruptly. They wept because they knew what was expected of them and were not going to be outdone by their neighbours.

Ginzburg herself collapsed in tears, but on account not of Stalin but of her own suffering and losses during her long years in the Gulag, and also from relief.36 The former Gulag inmate Janusz Bardach, who by 1953 was studying medicine in Moscow, was shocked by Stalin's death, noting 'how much I had come to believe in Stalin's immortality.' He shared the general anxiety and was careful not to reveal his true feelings. Of the grief on the streets, he observed:

> Certainly, a great deal of it was raw grief, even terror of being abandoned, but much of it was a mask that had to be put on because the occasion called for it ... no-one knew what would happen next or how his or her behaviour would later be interpreted by the Party and secret police.37

Soviet intellectuals remained more sceptical about the universal demonstrations of grief (at least in memory) attributing them to fear, confusion, and disorientation rather than sorrow and to the careful observance of prescribed conduct and social norms. Nonetheless, many testimonies of the period, including letters to the authorities, indicated that for many people, as for Ginzburg, Stalin's death marked the passing of a tumultuous era which had framed their personal lives, so that mourning the dead dictator was intertwined with their private understanding and memories of their individual destinies: to mourn Stalin was to grieve too for the passing and tribulations of their own lives.

Letters and wreaths continued to pour in to the Central Committee and Soviet authorities from all over the country: two hundred thousand messages of condolence were reportedly received.38 Tributes from key Party and state bodies were sent to the Central Committee for clearance. Even the Orthodox Patriarch's letter of 4 March expressing his condolences on Stalin's illness, urging his flock to pray for the dictator's recovery, was sent for approval by the Central Committee.[39] The superabundance of tributes was inevitable in a culture of the gift, of which patronage and tribute were essential components, and where omissions were as significant as commissions. Emulation was vital: one could not afford to be the only fiefdom, factory or institute which failed to express reverence and grief, for this signalled not so much a lack of proper feeling (though this was also an issue) as questionable loyalty to one's superiors, and ultimately to the regime and its official values.

The copious correspondence to the Central Committee and government expressed not only grief but also the hope of cashing in on the opportunities afforded by Stalin's death. Activists, devout Party and Komsomol members, writers and students, the naïve and the officious, all wrote in with suggestions about how to glorify Stalin's memory, displaying an impressive command of the obligatory language of the cult. Correspondents included not only military men, engineers and teachers, workers and villagers, but also an elderly widow who had lost five sons in the war, and even someone writing from the famous Matrosskaya Tishina prison in Moscow (who suggested renaming Red Square after Stalin). Proposals ranged from relatively modest initiatives (such as new and fuller editions of works about and by Stalin, and imprinting his profile on coins) to more ambitious ventures, including the inauguration of Stalin monuments and Stalin museums. The idea of a Stalin mausoleum found favour, as did the projected Pantheon, while several people proposed that Moscow should be renamed after Stalin; one M.D. Molotov even suggested that Georgia should henceforth be called the 'Stalinist Soviet Socialist Republic.'[40] Others were inspired to verse. N.V. Nikanovich, a Red Army schoolboy, wrote a poem about Stalin's portrait in his room, a recurrent theme in the literature of the Stalin cult: 'From the portrait/ Our beloved Leader and Teacher/ Quietly looks at me/ And it seems one can hear/ How he speaks/ 'Grow up and study/ As the Fatherland commands'/And with a paternal look/He consoles me.'[41] While this boy was as proficient as any star versifier in the officially approved style and sentiment, others struck a rather more personal note. One Leningrader, who wanted a statue to Stalin to be erected in Leningrad, explained:

> Thanks to Soviet power and the paternal care of our beloved and close father Comrade Stalin, I, the simple son of a worker, like thousands of others, received a higher education, which it

would not even have been possible to dream about under Tsarism.42

Like others in the category of Soviet citizens to whom Sheila Fitzpatrick drew attention – those who benefited from Stalinist modernization through educational and career opportunities hitherto closed to them – his attitude to Stalin was, if this letter is to be believed, quite positive.

Some suggestions were open to questionable interpretation, like that of the invalid from a village in the Stavropol area who suggested a fountain of tears in Moscow. Other ideas verged on (or tipped over into) the ludicrous: one A. Ya. Yelkin wanted a song about Stalin to be commissioned from writers and composers, which would then be broadcast daily at a fixed time, when the entire nation would be required to stand to attention. Less redolent of fanatical reverence (or rather suggestive of the desire for a holiday) was the proposal that the anniversaries of the death of both Lenin and Stalin be marked by public holidays.43 The Pantheon announced by the Presidium (an idea quickly and quietly quashed) elicited innumerable eccentric proposals, inspired presumably not only by devotion but by the expectation of rewards (monumental artists proved enthusiastic supporters of the Pantheon.) Someone suggested expanding Red Square to accommodate it, demolishing the walls of the Kremlin and other monuments to make way for it. Another proposal envisaged a vast baroque temple to Lenin and Stalin, surmounted by a chained globe (functioning as a cupola), a vase bearing the portraits of Lenin, Stalin and workers, the ensemble topped off by a star.44 Most eccentric of all, however, was the proposal by Petr Kravchuk from Odessa, who suggested keeping the memory of Lenin and Stalin alive by projecting the image of the leaders onto the walls of the Kremlin towers or the Pantheon every midnight, while the national anthem played.45

However, while ordinary Russians still entertained these illusions, a change of course was being sponsored from above. At the first Presidium meeting after the funeral, on 10 March, Malenkov affirmed that it was 'necessary to put an end to the politics of the cult of personality': P.N. Pospelov was given the responsibility for overseeing this process in the press and Khrushchev that of handling popular comments on Stalin's memory.46 The motive for this was the fear that any one character – especially the head of the secret police, Lavrenty Beria – would attempt to capture the totality of Stalin's power. In the interests of their own security, the new leadership counterposed the principle of collective leadership to the cult of personality. The first amnesties from the camps were introduced in the early summer. The innumerable references to Stalin in the press rapidly diminished and the first signs of the Thaw became apparent despite the divergences of policy and vicious infighting in the party leadership. When Beria was arrested and executed later in 1953, a propaganda campaign cast aspersions on aspects of the hitherto glorified Stalin era. These developments were not wholly popular and met with some resistance and disapproval. Not until Khrushchev's famous secret speech in February 1956 was this attack explicitly and dramatically extended to Stalin himself. The burden of this speech soon became known to the wider Party membership, provoking considerable confusion. How should history now be taught? What should be done with the dictator's images and monuments? After an initial period of iconoclasm in March 1956, the Party – to many *apparatchikis'* relief – began to back-pedal as the intelligentsia, in particular, began to demand the political reforms which were the logical corollary of Khrushchev's attack on Stalin's tyranny. By 1957, Khrushchev himself had called a halt to the initial phase of de-Stalinization which had by then served his purposes but threatened to destabilize the regime.

Stalin, it was frequently observed, remained a conspicuous presence in the public sphere, in offices, railways, squares and streets, and above all, in the mausoleum beside Lenin.[47] Not until the 22nd Party Congress in October 1961 was Stalin finally dislodged from his prominent place in public life. Khrushchev renewed his attack on Stalin as a means of defending himself and the new Party programme from his critics, including Molotov. The Congress, on the penultimate day, resolved that it was 'unsuitable' to preserve Stalin alongside Lenin, after an old Party member declared that she had consulted Ilyich who complained about Stalin's presence in the mausoleum. Stalin was quietly removed that night and buried under the Kremlin walls.[48] It was only then that his image and name disappeared from the streets and cities of the Soviet Union and that Stalin became invisible. If it is true, as Louis Marin observed of Louis XIV, that 'the king is truly king ... only in his images. They are his real presences', only when his images disappeared was Stalin ejected from public life. It did not matter that Stalin the *vozhd'* did not resemble Stalin the man, at least until the discrepancy was exposed by his heirs in their attempt to undermine his authority and claim the body politic for themselves. Stalin's absence from public view did not mean, however, his complete eclipse in Russian political culture. De-Stalinization was never fully completed, even under

Gorbachev. As a result, Stalin has returned to the scene under President Putin: a museum to Stalin opened in Dagestan in February 2006; Volgograd has debated reverting to Stalingrad, while his bronze effigy has, since the start of the millennium, commemorated the Commander-in-Chief of the Soviet Armed Forces at the Museum to the victory in World War II in Poklonnoe Gore, where he occupies pride of place of the right of the ceremonial entrance alongside Zhukov and Kutuzov.

What does the handling of and reaction to Stalin's death tell us about attitudes to death in the public culture of Soviet Russia in the 1950s? Stalin's death was significant above all for the way it was used in the political culture: in his obsequies, he was celebrated not as a man, or as a great revolutionary leader (despite the regime's revolutionary claims) but as a quasi-Tsar, as a symbol of the great Russian state, its endurance and power. After his death, however, another model of public funeral became available: the public (if not the state) funeral was reinterpreted by the intelligentsia in the ceremonies surrounding the death and burial of the poet Boris Pasternak in 1960. On this occasion, the ceremonies became a spontaneous and public demonstration of the intelligentsia's support for the condemned and hounded writer and an implicit criticism of the Party leaders (who indeed saw it as a challenge to their authority). This funeral reinvented a Russian tradition, inaugurated with the burial in 1837 of Pushkin, the great poet who had been seen as the victim of the intrigues of the court and of an oppressive autocracy. It marked the distance travelled since Stalin's death, which had also coincidentally been the day of Prokofiev's funeral, when no flowers were available for the composer, whose death – like that of so many millions of other private Soviet citizens – passed unnoticed.

Bibliography

Alexandrov, Grigory, *Bright Path* (Mosfilm, 1940).
Alliluyeva, Svetlana, *Twenty Letters to a Friend* (London: World Books, 1968).
Applebaum, Anne, *The Gulag: a History of the Soviet Camps* (London: Allen Lane, 2003).
Bardach, Janusz and Kathleen Gleeson, *Surviving Freedom: after the Gulag* (Berkeley: University of California Press, 2003).
Chuev, Felix, *Molotov Remembers*, ed. Albert Resis (Chicago: Ivan Dee, 1993).
Field, Daniel, *Rebels in the Name of the Tsar*, 2nd edn (London, Boston: Unwin Hyman, 1989).
Ginzburg, Eugenia, *Within the Whirlwind*, translated by Ian Boland (London: Collins and Harvill Press, 1979).
Jones, Polly, 'From Stalinism to Post-Stalinism: De-Mythologising Stalin, 1953-56,' in *Redefining Stalinism*, ed. Harold Shukman (London: Frank Cass, 2003), 130-41.

Kantorowicz, Ernst, *The King's Two Bodies. A Study in Medieval Political Theology* (Princeton NJ: Princeton University Press, 1957).
Knight, Amy, *Beria: Stalin's First Lieutenant* (Princeton: Princeton University Press, 1993).
Khrushchev Remembers, translated by Scott Talbott (London: Andre Deutsch, 1971).
Kuromiya, Hiroaki, *Freedom and Terror in the Donbass* (Cambridge: Cambridge University Press, 1998).
Maryamov, G., *Kremlevskii tsenzor: Stalin smotrit kino* (Moscow: Kinotsentr, 1992).
Merridale, Catherine, *Night of Stone: Death and Memory in Russia* (London: Granta, 2000).
Sakharov, Andrei, *Memoirs,* translated by Richard Lourie (London: Hutchinson, 1990).
Service, Robert, *Stalin: a Biography* (London: Macmillan, 2004).
Shepilov, Dmitri, *The Kremlin Scholar: a Memoir of Soviet Politics under Stalin and Khrushchev,* edited by Stephen V. Bittner, translated by Anthony Austin (New Haven, London: Yale University Press, 2007).
Tumarkin, Nina, *Lenin Lives! The Lenin Cult in the Soviet Russia* (Cambridge / Mass., London: Harvard University Press, 1997).
Volkogonov, Dmitri, *The Rise and Fall of the Soviet Empire*, edited and translated by Harold Shukman (London: Harper Collins, 1999).
Weber, Max, 'Economy and Society' (1925), in *Max Weber on Law in Economy and Society*, ed. Max Rheinstein (Cambridge, MA: Harvard University Press, 1969), 335-7.
Wortman, Richard, *Scenarios of Power: Myth and Ceremony in Russian Monarchy,* vol. I (Princeton NJ: Princeton University Press, 1995).
Wortman, Richard, *Scenarios of Power: Myth and Ceremony in Russian History,* vol. II (Princeton, NJ: Princeton University Press, 2000).
Yevtushenko, Yevgeny, *A Precocious Autobiography* (London: Collins and Harvill Press, 1963).
Zbarsky, Ilya and Samuel Hutchinson, *Lenin's Embalmers* (London: Harvill, 1997).
Zubkova, Yelena, *Russia after the War* (Armonk, New York: M.E. Sharpe Inc., 1998).

---

[1] Richard Wortman, *Scenarios of Power: Myth and Ceremony in Russian History,* vol. II (Princeton, NJ: Princeton University Press, 2000); Max Weber, 'Economy and Society' (1925), in *Max Weber on Law in Economy and Society*, ed. Max Rheinstein (Cambridge, MA: Harvard University Press, 1969), 335-7; Daniel Field, *Rebels in the Name of the Tsar* 2nd edn (London, Boston: Unwin Hyman, 1989), 1-26, 208-11.

[2] Svetlana Alliluyeva, *Twenty Letters to a Friend* (London: World Books, 1968), 13-14; *Khrushchev Remembers,* trans. Scott Talbott (London: Andre Deutsch,1971), 315-24; Felix Chuev, *Molotov Remembers,* ed. Albert Resis (Chicago: Ivan Dee, 1993), 236-7. Molotov was sceptical about the Beria thesis. Amy Knight, *Beria: Stalin's First Lieutenant* (Princeton: Princeton University Press, 1993), 176-8; Robert Service, *Stalin: a Biography* (London: Macmillan, 2004), 582-9; Dmitri Volkogonov, *The Rise and Fall of the Soviet Empire,* ed. and trans. Harold Shukman (London: Harper Collins, 1999), 171-9.

3 Alliluyeva, *Twenty Letters*, 17-19.
4 Yelena Zubkova, *Russia after the War* (Armonk, New York: M.E. Sharpe Inc., 1998), 151-2; Hiroaki Kuromiya, *Freedom and Terror in the Donbass* (Cambridge: Cambridge University Press, 1998), 324 for similar reactions there.
5 Yevgeny Yevtushenko, *A Precocious Autobiography* (London: Collins and Harvill Press, 1963), 89.
6 Yevtushenko, *Autobiography*, 89; G. Maryamov, *Kremlevskii tsenzor: Stalin smotrit kino* (Moscow: Kinotsentr, 1992), 50.
7 Anne Applebaum, *The Gulag: a History of the Soviet Camps* (London: Allen Lane, 2003), 429.
8 Grigory Alexandrov, *Bright Path* (Mosfilm, 1940). For an example of this style of painting, Yuri Kugach, *Glory to Great Stalin* (1950).
9 Nina Tumarkin, *Lenin Lives! The Lenin Cult in the Soviet Russia* (Cambridge Mass., London: Harvard University Press, 1997), especially 134-207.
10 Ilya Zbarsky and Samuel Hutchinson, *Lenin's Embalmers* (London: Harvill, 1997), 114.
11 Catherine Merridale, *Night of Stone: Death and Memory in Russia* (London: Granta, 2000), 106-108, 114-15.
12 *Three Songs of Lenin* (Mezhrabpomfilm, 1934) directed by Dziga Vertov: Vertov believed in the revolutionary potential of documentary footage and devoted the second part of this film to (edited) footage of Lenin's funeral shot in January 1924.
13 For a discussion of the funeral arrangements for Lenin, see Tumarkin, *Lenin Lives*, 135-42, 145-51, 160-4.
14 Rossiiskii gosudarstvennyi arkhiv sotsial'no-politicheskoi istorii (henceforth RGASPI): f.558: op.11: d.1487: ll.1-2.
15 RGASPI: f.558:op.11: d.1487: ll.45-54 for the security arrangements for the funeral. For an account of the tragedy by a highly placed observer, see Dmitri Shepilov, *The Kremlin Scholar: a Memoir of Soviet Politics under Stalin and Khrushchev*, ed. Stephen V. Bittner, trans. Anthony Austin (New Haven, London: Yale University Press, 2007), 18-19, 30-3. Reporting of the funeral was cleared by the Central Committee. Presidium member Pospelov cleared TASS reports on the crowds visiting the Hall of Columns on 6 March: *Rossiiskii gosudarstvennyi arkhiv noveishei istorii* (henceforth RGANI): f.5: op.30: d.41: ll. 40-3.
16 RGASPI: f.558: op.11; d.1487: ll.58-64 for the outline of the funeral arrangements (which ran to plan).
17 RGASPI: f.558: op.11: d.1487: ll.38-44 for the radio schedule.
18 Rossiiskii gosudarstvennyi arkhiv kinofotodokumentov, Krasnogorsk (henceforth RGAKFD): I-7132: *Proshchanie s vozhdem* (1953).
19 For documentary footage of this kind see, RGAKFD, Krasnogorsk: 0: 16060-25: Stalin's funeral.
20 Shepilov, *Kremlin Scholar*, 31; Yevtushenko, *Autobiography*, 89-92, for another first-hand account from a different perspective. For Yevtushenko, the episode changed his outlook on life and gradually on Stalin.
21 Richard Wortman, *Scenarios of Power: Myth and Ceremony in Russian Monarchy*, vol. I (Princeton NJ: Princeton University Press, 1995), 75-8.
22 Wortman, *Scenarios*, vol. I (1995), 271-3, 415; vol. II (2000), 198-200, 298-300. The famous poster by V. Gorokov *In the Kremlin, Comrade Stalin*

Takes Care of Us (1940) showed the leader in his study in the Kremlin, working by lamplight late at night on behalf of the labouring masses.

23 Wortman, *Scenarios*, vol. II, 270.
24 Merridale, *Night of Stone*, 35. She provides a detailed description of Alexander III's obsequies, 34-7.
25 Nina Tumarkin, *Lenin Lives*, 167-8.
26 *Stalin v sertse* (1953), 20-34. 'Vechno s nami' by one Kirsanov, 'Net, on ne umer' by a Spaniard, and 'Bessmertie vozhdya'.
27 'No velikii genii/ ne ugas -/ Stalin vnov'/izvechnogo bessmertiya/Uchit nas/ i napravlyaet nas [...]/Stalin umer -/Stalin vechno s nami/ Stalin zhizn',/ a zhizni net kontsa' in *Stalin v sertse*, 18-19.
28 Dmitri Volkogonov, *The Rise and Fall of the Soviet Empire*, 178; Shepilkov, *Kremlin Scholar*, 17; Ogonek.
29 RGANI: f.5: op.30: d.41: l.28.
30 RGANI: f.5: op.30: d.41: ll.36-9: Khrushchev memorandum to Malenkov, 27 March 1953.
31 Ilya Zbarsky, *Lenin's Embalmers* (1997), 165-7. The art historian Marina Chegodaeva recalled being brought along to visit the embalmed leader as a young woman and being struck by his unimposing figure in death.
32 Ernst Kantorowicz, *The King's Two Bodies. A Study in Medieval Political Theology* (Princeton NJ: Princeton University Press, 1957).
33 RGASPI: f.558: op.11: d.1487: ll. 78-80, 83-5, 87-8.
34 Shepilov, *Kremlin Scholar*, 19-21.
35 Andrei Sakharov, *Memoirs*, trans. Richard Lourie (London: Hutchinson, 1990), 163-4.
36 Eugenia Ginzburg, *Within the Whirlwind*, trans. Ian Boland (London: Collins and Harvill Press, 1979), 356-7.
37 Janusz Bardach and Kathleen Gleeson, *Surviving Freedom: after the Gulag* (Berkeley: University of California Press, 2003), 240-1.
38 RGASPI: f.82: op.2: d.984: l.105.
39 RGANI: f.5: op.30: d.41: ll.5-11.
40 RGANI: d.5: op.16: d.593a:ll.1-13, 18; f.5: op.30: d.41: ll.48-9.
41 RGANI: d.5: op.16: d.593a:ll.a:l.253.
42 RGANI: d.5: op.16: d.593b: ll. 35-6.
43 RGANI: f.5: op.16: d.593a: ll. 1-10; f.5: op.30: d.41: ll.45-50, 69-70.
44 RGANI: f.5: op.16: d.593a: ll.25-37, 155-9. Zubkova, *Russia after the War*, 153.
45 RGANI: f.5: op.16: d.593a: ll.193-1950b.
46 Zubkova, Russia after the War, 178.
47 Polly Jones, 'From Stalinism to Post-Stalinism: De-Mythologising Stalin, 1953-56,' in *Redefining Stalinism*, ed. Harold Shukman (London: Frank Cass, 2003), 130-41.
48 William Taubman, *Khrushchev: the Man and his Era* (London: Free Press, 2004), 514-5.

Fig. 3.1) Joseph Stalin lying in state in the hall of Trade Union House, Moscow, 12th March 1953. Hulton Archive / Getty Images.

Fig. 3.2) The Bodies of Lenin and Stalin in the Kremlin Mausoleum.

4 | The Mutilation and Non-Burial of the Dead in Homer's *Iliad*[1]

Bridget Martin

Homer's *Iliad* recounts the ten-year, mythical war which was fought between the Greeks and Trojans following Trojan Paris's abduction of the beautiful Helen. During the ten years of fighting hundreds of warriors die on the Trojan plain. The lucky among these are taken from the battlefield and given burial rites. In Homer these rites are referred to as the *geras thanonton* (*Il.* 16.457; 16.675), the honour or privilege of the dead. Various actions are described as a *geras* for the dead, ranging from the simplistic closing of the eyes (*Od.* 24.292-296), the cutting of hair and weeping (*Od.* 4.197-198) to the practical washing and laying-out of the corpse (*Od.* 24.188-190) and finally to the mourning of the dead (*Il.* 23.6-9) and the burial and the erection of a tomb (*Il.* 16.456-457; 16.674-675).[2] Such is the importance of these rites that both sides readily agree to a ceasefire in *Iliad* 7 so that the dead may be collected for burial. As Agamemnon, the leader of the Greeks, states: 'There can be no grudging the bodies of the dead their swift appeasement by the fire, once they have died' (*Il.* 7.409-410). Unfortunately, Agamemnon's axiom is not a guiding principle in the *Iliad* as the dead, more specifically the common – as opposed to the heroic – dead, are often left unburied and mutilated, either as a direct consequence of non-burial or as a separate act of aggression performed by their victorious opponents.[3] This is a fate which the Homeric warriors fear far more than death and it is the aim of this chapter to determine the reasons for this fear. It will be argued that non-burial, and the consequential post-mortem mutilation by wild animals, jeopardizes the status and honour of the deceased among his living peers and also denies him full integration into the society of the Underworld. Owing to this lack of integration the deceased must remain in a state of social liminality in the Underworld, which mirrors his dishonour and reduced status in the world of the living. The denial of burial, therefore, divests the warrior of his honour and status in the world of the living and, for eternity, in the world of the dead.

Methods of Mutilation and Non-Burial

The mutilation and non-burial of the dead occur in three interconnected manners in the *Iliad*.[4] Firstly, the corpse of the fallen warrior is mutilated by his opponent as a consequence of the violence of warfare. Peneleos, Agamemnon and Ajax all decapitate the corpse of their fallen enemy on the battlefield (*Il.* 14.496-500; 11.261; 13.202-205) while Hippolochus extends the mutilation even further and not only beheads Peisandros but also cuts off his arms and sends his torso rolling through his comrades (*Il.* 11.145-147). While these actions could be attributed to the faceless violence of warfare, there is also a sense that they have their genesis in personal enmity. Ajax, for example, beheads Imbrios in anger at the death of Amphimachos (*Il.* 13.203) while Achilles repeatedly attempts to mutilate Hector's corpse in recompense for Patroclus's death (for example: *Il.* 22.395-404; 23.21; 24.14-18). Secondly, the mutilation of the dead occurs under the same conditions as the previous example but includes the removal of the warrior's armour. The removal of armour is a common feature on the Homeric battlefield (for example: *Il.* 4.465-466; 6.70-71; 7.146; 10.387), but it is not coupled with the act of mutilation until *Iliad* 16. As the battle rages for the possession of Sarpedon's corpse, Glaucus appeals to Hector and the Trojans not to allow it to be stripped of its armour and mutilated (*Il.* 16.545-546) while Patroclus desperately tries to perform just such an act (*Il.* 16.559-560). The combination of mutilation and the stripping of armour is found increasingly often in later books: Hector desires to perform such an action on Patroclus (*Il.* 17.125-127) but he is the one who ends up suffering such a fate at the hands of Achilles and the Greeks (*Il.* 22.367-371).

Thirdly, and most frequently, the corpse is mutilated by wild birds and animals as a direct result of non-burial. This does not mean, however, that the act of desecration is entirely divorced from the warriors; as Vermeule states: '[The dogs and birds] are spiritual extensions of the warrior making the taunt, a hunting image, in the realm of traditional rhetoric and exaggerated mockery'.[5] For example, Achilles's anger at Hector reaches such a point he wishes it would drive him to perform the ultimate mutilation and cannibalize Hector's corpse (*Il.* 22.346-347).[6] As this is not possible, Achilles 'dismembers and consumes [Hector] through the mediation of dogs and birds' or at least attempts to do so.[7] The act of non-burial therefore provides a means through which a warrior may desecrate his enemy to an extent beyond his own capabilities. Consequently, and not surprisingly, non-burial is met with fear and disgust in the *Iliad*.

The Use of Non-Burial as a Threat

Owing to this fear, the threat of non-burial is a commonly employed intimidation tactic on the battlefield. As they prepare to engage each other in combat, Hector warns Ajax that he will leave his corpse for the birds and animals to feast upon (*Il.* 13.829-832), while Diomedes prophesies that birds, and not women, will flock around Paris when he has fallen in battle (*Il.* 11.394-395).[8] These taunts are a characteristic aspect of psychological warfare and form part of what Emily Vermeule labels 'battle mockery', whereby the warrior employs 'formal taunting mockery' to lower the self-esteem of his opponent. Vermeule states of 'battle mockery':

> The man's physical weakness should be exposed to public laughter; he should be humiliated in front of his fighting comrades, his ancestry must be doubted (although not to the same degree of pungency as is common with us); and, most of all, the future of his body and the quality of his mind should be pictorialized in a manner certain to distress him. At least it might make his hand shake.[9]

Although the threat of non-burial and mutilation forms part of this regulated and stylized mockery, the prominence of the act within the epic sets it apart from the other aspects of 'battle mockery' and suggests that it has an importance above and beyond that of an inevitable and accepted consequence of war. The very opening lines of the *Iliad* establish the close connection between the death of a warrior and the possibility of his non-burial and post-mortem mutilation:

> Sing, goddess, of the anger of Achilles, son of Peleus, the accursed anger which brought uncounted anguish on the Achaeans and hurled down to Hades many mighty souls of heroes, making their bodies the prey to dogs and the birds' feasting: and this was the working of Zeus' will. (*Il.* 1.1-5)

This connection is most poignantly drawn by Priam, the King of Troy, who visualizes the future destruction of his city through the image of his own dogs feasting upon his flesh (*Il.* 22.66-71). Such is the horror associated with this end that a certain sense of sympathy can be discerned behind the harsh words of enemies. Take, for example, the taunts spoken by Odysseus above the fallen Trojan warrior, Sokos:

> Poor wretch, you will not have your father and honoured mother to close your eyes in death – no, carrion birds will fold their wings thick over you and tear your flesh. But I, if I die, will have full burial from the godlike Achaians (*Il.* 11.452-455).

In highlighting the contrast between their two fates, Odysseus follows a pattern which is later used by Achilles when he contrasts Hector's future non-burial with the funeral of Patroclus: 'Now the dogs and birds will maul you hideously, while the Achaians will give Patroclus full burial' (*Il.* 22.335-336). The contrast between the two fates points to an underlying truth concerning burial in the *Iliad*: burial is not the 'common share of the dead but the privilege of the victor'.[10] Yet, despite Odysseus's status as the victor and his boasts concerning his own future burial, it is possible to detect a certain amount of regret in Odysseus's words at the fate of his enemy, whom he identifies as a 'poor wretch'. It seems that the aversion to non-burial is strong enough to transcend the divide between enemies.

The Occurrence of Non-Burial?

The active presence of the threat and the fear of non-burial in the *Iliad* are easy to establish, although even a quick scan of the epic reveals that actual occurrences of the same are rare. Redfield states that:

> [N]o one is ever fed to the dogs in the *Iliad*. It is as if the poet, having established through general expressions and threats the limiting case of impurity, draws back from that limit.[11]

To a certain extent Redfield is correct; Homer does not describe any corpse being eaten by the wild animals. Prominent warriors such as Sarpedon and Patroclus are saved from this fate by the actions of their comrades who fight in defence of their respective corpses (*Il.* 16.563-683; 17.1-761). This is also sometimes the case with more common warriors: the Thracians defend the corpse of their companion, Peiros from the attack of an enemy (*Il.* 4.532-535) while Ajax is prevented from stripping the armour from the corpse of Amphios by a hail of Trojan arrows (*Il.* 5.617-626). Even the most prominent case of non-burial, Achilles's treatment of Hector's corpse throughout Books 22 and 23 whereby he drags him behind his chariot and tosses him in the dust for the dogs to feast upon (*Il.* 22.395-404; 24.14-21), is quickly resolved. The gods Apollo and Aphrodite prevent Achilles's actions from marring Hector's beauty (*Il.* 23.184-191), and the *Iliad* concludes with the hero's elaborate and over-due burial (*Il.* 24.782-804).[12] These examples provide compelling proof for Redfield's declaration that 'no one is ever fed to the dogs in the *Iliad*' but, while it is true that Homer does not dwell upon such instances, not every warrior can be carried from the battlefield and given burial.

Despite the fact that Homer offers an extensive list of bloody and innovative ways to die in his epics (for example: *Il.* 5.290-296; 13.616-617; 16.740-742; 16.345-350), he can be oddly squeamish about, and thus avoid, certain issues. The production of four children from the incestuous union of Oedipus and his mother, Epicaste is, for example, studiously ignored in the *Odyssey* (*Od.* 11.271-274) and the same may be said for the inexorable destruction of exposed corpses by scavenging animals. The very prevalence of the threat of non-burial highlights its inevitable occurrence as it would lose all power if the logical outcome of the threat was not to be seen scattered about the battlefield. Also, certain hints that this is occurring do find their way through Homer's reticence. Take for example the fate of Asteropaios, who dies at the hands of Achilles in the River Scamander: 'And the eels and fish were his busy attendants, tearing and nibbling at the fat around his kidneys' (*Il.* 21.203-204). While the act is being performed by fish instead of wild animals, the result is still the same. In *Iliad* 10 a meeting is called by the Greek leaders and they chose to sit in a clear space 'where room could be seen free of fallen corpses' (*Il.* 10.199). Garland concludes that these are the corpses of common warriors who are left to rot on the battlefield, he states that '[i]t is almost as if ordinary soldiers do not qualify as proper dead'.[13] Based upon this evidence, it can be taken as a reasonable certainty that non-burial was a regular occurrence and, as such, a legitimate fear for the Homeric warriors. It therefore remains to determine the basis of this fear.

The Fear of Non-Burial

On a fundamental level, the revulsion associated with non-burial is an understandable reaction; an exposed corpse is a source of horror and, more importantly, of contagion. Yet, there is no indication that the corpse is viewed in such a manner in the *Iliad*. The presence of a corpse, or even the touching of one, does not produce anxiety or apprehension. Hector's corpse is described as being 'dewy fresh' (*Il.*

24.757; 24.419) and both Patroclus and Hector are touched, without horror, by the mourners at their respective funerals (*Il.* 23.135-137; 24.710-712). Additionally, the strong connection between the unburied corpse and the spread of contagion or pollution is either not a concern or is largely suppressed in the *Iliad*. It could even be argued that non-burial offers a means of *preventing* the pollution associated with an exposed corpse.[14] Vermeule posits that there are three means of negating the pollution of a corpse, namely 'scavenging, burial and fire'.[15] As the wild animals consume the corpse in a similar manner to fire it may be argued that they play a role in preventing pollution. The close connection between fire and scavenging can be seen when Achilles states: 'But for Hector's devouring, the son of Priam, I shall not give him to the fire, but to the dogs' (*Il.* 23.182-183). As the animals work in some measure to prevent pollution the contagion of a corpse cannot explain the fear of non-burial. Rather, the fear of non-burial is intensely personal and reflexive; the warrior is concerned for the fate of his own corpse and the impact which his own non-burial will have upon himself, not that he will chance upon the corpse of another and suffer as a consequence of this.[16] Owing to this intense personal fear, it is logical to assume that non-burial has an adverse effect upon a central tenet of a warrior's psyche and there is nothing more important to a warrior's sense of self than his honour (*timē*) and his status among his peers.

The Loss of Honour (*Timē*)

Honour is not an unalterable aspect of a Homeric warrior's character; rather it is something which can be both given and taken away. Consequently, the Homeric warrior is constantly aware of the possibility that he may be deprived of his honour. As Adkins states, the

> Homeric hero not merely feels insecure, he is insecure. To be deprived of *timē*, even in the slightest degree, is to move so much nearer to penury and nothingness...[17]

Perhaps the most obvious example of the removal of honour occurs in *Iliad* 1 when Agamemnon claims Achilles's war-prize Briseïs to compensate for the loss of his own prize, Chryseïs. In taking Briseïs, Agamemnon also takes honour from Achilles and as a result Achilles withdraws from the fighting and allows near-destruction to fall upon his comrades. During this exchange Agamemnon refers to Chryseïs as his *geras* (*Il.* 1.120), his 'prize of honour' which, by extension, suggests that Briseïs is Achilles's *geras* and the loss of the same results in the loss of his honour. As mentioned earlier, burial rites are referred to as the *geras thanonton*, which suggests that they are inextricably linked with the honour of the warrior. Redfield explains this connection as follows:

> The funeral is the *geras* of the dead; *geras* is the name of those marks of honour which a man is entitled to claim in virtue of his status or social role. In one sense the *geras* marks the status; in another sense it confers status, so that the loss of *geras* (as in the case of Chryseis or Briseis) threatens a loss of status. The funeral may thus be thought of as a ceremony by which a definite social status is conferred upon the dead.[18]

As burial rites are considered to be a *geras* for the deceased, the lack of those burial rites must logically result in dishonour. This dishonour manifests itself in two specific but interconnected manners: Firstly, the physical desecration of the warrior's corpse jeopardizes the continuance of his status among his peers as the corporeal symbol of that status has been removed. Secondly, the absence of burial rites means that the deceased's passage from the world of the living to the world of the dead is incomplete and, consequently, he cannot become fully integrated into the world of the dead. This results in the social liminality of the deceased whereby he is either denied access to the society of the dead or he cannot replicate his former social position within the social hierarchy of the Underworld. The adverse effects of non-burial in the world of the living will be considered firstly before moving on to the world of the dead.

The Loss of Honour and Status in the World of the Living

Physical beauty is a defining characteristic of a Homeric hero. This is not the 'feminine' physical beauty which Diomedes ridicules in Paris (*Il.* 11.385) but rather the pronounced presence of strength and physicality which acts as a visible indicator of a warrior's heroism, status and, by extension, his honour. Achilles, the foremost hero in the *Iliad*, is described as the most handsome of all the Greeks (*Il.* 2.672-674) while Thersites, who wishes to abandon the war and head for home, is described as the ugliest of the Greeks (*Il.* 2.216-219). Death did not spell the end for a warrior's beauty, rather it could be maintained if timely and correct burial rites were performed. Jean-Pierre Vernant suggests that a Homeric warrior may achieve a *kalos thanatos*, or 'beautiful death' by dying gloriously in battle 'in the fullness of their masculine nature', and the beauty of the corpse acts as a symbol of this *kalos thanatos*.[19] The Greeks, for example, are described as admiring 'the size and wonderful looks' of Hector's corpse (*Il.* 22.370-371), and the fact that Aphrodite and Apollo do not allow Hector's corpse to bear the marks of his mistreatment (*Il.* 23.184-191) is a testament to the necessity of maintaining the warrior's beauty in death. This necessity is further evidenced in Achilles's concern that Patroclus's corpse will be marred by the natural process of decay before he can be given burial (*Il.* 19.23-33).

If the preservation of a warrior's beauty symbolizes his *kalos thanatos* and, by extension, the preservation of his honour and status, it is logical to assume that the destruction of a warrior's beauty functions as a symbol of the warrior's *kakos thanatos*, or 'terrible death', and the reduction in his honour and status.[20] This reduction is exacerbated by two further actions. The first of these is the removal of the warrior's armour prior to his non-burial, which both visually and symbolically strips him of his status. This can be seen in the example of Hector whereby Achilles strips him of his armour before the Greeks desecrate his corpse and before Achilles tosses it in the dirt, unburied (*Il.* 22.370-371).[21] The second and, arguably, more far-reaching act is the denial of a tomb, the erection of which would form the logical conclusion of burial rites. The erection of a tomb acts as a physical stimulant to memory and thus promotes the continued presence of the warrior within societal memory.[22] Vernant suggests that the erection of a tomb is one of the two necessities for the warrior's exploits to remain in societal memory, the other being memorialized in epic song.[23] While only the foremost warriors may hope for the latter, even the most humble warrior can achieve a measure of immortality through the erection of a tomb in his honour. Therefore, the desecration of the warrior's corpse, combined with the removal of his armour and the absence of a tomb, results in the loss of his honour and status among his living peers and jeopardizes the continuance of his presence within societal memory. It remains to be seen if this dishonour and lack of status is also transferred to the world of the dead.[24]

The Loss of Honour and Status in the World of the Dead

In his seminal work on societal rites of passage, Arnold van Gennep theorizes that a man's life is made up of a series of stages, such as birth, marriage, fatherhood and death, and that the transition from one stage to another is subject to certain ceremonies, identified as rites of passage.[25] These rites can be divided into rites of separation (preliminal), rites of transition (liminal) and rites of incorporation (postliminal).[26] The process of death may be accommodated within this framework in the following manner: the rites of separation cover the act of dying, the rites of transition refer to the burial rites, and the rites of incorporation refer to the integration of the deceased into the society of the Underworld.[27] If the transitional – that is the burial rites – are not complete then the move to integration is not possible and the deceased must remain in a state of liminality. By applying this theory to the act of non-burial in Homer it can be argued that the act places the deceased warrior in a perpetual liminal state whereby he is neither alive nor fully dead. Although this is not a new theory, for the most part scholarship tends to accept this liminality as a *physical* state whereby the deceased is denied access to the Underworld proper. This is opposed to a *social* state whereby the deceased is denied access to the society of the deceased, as will be argued for below.[28]

The theory of conditional physical admittance to the Underworld is based largely upon the requests for burial from the ghosts of Patroclus in *Iliad* 23 and Elpenor in *Odyssey* 11. Following his death on the battlefield, Patroclus appears to Achilles as a dream-figure in order to ask for burial:

> Bury me as quickly as can be, so I can pass through the gates of Hades. The ghosts, the phantoms of the dead, are keeping me away, they will not let me cross the river to join their number, but I am left wandering in vain along the broad-gated house of Hades. (*Il.* 23.71-75)

Patroclus's words certainly suggest that, in his unburied state, he has been denied some manner of access and that this is policed by the dead themselves. However, he does not explicitly claim that the dead prevent him from entering the Underworld proper, merely that they prevent him from mingling (*misgesthae*) with them beyond the river. This river is not given a name by Patroclus, and the River Styx, as a barrier between the world of the living and the dead, is not a fixed concept in the Homeric epics. As such, Patroclus's words need not be taken as an indication that the river presents a barrier in admittance to the Underworld proper. Rather, Patroclus's suggests that he has entered the Underworld but has not been successfully integrated into the society of the deceased. Patroclus suffers from social as opposed to physical liminality.

Elpenor, the second ghost, asks Odysseus for burial when the hero raises the dead in *Odyssey* 11 using a necromantic ceremony:

> I beg you, master, to remember me then and not to sail away and forsake me utterly nor leave me there unburied and unwept, in case I bring down the gods' curse on you. So burn my body there with all the arms I possess, and raise a mound for me on the shore of the grey sea, in memory of an unlucky man, so that men yet unborn may learn my story. (*Od.* 11.71-76)

As with Patroclus, there is no overt indication that Elpenor has been denied access to the world of the dead, especially as he emerges at the same time, at the same place and in response to the same ceremony as the rest of the dead. Certainly Elpenor's preoccupation is not with entry to the Underworld but rather with his desire to remain within societal memory by the erection of a tomb. Elpenor's entire request to Odysseus concentrates upon the perpetuation of his name and thus his honour and status in the world of the living. In contrast, Patroclus is preoccupied with his honour and status in the world of the dead. However, neither shows a concern for physical entry to the Underworld.

According to Vernant's theory of the *kalos thanatos* the timely burial or cremation of the warrior when his beauty is still intact allows for the perpetuation of his honour and status among his peers and within societal memory. Vernant further suggests that the fire of cremation allows for the transference of the warrior's physical appearance to the Underworld whereby it is 'saved from corruption by disappearing into the invisible'.[29] By combining these two theories and extrapolating a little further it may be suggested that the honour and status of the warrior, of which his physical beauty is a symbol, is also transferred to the Underworld and thus perpetuated in the afterlife. In this way, the warrior may expect to occupy a social position within the society of the deceased analogous to that which he held during life. If, however, the warrior is not given burial or if he suffers some manner of ignoble desecration then not only can he not replicate his social position among the dead but, as Patroclus suggests, he is denied full integration into the society of the deceased.

The ability to partake in a social hierarchy is one of the defining characteristics of the Homeric dead, as seen especially in *Odyssey* 11. When Odysseus encounters Achilles in the Underworld he attempts to placate the hero about his early death by praising the superior status which he holds within the society of the deceased:

> But you, Achilles, you are the most fortunate man that ever was or will be! For in the old days when you were on Earth, we Argives honoured you as though you were a god; and now, down here, you have great power among the dead. Do not grieve at your death, Achilles. (*Od.* 11.483-486)

Achilles laments the futility of such power but he does not deny that he holds such a superior position (*Od.* 11.488-491). As Achilles has achieved Vernant's *kalos thanatos* by dying gloriously in battle at the height of his masculinity and as he was offered extensive funeral rites (*Od.* 24.43-95) it may be suggested that he transferred his heroic status and honour to the Underworld. As a result of this, Achilles enjoys a high social position within the hierarchy of the deceased and may be assured of the continuance of his presence within societal memory; as Agamemnon states: 'So even death, Achilles, did not destroy your name, and your great glory will last forever among all mankind' (*Od.* 24.93-95).

While Achilles offers an insight into the perpetuation of honour in the Underworld, Agamemnon's status reveals the results of a shameful death and corrupt burial. Theoretically, Agamemnon should enjoy a similar, if not a higher, social position to that of Achilles as he was a king during life and the heroic leader of the Greek forces during the Trojan War. Yet, when Odysseus meets Agamemnon in the Underworld there is no indication that he has replicated his former social position within the society of the deceased. Admittedly, many of the dead flock around Agamemnon but these are the warriors who also fell victim to Agamemnon's wife Clytemnestra and her lover Aegisthus (*Od.* 11.388-389, cf. *Od.* 24.21-22), not those who see him as their leader. This anomaly in Agamemnon's status may be explained by the ignoble manner of his death and burial, the nature of which he explains to Odysseus:

> It was Aegisthus who plotted my destruction and with my accursed wife put me to death. He invited me to the palace, he feasted me, and he killed me as a man fells an ox at its manger... And I, lying on the ground, trying to raise my arms, tossed dying upon Aegisthus' sword. But [Clytemnestra], bitch that she was, turned away, and did not deign, though I was going to the house of Hades, either to draw down my eyelids with her fingers or to close my mouth. (*Od.* 11.409-426)

Although there is no indication that Agamemnon was denied burial, his rites did suffer a certain amount of corruption. As stated earlier, the closing of the eyes was considered to be a *geras* for the dead and this is the very thing which Clytemnestra refuses to perform for her husband. When this corruption is combined with Agamemnon's ignoble death, the resulting dishonour renders him unable to hold a social position in the Underworld on a level with that of Achilles or akin to his own former status. There is further evidence of this in *Odyssey* 24 when Achilles laments the fact that Agamemnon died a wretched death at the hands of his wife and her lover and did not die in Troy where he would have been honoured with a tomb, and his son would have inherited a proud name (*Od.* 24.32-34).[30] Agamemnon and Achilles were equals in life (even if Agamemnon considered himself to be Achilles's superior) but they are manifestly not so in the Underworld and the only way to account for this is the manner of their respective death and burial. Achilles died a *kalos thanatos* and thus replicates his honoured social position in the Underworld; Agamemnon died a *kakos thanatos* and thus cannot replicate his social position but must remain dishonoured.

The contrasting afterlives of Achilles and Agamemnon, in conjunction with Patroclus's desire for integration with the dead, strongly suggest that the manner of a warrior's burial has a fundamental effect upon his existence in the Underworld. Due to a lack of burial rites, the deceased is not given the opportunity to fully disengage from the world of the living and, as a direct result of this, cannot be fully integrated into the world of the dead. As such, the decrease in honour and status which the deceased suffers in the world of the living is mirrored by his social exclusion or reduced status in the Underworld. It is clear, therefore, that non-burial and mutilation result in lasting and harmful consequences for the deceased, reaching even into the Underworld itself. The loss of a warrior's honour and status in the world of the living jeopardizes his presence in societal memory. This divests the warrior of his past, whereby his deeds are remembered and of his future, whereby succeeding generations speak of his glory. This loss of a future also extends into the Underworld where the warrior is prevented from taking any enjoyment from his eternity among the dead as he is ostracized or, at the very least, dishonoured with a lowly social position. Owing to these extensive and far-reaching consequences it is not surprising that non-burial is used widely as a threat in the *Iliad* and that it is viewed by the warriors, quite literally, as a fate worse than death.

Bibliography

Adkins, A. W. H., 'Homeric Values and Homeric Society,' *The Journal of Hellenic Studies* 91 (1971), 1-14.

Aeschylus, *Choephori, Aeschylus' Agamemnon, Libation-Bearers, Eumenides*, translated by Alan H. Sommerstein (Cambridge, Mass.; London: Harvard University Press, 2008).

Bremmer, Jan, *The Early Greek Concept of the Soul* (Princeton, Guildford: Princeton University Press, 1983).

Garland, Robert, '*Geras Thanonton*: An Investigation into the Claims of the Homeric Dead,' *Bulletin of the Institute of Classical Studies*, Vol. 29 (1982), 69-80.

Gennep, Arnold van, *The Rites of Passage*, translated by Monika B. Vizedom and Gabrielle L. Caffee (Chicago: University of Chicago Press), 1960.

Griffin, Jasper, *Homer on Life and Death* (Oxford: Clarendon Press, 1980).

Homer, *The Iliad*, translated by Martin Hammond (Harmondsworth: Penguin, 1987).

Homer, *The Odyssey*, translated by E.V. Rieu (London: Penguin, 1991).

Martin, Bridget, 'The Return of the Dead in Greek Tragedy,' PhD thesis, University College Dublin, Ireland, 2012.

Redfield, James M., *Nature and Culture in the 'Iliad': the Tragedy of Hector* (Chicago; London: University of Chicago Press, 1975).

Rohde, Erwin, *Psyche: the Cult of Souls and Belief in Immortality Among the Greeks*, Vol. 1, translated from the eighth German edition by W.B. Hillis (New York, Harcourt: Brace & Co., 1925).

Segal, Charles, *The Theme of the Mutilation of the Corpse in the Iliad* (Leiden: Brill, 1971).

Sourvinou-Inwood, Christiane, 'To Die and Enter the House of Hades: Homer, Before and After,' in *Mirrors of Mortality: Studies in the Social History of Death*, ed. Joachim Whaley (London: Europa, 1981), 15-39.

Sourvinou-Inwood, Christiane, *Reading' Greek Death: to the End of the Classical Period* (Oxford: Clarendon Press, 1995).

Vermeule, Emily, *Aspects of Death in Early Greek Art and Poetry* (Berkeley; Los Angeles; London: University of California Press, 1979).

Vernant, Jean-Pierre, 'A "Beautiful Death" and the Disfigured Corpse in Homeric Epic,' in *Mortals and Immortals: Collected Essays*, ed. Froma I. Zeitlin (Princeton, New Jersey: Princeton University Press, 1991), 50-74.

TABLE 4.1: Post-mortem mutilation in Homer's *Iliad* incorporating threats, allusions and actual occurrences

Post-mortem mutilation by man	Post-mortem mutilation coupled with the stripping of armour	Post-mortem mutilation as a consequence of non-burial (i.e by wild dogs/birds/fish)
		1.3-5
		2.391-393
		4.237-238
		8.379-380
11.145-147		
11.261		11.161-162
		11.393-395
		11.452-454
		11.816-818
13.202-205		13.831-832
14.498-500		
		15.348-351
	16.544-547	
	16.559-561	
		16.836
17.125-127	17.125-127	17.125-127
		17.240-241
		17.254-255
		17.272-273

18.176-177		
		18.271-272
		18.283
	18.334-335	
		19.23-27*
		21.203-204
		22.42-43
		22.66-76
		22.89
		22.256-259
		22.335-336
		22.338-343
22.346-347 (?)		
		22.348-354
	22.367-375	
22.395-404		
		22.508-509
23.21		23.21
		23.182-183
24.14-18		
24.50-52		
		24.211
24.408-409		24.408-409
		24.411-415
24.416-417		

*This is an unusual example as it refers to the natural process of decay rather than the result of non-burial.

1. This chapter is based in part upon chapter one of my PhD thesis 'The Return of the Dead in Greek Tragedy' (PhD thesis, University College Dublin, Ireland, 2012), which examined the awareness of the dead in the Homeric Underworld in detail. While this chapter concentrates upon Homer's *Iliad* (*Il.*), his second epic, the *Odyssey* (*Od.*) is also referred to throughout and used as a source of illustrative examples. Unless otherwise indicated all extracts from the *Iliad* are taken from Martin Hammond's Penguin translation (*The Iliad*, transl. Martin Hammond (Harmondsworth: Penguin, 1987)) and all the extracts from the *Odyssey* are taken from E.V. Rieu's Penguin translation (*The Odyssey*, transl. E.V. Rieu (London: Penguin, 1991)), although the Greek names have been Latinised throughout.
2. For a full and detailed discussion on the *geras thanonton* in Homer, see: Robert Garland, '*Geras Thanonton*: An Investigation into the Claims of the Homeric Dead,' *Bulletin of the Institute of Classical Studies* 29 (1982), 69-80.
3. For a full discussion on the mutilation of the dead in Homer, see: Charles Segal, *The Theme of the Mutilation of the Corpse in the Iliad* (Leiden: Brill, 1971); Jasper Griffin, *Homer on Life and Death* (Oxford: Clarendon Press, 1980); Bridget Martin, 'The Return of the Dead,' 36-43. The absence of burial, or non-burial as it will be more commonly named, does not solely refer to the completion of internment or cremation. The absence or denial of the accompanying rites such as lamentations and the offering of gifts also falls under the umbrella term of 'non-burial'.
4. See Table 4.1 for a complete breakdown of these occurrences in the *Iliad*.
5. Emily Vermeule, *Aspects of Death in Early Greek Art and Poetry* (Berkeley; Los Angeles; London: University of California Press, 1979), 103.
6. Hecuba expresses a similar desire to devour Achilles's liver (*Il.* 24.212-213) while Zeus suggests that Hera's anger against the Trojans can only be assuaged by her eating the raw flesh of their King, Priam (*Il.* 4.34-36).
7. Jean-Pierre Vernant, 'A 'Beautiful Death' and the Disfigured Corpse in Homeric Epic,' in *Mortals and Immortals: Collected Essays*, ed. Froma I. Zeitlin (Princeton, New Jersey: Princeton University Press, 1991), 67.
8. See also *Il.* 11.452-455; 22.335-336.
9. Vermeule, *Aspects of Death in Early Greek Art and Poetry*, 99.
10. James M. Redfield, *Nature and Culture in the 'Iliad': the Tragedy of Hector* (Chicago; London: University of Chicago Press, 1975), 168.
11. Ibid., 169.
12. It is interesting to note that the opening lines of the *Iliad* incorporate references to the non-burial of the dead while the closing line speaks of burial: 'Such was the burial they gave to Hector, tamer of horses' (*Il.* 24.804).
13. Garland, '*Geras Thanonton*,' 70.
14. In later literature, most notably fifth-century, Greek tragedy, non-burial is a dangerous source of pollution. This is especially evident in Sophocles's *Antigone* in which the contagion occasioned by the non-burial of Polyneices spreads to neighbouring cities as birds drop parts of his corpse onto the holy altars (Soph. *Ant.* 1005-1022).
15. Vermeule, *Aspects of Death in Early Greek Art and Poetry*, 109.
16. However, the distress which non-burial and mutilation would cause the deceased's family must also play some role.
17. A. W. H. Adkins, 'Homeric Values and Homeric Society,' *The Journal of Hellenic Studies* 91 (1971), 10.

[18] Redfield, *Nature and Culture in the 'Iliad'*, 175.
[19] Vernant, 'A 'Beautiful Death' and the Disfigured Corpse in Homeric Epic,' 50-74.
[20] *Ibid.*, 68.
[21] For more examples see the column entitled 'Post-mortem mutilation coupled with the stripping of armour' in Table 4.1.
[22] Vernant, 'A "Beautiful Death" and the Disfigured Corpse in Homeric Epic,' 68-69.
[23] *Ibid.*, 68-69.
[24] Two distinct images of the dead may be found side by side in the Homeric epics. On the one hand the dead are portrayed as witless wraiths, devoid of all perception and awareness, that flit about like shadows or smoke. On the other hand, the dead are portrayed as consciously aware beings that interact with one another within a hierarchically structured Underworld and may converse with the living when properly evoked. It is not the aim of this chapter to determine which, if either, of these two depictions may be considered the true image of Homeric eschatology, nor to argue the merits of either depiction. Nevertheless, the latter image of the sentient dead is certainly the more consistent and ubiquitous and, as such, is the depiction upon which the argument in this chapter rests.
[25] Arnold van Gennep, *The Rites of Passage*, transl. Monika B. Vizedom and Gabrielle L. Caffee (Chicago: University of Chicago Press, 1960), 3.
[26] Van Gennep, *The Rites of Passage*, 11.
[27] *Ibid.*, 146-165.
[28] For the belief that non-burial presents a barrier in admittance to the Underworld see Christiane Sourvinou-Inwood, 'To Die and Enter the House of Hades: Homer, Before and After,' in *Mirrors of Mortality: Studies in the Social History of Death*, ed. Joachim Whaley (London: Europa, 1981), 18; Christiane Sourvinou-Inwood, *'Reading' Greek Death: to the End of the Classical Period* (Oxford: Clarendon Press, 1995), 63; Vermeule, *Aspects of Death in Early Greek Art and Poetry*, 12; Jan Bremmer, *The Early Greek Concept of the Soul* (Princeton, Guildford: Princeton University Press, 1983), 89-108; Griffin, *Homer on Life and Death*, 47.
[29] Vernant, 'A "Beautiful Death" and the Disfigured Corpse in Homeric Epic,' 69-70.
[30] The theme of Agamemnon's dishonour in the Underworld is also dealt with in Aeschylus's fifth-century, Greek tragedy, the *Choephori*. Lines 345-362 share many similarities with the words of Achilles concerning Agamemnon's ignoble burial.

5 | Identity and the Act of Dying: Sketching a Philosophical Perspective

Dan Farrelly

Preoccupation with this material arises from my work as translator of several books of the German philosopher Josef Pieper (1904-1997) for St Augustine's Press (Indiana).[1] What is most impressive in Pieper's work is not only his scholarly grasp of the Western tradition of philosophy – from Plato and Aristotle, Augustine and Aquinas, right down to the most modern philosophers of the 20th century – but also his handling of the problems of faith. Pieper writes as a philosopher but makes no attempt to separate out his Christian belief in the role of a Creator. To any modern person who does not believe in a Creator/creature relationship, Pieper's fundamental idea may seem gratuitous. His philosophy is always on the brink of theology. Yet we may ask to what extent he crosses the boundary between the two disciplines and whether it matters. How strict is this division between the disciplines, especially since both are involved not just with theories but with interpreting *experience*? Pieper himself is not concerned with rational proof but with evidence of a completely different kind. The sphere of lived experience of the transcendental can hardly be the preserve of any one discipline.

It is useful to introduce here some of the common ground shared by Josef Pieper and the Evangelical theologian of the same era, Rudolf Bultmann. While he bases much of his thinking on the philosophy of Martin Heidegger, Bultmann continually distinguishes between Heidegger's 'existentialia' – the conditions of man's actual existence insofar as he exists, for instance, in time and place and history – and what Bultmann himself refers to as the 'existenziell'.[2] Heidegger's 'existentialia' are structures of existence which apply to every human being, whereas what is 'existentiell' concerns the individual's own personal experience at a particular moment in time and in a particular situation.

For both Pieper and Bultmann a central concern is the point of intersection between what the philosopher, as philosopher, can know, and what the Christian believer accepts about death and the afterlife. Pieper quotes St Augustine, who, at the age of nineteen, after the death of a young friend, wrote:

> Then it became dark in my heart, and wherever I looked I only saw death ... I hated everything ... I had become a big question to myself' (factus eram ipse mihi magna quaestio). It has been said: here is 'the birth of existential philosophy' from the experience of man's fate in confrontation with death.[3]

The *Sturm und Drang* movement in Germany in the 1770s and 1780s, with its special emphasis on highly personal concerns as expressed in the early works of Goethe, Lenz, and Schiller, is part of the broadly existential stream that culminated in the works of Schopenhauer, Nietzsche, and Kierkegaard, followed by Heidegger, Jaspers, Gabriel Marcel, Sartre and Camus and others in the 20th century. But while these 'existential' themes are understood as relatively new, their emphasis on experience as opposed to ideas and concepts is far from new. From medieval times there was always the conflict – in the Christian Church – between, on the one hand, the authority of the teaching Church and, on the other hand, the mystics whose main source of knowledge was not what the Church taught but what they experienced directly of the divine. Some of these mystics, against all the odds, eventually gained recognition by the Church authorities, and even became founders of accepted religious orders within the Church. Their experience of the divine brought new, rich impulses to the Church.

Let me turn briefly to Goethe. Sometimes amongst Germans one hears the phrase: 'That is the Gretchen question'. In many contexts it merely means: that is the fundamental question. But in Goethe's *Faust* it means something very particular. Worried by her lover's seeming lack of religion, Gretchen asks him: 'Do you believe in God?' Like many another person, Faust avoids giving a simple yes/no answer to this question. Instead, he produces a flood of rhetoric – the scholar's semi-pantheistic response that leaves Gretchen confused.

> **Gretchen:** Do you believe in God?
> **Faust:** My dear, who dare say
> 'I do believe in God'?
> Ask philosophers and priests about God:
> Their answers only seem to mock the questioner.
> **Gretchen:** So, you don't believe?
> ...
> **Faust:** Who can have real feelings
> And bring oneself to say
> 'I don't believe'?
> He who embraces all
> And keeps all things in being –
> Does he not embrace and keep
> You, me, himself in being?
> Up there you see the heavens' vault,
> And here below the earth stands firm.
> And don't the eternal stars ascend all around the sky?
> We gaze into each other's eyes –
> And doesn't the visible, invisible secret
> Penetrate our hearts and minds,
> Encompass them?
> Fill your heart with it, as much as you can take,
> And once you know the bliss it generates,
> Call it what you like –
> Call it joy, heart, love, God.
> I find no name for it.
> To feel is everything.[4]

While Gretchen's question is a traditional one, Faust's response is one of the modern answers. Faust understands the basis of Gretchen's question and builds his answer on it. He takes up her simple belief by using the words: 'He who embraces all and keeps all things in being'. Here he is alluding to the doctrine she would have learnt in her catechism lessons and in the sermons at church on Sunday: simply, God is the creator of all things, and we are his creatures – brought into being and kept in being, every moment of our lives, by the direct will of this creator. That is where Gretchen is coming from. But Faust gives his answer without any actual or theoretical commitment to the definite teaching of the Catholic Church to which Gretchen belongs. He is 'liberal' in that he does not accept the dogmas of the Church, but Goethe, in his Faust figure, is a child of his time – with a genuine belief in and acceptance of an intrinsic relationship between the creator and the created world.

The most up-to-date rejection of even this notion of creation is found in Stephen Hawking's recent book, *The Grand Design*, co-authored with the US physicist Leonard Mlodinow.[5] Here Hawking and Modlinow write that a new series of theories made a creator of the universe redundant. Simultaneously with reading this book, I found the opposite theme expressed in a performance of Newman's *Dream of Gerontius* given in Dublin's National Concert Hall. What is striking is the profoundly personal, existential nature of Newman's poem. For example, Gerontius, on the point of dying, exclaims:

> And Thou art calling me; I know it now.
> Not by the token of this faltering breath,
> This chill at heart, this dampness on my brow ...
> 'Tis this new feeling, never felt before ...
> That I am going, that I am no more.'
> Tis this strange innermost abandonment, ...
> This emptying out of each constituent
> And natural force, by which I come to be.[6]

With Hawking and Newman we are confronted with two opposite ends of the spectrum. While listening to the voice of Newman – and Pieper, and others closely related to Pieper's thinking – we cannot but hear the voice of Stephen Hawking, the voice of the rational scientific mind, in the background.

As with Pieper, there is no doubt that in Gerontius's existential encounter with death we are dealing not with a speculative problem about a creator but with a personal confrontation with the very foundation of our being. It is in this context that our act of acknowledging or rejecting our status as creature is, arguably, fundamental to our choice of identity. For the believer and the non-believer alike, this choice of acceptance or rejection is accompanied by a radical fear of what happens at the point of death. To the mind of the non-believer, death is total annihilation of the person. Even the thought of living on for a generation or two in the memory of a relatively small number of people can be of no significance to the person who sees no alternative to annihilation. And for the believer who sees himself, in every aspect and in every fibre of his being, as entirely in the hands of the creator who also keeps him in being, even non-annihilation after death can be a terrifying idea. In the face of both of these frightening alternatives we face the questions: Who am I? What am I? What is my future?

The Act of Dying

Pieper focuses on life as a journey, a kind of pilgrimage. He uses the term 'status viatoris'.[7] At the end of life's journey is death – and here Pieper distinguishes between 'death' and the 'act of dying'. The obvious meaning of 'death' is the event where the person becomes lifeless before us, after which the body will be either buried or cremated. But at this very point of dying, as the person draws his last breath, what is, for him, the meaning of this 'event'? In conjunction with his analysis of the real meaning of the 'journey', Pieper analyses the 'act' of dying in which he sees an element of free choice. Not, of course, the choice to die or not to die. Rather, confronted with our awareness of actually dying, he says we have a free personal response. In the end we choose a turning to God, or, equally, we can choose the course of denial – a turning away from God.

But, in analysing this moment of free choice the philosopher arrives at a frontier where his philosophical knowledge encounters its limits. What does he know about the existence of an afterlife: whether there is one, and, if there is, what does it mean for the individual who dies? This is a very abrupt halt. Across the barrier at the frontier of his knowledge, the philosopher sees, in the distance, the theologian/believer, who is buoyed up by his faith in Christ and his belief in the resurrection of the body and an afterlife.

Reaching back into tradition, Pieper examines what he calls Plato's eschatological myths, which reflect an extraordinary level of belief that predates Christianity by several centuries. These myths, according to Pieper, are not of Plato's own creation.[8] Neither he nor Socrates claim ownership of them. In relating the myths about death, judgement after death, punishment and reward, and even a form of purgatory in the afterlife, Plato is handing down the wisdom of the ancients: not the ancients who can be identified and whose opinions could now be relativized as merely reflecting current beliefs, but he is reaching much further back: to time immemorial when men heard the 'truth' from the gods themselves. Acceptance of this 'wisdom' itself implies and requires a certain level of belief – belief in something that no philosopher can prove, whether by rational deduction or empirical proof.

With regard to the theme of 'turning to or away from God' Pieper is thinking explicitly within a particular tradition and – despite his very broad knowledge – he has relatively little to say, in this context, about modern and ancient cultures apart from the culture of the West. It is the philosophy – and the religion – of what we call Western civilization that Pieper draws on and that concerns us here. The idea of a creature/creator relationship, whether we believe in it or not, is part of our tradition. If we reject it, we know what we are rejecting. We will recognize it as belonging to the Old and New Testaments as well as to Greek philosophy – represented mainly by Socrates, Plato, and Aristotle – and also to the Christian tradition represented especially by Augustine and Thomas Aquinas. So Pieper is talking to us as people who belong, in some way, to this particular tradition of Western Christendom, where there is general acceptance of the idea that we are involved in a world that transcends the world of appearances. It is not enough to dismiss this 'other' world as if it were merely one imagined by generations of unenlightened people deluded by religion. As Regine Kather points out in her book on *Hildegard von Bingen interkulturell gelesen*:

> Worldwide most people believe in a fundamental reality that transcends space and time and gives life meaning and an ethical orientation.[9]

According to Kather, the modern philosophies that deny the existence of a transcendence sphere form a tiny minority in the context of convictions shared currently – and historically – by world civilizations.

A Higher Consciousness

It is not just the conviction of some of the major religions of the world – Judaism, Christianity, Islam, to name the most obvious ones that spring to mind – that there is a real sphere beyond, or behind, or within the material world in which we live. Awareness of this sphere is often called a 'higher consciousness' – precisely one that transcends what since Plato and Kant is usually referred to as the world of appearances, the world characterized by its subjection to the conditions of time and place.

The 'higher consciousness' is not something shared only by an esoteric elite. It may be something which, for many, is drowned out in a frenzy of activity and in the many forms of escapism. Ironically, the term 'escapism' is usually applied to traffic in the opposite direction: for instance, people who use the arts to escape from the humdrum conditions of their daily lives or from the prevailing political and social conditions are said to be escapists. But the escapist, more fundamentally, is the one who, arguably, 'escapes' by suppressing the higher consciousness or refusing it entrance. Everywhere people experience the invitation to 'see' beyond the most obvious phenomena. They experience nature, love, art, music, and – as Goethe had his

Wilhelm Meister say – we become aware here of something more than what we see immediately before our eyes. In Natalie's house Wilhelm is admiring the paintings in her gallery. First we hear the 'objective' voice of the narrator and then the more 'subjective' voice of Wilhelm himself – one voice reinforcing the other:

> It was a world, it was a heaven that here surrounded the beholder, and apart from the thoughts inspired by those shapes and forms, apart from the feelings they engendered, something else seemed to be present that seemed to grip the whole of the person. Wilhelm noticed it, too, without being able to account for it. 'What is it,' he exclaimed, 'that independently of all meaning, free from all sympathy that human events and fates inspire in us, is able to have such a strong yet charming effect on me. It appeals to me in its wholeness, in its every part, but in such a way that I am unable to understand the former and cannot specially assimilate the latter! I feel it is possible to dwell here, to rest, to take in everything with my eyes, to be happy, and to feel and occupy my mind with something quite different from that which is before my eyes.'[10] (My translation)

Of course, it is obvious that there is a similar experience with regard to the sublime music of the great classical composers. The succession and organization of notes is not simply just that; nor can its significance be reduced to the emotions it generates. To the 'higher consciousness' this music is saying something that has profound meaning. It gives us the impression of being in the presence of a higher world. This conviction is expressed by Schubert, for example, in his famous setting of Franz Schober's poem, 'An die Musik':

> Charming art,
> In how many dark hours
> Which have me caught up in life's wild turmoil
> Have you warmed my heart, kindling love in it,
> And carried me off into a better world!
> Often through a sweet, sacred harmony
> You have opened to me
> The heavenly prospect of better times.[11]

This is not an isolated example in the songs of Schubert. Instead, it is a typical example of his openness to a transcendence dimension – a dimension in which, as his songs continually indicate, he constantly lived while in the process of creating his songs. It is, for example, hardly conceivable that Schubert could write his fine settings of Novalis's religious songs, interpreting the words which express the intimate relationship between our concrete world and a higher, other, sphere, without sharing in the experience which inspired the poem in the first place.

It is not by chance that Schubert was drawn to Novalis's poetry. Here we encounter a consciousness which, while it is imbued by Christian faith, is also characterized by a conviction that the person lives simultaneously in two interpenetrating spheres. While living and working in the concrete world, Novalis's heroes – as in his novel *Heinrich von Ofterdingen*[12] – are aware of a transcendence dimension which is not presented to the reader as a figment of the author's imagination but as something actually experienced. Novalis's Heinrich has constant access to 'another' dimension of his existence. This consciousness arose for Novalis personally as a result of the premature death of his fiancée, Sophie von Kühn. After her death he lived – and wrote – in the conviction that only his own death separated him from her and that the bond that tied him to life would be released by something as gentle as a dream – an image which suggests the intimacy of the relationship between the sphere of his concrete world and the other sphere which is only fully attainable in death. Meantime, he lives with the premonition (Ahndung) of the higher sphere.

Clearly, our experience of death, especially of that of a person close to us, involves a confrontation with the basic question of what our own death will mean. 'What has happened to our beloved one?' is the first question. We also ask: 'What happens to anyone?' A further question is: 'What will happen to me?' These are metaphysical questions, very different from the questions which normally occupy us on a daily basis, such as: 'Do I have time to catch that train?' or 'Is it worth my while applying for that job?'

Our deliberate openness – or otherwise – to the higher consciousness, our willingness to engage with and affirm the truth we are confident it reveals is intrinsically related to our willingness to accept, at the point of our own death, the truth about our status as creature in relation to the all-powerful creator. Opening to what one is convinced is the truth offered in this 'higher consciousness' means already opening to the final truth about the meaning of our existence as it will be revealed to us at the point of death. Ultimately it means the affirmation of our creature status.

Creature Status

Does reference to this already imply a gratuitous introduction of theology? Thinking and writing outside the explicit context of the biblical world, artists and others who look beyond immediate concrete reality are not likely to speak in terms of creator and creature. Those who do use these terms would usually be understood to be working and thinking within the traditional context of revealed religion – as if accepting as authentic and binding, for instance, the theological interpretation of the creation story in the Book of Genesis. These would be seen as traditional believers with the 'privileged' knowledge available only to those who have traditional faith. But in fact it is more than plausible that the experience of our dependence on forces that exist in another world is available outside the context of 'revealed' religion. Accordingly, depending on the intensity and continuity of the alternative experience of the 'other' world, it is feasible that the human person, at the hour of death, is found to be in the same situation – where it is possible either to affirm one's dependence on this higher reality or, by despairing, to deny it. We should not forget that even for the firmest believer, the person most buoyed up by faith in the God of revelation, death brings the inevitable encounter with the most terrifying mystery. St Thomas Aquinas, with all his profound knowledge of theology and philosophy, insisted that the thing we know best about God is that we know nothing at all about him. Pseudo-Dionysius, a mystic of the 5th-6th century AD whose writings made a substantial impact on medieval theology, and expecially on Aquinas, is known for a radical statement which is scarcely distinguishable from the most profound agnosticism:

> God is not soul or mind, nor does God possess imagination, conviction, speech, or understanding. Nor is God speech *per se*, understanding *per se*. God cannot be spoken of and cannot be grasped by understanding. God is not number or order, greatness or smallness, equality or inequality, similarity or dissimilarity. God is not movable, immovable or at rest. God has not power; God is not power, nor light. God does not live nor have life. God is not a substance nor eternity nor time. God cannot be grasped by the understanding since God is neither knowledge nor truth. God is not kingship. God is not wisdom. God is neither one nor oneness, divinity nor goodness. Nor is God a spirit in the sense in which we understand that term. God is not sonship nor fatherhood, and is nothing known to us or any other being. Existing beings do not know God as God actually is and God does not know them as they are. There is no

speaking of God, nor name nor knowledge of God. Darkness and light, error and truth – God is none of these. God is beyond every assertion and denial. We make assertions and denials of what is next to God, but never of God, for God is both beyond every assertion, being the perfect and unique cause of all things, and, by virtue of a preeminently simple and absolute nature, free of every limitation; God is also beyond every denial.[13]

Having suggested that there is no unbridgeable gap between the two groups of people who share the higher consciousness – though in such different ways – I would like to return to the more accessible approach to discussing relationships between creator and creature.

Fundamental Identity

Here I suggest that our final choice – but also our daily choice – concerns the idea that we are creatures, the product of an all-powerful creator, who makes us out of nothing, i.e. gives us being and keeps us in being. If, while we are alive, we accept the creator/creature relationship, we have the key to a fundamental understanding of our identity. If we doubt or reject this relationship, we have to look elsewhere for understanding our identity and for establishing it. Expression of belief in our status as creature is already to be found in Plato and Aristotle. It is perhaps most clearly expressed in the Old Testament – in the accounts of creation in Genesis, for example. It is also expressed in the early Church councils. The text of the Nicene Creed says: 'I believe in God, the creator of heaven and earth, creator of all things visible and invisible.' In a slightly different context, Pieper again quotes Augustine's *Confessions Book X*:

> Men go and look with astonishment at the peaks of the mountains, the unlimited waves of the sea, the broad flow of mighty rivers, the endless expanse of the ocean, and the course of the stars.[14]

The sense of wonder expressed in that text goes hand in hand with the perhaps crushing experience of our own fundamental insignificance – of, personally, being a tiny atom in an immense universe: if, for example, I think of myself as one single person amongst the billions who inhabit our planet at this moment, to say nothing of those who have gone before for some millions of years, I pose the disturbing question: 'What am I?' I think of the single grain of sand lost in the vast expanse of our sandy beaches and oceans. I think of my mind, that minuscule light which could, like a tiny spark, be suddenly extinguished and entirely lost. The question is: what significance can we attach to ourselves? If we are so insignificant in ourselves, in the immense scheme of things, what does death mean to us? And for that matter: what does life mean to us?

The experience of absolute helplessness, absolute dependence on another force – not only for one's human existence in this life but, even more deeply, for one's being at all – produces a most radical fear. It is at this point that Pieper identifies the challenge of the individual to make a free choice in the act of dying: either to face the fear in a spirit of hope – turning to the ultimate foundation of being – or to turn away in despair. This is the point where the individual makes the final choice about his fundamental identity. One has no choice about whether one will be or not be. But one has a certain freedom, deep within oneself, to accept or reject absolute dependence, one's real status as creature, having nothing but what one receives from the hand of the creator. Acceptance is based on hope, while rejection means despair.

But what is this hope if not hope based on a belief in an afterlife? The possibility of life after death is linked with possible concepts of immortality – but here again we are staying within the Western tradition. Perhaps the two most familiar concepts are those of Plato and Aristotle (and Aristotle's interpreter, Aquinas). For Plato, as Pieper points out, soul and body are related to one another like the guest in the house that accommodates him; like the prisoner in jail; like the boatman in his boat.[15] When death occurs, the guest leaves the house, the prisoner leaves the jail, the boatman steps off the boat – and walks away. This view of the relationship between soul and body was shared by Christian thinkers from Augustine down to the time of Aquinas. But Aquinas himself represents the other school of thought which concerns us here. Following Aristotle, Aquinas considers that man, in reality, is not the soul that uses the body but is the living unity made up of body and soul. This means not only that the human person has a bodily aspect, but that the soul itself also has a bodily aspect. The soul, by its very nature – and this is what makes it to be soul – is what gives the body its essential form: 'anima forma corporis' [Pieper].[16] This intrinsic interrelationship of body and soul has, according to Aquinas and Pieper, an important bearing on the status of the soul when death separates it from the body.

Aquinas, again according to Pieper, does not argue for the immortality of the soul, because, in his interpretation, it has no independent existence outside of its relation to the body. Instead,

Aquinas talks about the 'indestructibility' of the soul.[17] He reserves the term immortality or immortal life mainly for the resurrected Christ and for those living a bodily existence in paradise after the resurrection. The human soul, when separated from its body in death, does remain indestructible, but, by its very nature, requires union – or reunion – with its body. In this requirement Pieper senses a philosophical basis for saying that life continues in a physical form after death.

But what is the basis for saying that the person's soul is indestructible? For Pieper the most convincing argument here is the person's ability to grasp truth:

> The argument for the indestructibility of the soul, the argument from the possibility of truth, is as follows: because the human soul is capable of grasping truth [capax veritatis], because it is able to do something that is, in principle, beyond and independent of every conceivable material process, it must also have ... being that is independent of matter, independent of the body; it must necessarily be something that survives as real during the disintegration of the body and beyond.'[18]

These two philosophical interpretations bring us about as far as we can go without recourse to theology and revelation. They are both the fruit of speculation and seem far removed from anything we can experience. Here the philosopher, as philosopher, reaches his limit. Yet Plato, a kind of theologian in his acceptance of the great myths, describes in the *Timaeus* how the Father – yes, Plato says 'Father' – creates the gods, which are earth and heaven; and, as their offspring, the next generation of gods, who then have the task of bringing mortals into being.[19] But here, as in the Old Testament, there seems to be no focus on the personal creature/creator relationship as such, let alone on the need, at the point of death, to affirm or deny this relationship once and for all.

Conclusion

Given our starting point in this paper: the notion of our creation out of nothing; and given the final point, namely, our death in which we are confronted with either the ultimate acceptance or rejection of our creature status, we may see ourselves as on a journey which had its beginning and will have its end. Our affirmation or negation of the creature/creator relationship at the end of our lives is not an isolated decision. It is anticipated in our personal decisions every step of the way. Acknowledging our creature status alongside the status of others who are equally products of the creator – and this is where we find a basis for personal ethics, for social ethics and, strange as it may seem, for political ethics – consists partly in affirming all that is good in ourselves, first of all, and then finding and affirming what is good in others. Affirming all that we are, including our gifts and limitations, is an ongoing process of affirmation and acceptance of our status as creature: the status which we are, according to our basic assumption here, called on to affirm – or deny – right throughout life and at the point of death.

Bibliography

Bultmann, Rudolf, *Neues Testament und Christliche Existenz* (Tübingen: Mohr Siebeck, 2002).
Hawking, Stephen and Leonard Mlodinov, *The Grand Design* (Kindle Edition, 2010).
Goethe, Johann Wolfgang von, *Wilhelm Meisters Lehrjahre*, Hamburger Ausgabe, Bd. 7 (Hamburg: Christian Wegner, 1962).
Kather, Regina, *Hildegard von Bingen interkulturell gelesen* (Amazon Kindle Edition, 2011).
Novalis, *Schriften*, Erster Band, edited by Paul Kluckhohn and Richard Samuel (Stuttgart: W. Kohlhammer Verlag, 1960).
Pieper, Josef, *Tradition als Herausforderung* (Munich: Kösel-Verlag, 1963).
Pieper, Josef, *The Silence of Goethe* (South Bend, Indiana: St. Augustine's Press, 2009).
Pieper, Josef, *The Christian Idea of Man* (South Bend, Indiana: St. Augustine's Press, 2011).
Pieper, Josef, *The Platonic Myths* (South Bend, Indiana: St. Augustine's Press, 2011)
Pieper, Josef, *The Challenge of Tradition* (South Bend, Indiana: St. Augustine's Press, 2012).
Ruppert, Frank, *Franz Schubert and the Mysterium Magnum*, (Pittsburgh: RoseDog Books, 2009).

---

[1] The titles of these works are: *The Silence of Goethe* (2009), *The Platonic Myths* (2010), *The Christian Idea of Man* (2011); *The Challenge of Tradition* (2013). A selected list of other works of Pieper published by St Augustine's Press gives a glimpse of the range of thinking and writing of this distinguished 20th century philosopher, who, though deeply cognizant of the Christian and Catholic streams of thought, maintained a fiercely independent stance both as writer and teacher. See *The Concept of Sin*; *Death and Immortality*; *Enthusiasm and Divine Madness: On the Platonic Dialogue Phaedrus*; *Happiness and Contemplation*; *In Tune with the World: A Theory of Festivity*.

[2] For this distinction see Rudolf Bultmann, *Neues Testament und Christliche Existenz* (Tübingen: Mohr Siebeck, 2002), 63 and 66.

[3] Quoted by Pieper in *Tradition als Herausforderung (*Munich: Kösel-Verlag, 1963*)*, 68. English translations from this work are mine.

[4] Goethe's early *Faust* version, a fragment later to be included in his *Faust. Erster Teil* (1808) was written before 1775. The lines quoted here (1117-1148) were already in the pre-1775 version, now called *Urfaust*. The translation is mine.

[5] Stephen Hawking and Leonard Mlodinov, *The Grand Design* (Kindle Edition, 2010).

[6] 'The Dream of Gerontius,' *Newman Reader – Works of John Henry Newman*, National Institute for Newman Studies, Pittsburgh, no. 177, p.323, ll. 2-9.

[7] Pieper, *Tradition als Herausforderung*, 79.

[8] Pieper, *The Platonic Myths* (South Bend, Indiana: St. Augustine's Press, 2011), 11.

[9] Weltweit glauben ... die meisten Menschen an einen Raum und Zeit überschreitenden Seinsgrund, der dem Leben Sinn und eine ethische Orientierung verleiht. Regina Kather, *Hildegard von Bingen interkulturell gelesen* (Amazon Kindle Edition, 2011), 68.

[10] Es war eine Welt, es war ein Himmel, der den Beschauenden an dieser Stätte umgab, und außer den Gedanken, welche jene gebildeten Gestalten erregten, außer den Empfindungen, welche sie einflößten, schien noch etwas andres gegenwärtig zu sein, wovon der ganze Mensch sich angegriffen fühlte. Auch Wilhelm bemerkte es, ohne sich davon Rechenschaft geben zu können. 'Was ist das', rief er aus,'das, unabhängig von aller Bedeutung, frei von allem Mitgefühl, das uns menschliche Begebenheiten und Schicksale einflößen, so stark und zugleich so anmutig auf mich zu wirken vermag? Es spricht aus dem Ganzen, es spricht aus jedem Teile mich an, ohne daß ich jenes begreifen, ohne daß ich diese mir besonders zueignen könnte! ... Ja, ich fühle, man könnte hier verweilen, ruhen, alles mit den Augen fassen, sich glücklich finden und ganz etwas andres fühlen und denken als das, was vor Augen steht.' Goethe, *Wilhelm Meisters Lehrjahre*, Hamburger Ausgabe, Bd. 7 (Hamburg: Christian Wegner, 1962), 541 (emphases by the author).

[11] Du holde Kunst
In wieviel grauen Stunden,
wo mich des Lebens wilder Kreis umstrickt,
hast du mein Herz zu warmer Lieb' entzunden
hast mich in eine bessre Welt entrückt

...

Oft hat ... ein süßer, heiliger Akkord von dir
den Himmel bessrer Zeiten mir erschlossen.

[12] The first part of the novel was published in 1802 by Riemer in Berlin. See Novalis, *Schriften*, Erster Band, edited by Paul Kluckhohn and Richard Samuel (Stuttgart: W. Kohlhammer Verlag, 1960).

[13] Quoted by Frank Ruppert in: *Franz Schubert and the Mysterium Magnum* (Pittsburgh: RoseDog Books, 2009), 59.

[14] *Tradition als Herausforderung*, 254-55.

[15] *Ibid.*, 110.

[16] *Ibid.*, 111.

[17] *Ibid.*, 113.

[18] *Ibid.*, 89.

[19] Plato, *Sophist Dialogue*, 265c2, 266c5, 266b4. Quoted by Pieper in *The Platonic Myths* (South Bend Indiana: St Augustine's Press, 2011), 37.

6 | 'emotional rather than cerebral'?
Charles Villiers Stanford's *Requiem*

Wolfgang Marx

Charles Villiers Stanford's *Requiem* op. 63 is probably the first full setting of the Latin requiem mass by an Irish composer. After its first performance on 6 October 1897 at the Birmingham Musical Festival, the anonymous reviewer of the *Musical News* even stated that,

> Professor Villiers Stanford's Requiem ... is said, I know not with what truth, to be the first important setting of the Roman Catholic office ever composed by a prominent British musician.[1]

Indeed, there seems to be no earlier setting of the requiem by an Irish-born composer, yet we now know that there are some by British predecessors. While both Luc Voirin and Gilbert Chase's catalogues of requiem compositions [2] contain only references to earlier funeral compositions (yet not requiems) by British composers, the requiem database on www.requiemsurvey.org lists altogether four earlier British compositions: an undated setting by Nicholas Ludford (ca. 1485-ca. 1557), another undated one by William Hawes (1785-1846), one from 1816 by William Linley (1771-1816) and finally one from 1853 by Robert Lucas Pearsall (1795-1856).[3]

Stanford's *Requiem* is dedicated to the memory of Lord Frederick Leighton, one of the most famous and most respected British painters of his time. Leighton was born in 1830 and during the first 30 years of his life spent more time abroad than in his native country, living for an extended time in France, Germany and Italy. He became president of the Royal Academy in 1878, but had an interest in other arts beyond painting. He was also interested in music and close to many musicians and composers. His paintings had left a deep impression on the young Stanford so that when Leighton died on 25 January 1896 – a day after having become the first ever artist to receive a peerage –, he decided to commemorate him with a requiem mass. This is all the more surprising as neither the composer nor the painter were Roman Catholics (despite being not very religious himself, Leighton came from a Protestant family and was to receive a state funeral in St Paul's Cathedral); it indicates that Stanford did not regard writing a requiem as a primarily theological or probably even a religious exercise. He rather treated it as a suitable means of commemorating a great man as well as a means of presenting his own views of death and the afterlife in music.

This essay will consider Stanford's *Requiem* in the context of generic conventions of the mass of the dead as they existed in the nineteenth century. When Stanford finished his score in September 1896, among the most successful recent requiem compositions were Verdi's *Missa da Requiem* (premièred in Milan in 1873), Brahms's *A German Requiem* (premièred in its complete version in 1869 in Leipzig) and Dvořák's *Requiem* (also premièred in Birmingham six years before Stanford's composition in 1891). Gabriel Fauré's *Requiem* from 1888/9 is arguably equally well-loved and influential, yet differs from the other settings in its main function: Fauré wrote his piece for daily use in the liturgy; hence it is shorter, for smaller forces, more intimate and less dramatic. Verdi, Brahms, Dvořák and Stanford wrote for the concert hall and thus in a larger scale and for full orchestra. Unlike Fauré, these four composers do not primarily address grieving relatives and friends who have just lost a loved one but rather a paying audience less immediately affected by the death of the person to whom each work is dedicated. This means that the original liturgical and psychological functions of the requiem mass – intercession on behalf of the dead and consolation for those immediately affected by the loss (close relatives and friends) – are less relevant here. Yet while a concert-hall requiem is less likely to be an expression of grief (i.e. an individual emotional response to loss), it could still be an expression of mourning (connoting a public display of grief), and at the same time – or even instead of the latter – the celebration of the memory of a great man or woman.[4] If there is no personal emotional involvement on the part of the composer, the requiem could even be used for a quasi-philosophical reflection on the nature of death and mourning; this is arguably the case with Dvořák's *Requiem* which is not dedicated to anyone in particular while the composer experienced no significant personal loss at the time that might have triggered the composition.

Stanford's *Requiem* was often related to Italian models (most notably Verdi), but while there are some Verdian aspects to it I shall argue that Dvořák influenced Stanford more than the Italian master. In the sleeve notes accompanying the only available commercial recording of Stanford's *Requiem*, David Brown states that the work unites the composer's 'love of opera and song in its vocal ensembles with a reminder that he was a symphonist in its skilful, subtle and economical use of a relatively small number of thematic 'cells'.[5] This art of the symphonist goes back to Beethoven's model of relating the main thematic ideas of a composition to one another by way of shared motivic or rhythmic elements. What Brown calls 'cells' could also be described as a play with a particular three-note motif; I regard the way it is deployed in this composition as inspired by the use of a 'motto' in Dvořák's *Requiem*.

Introit

Stanford's 'Introit' begins with a three-note motif in the low strings that is repeated three times and descends in stepwise motion the A major scale, leading to a sustained A major chord before the choir enters:

Example 6.1: Stanford, *Requiem*, begin Introit[6]

Beginning a requiem composition in a low register is not uncommon, but this particular opening is certainly reminiscent of that of Verdi's *Missa da Requiem*. The Italian composer also starts with a descending three-note motif in the low strings, at first following the notes of the A minor triad, and in its second iteration descending by step. This is also followed by a chord confirming the opening key before the voices come in:

Example 6.2: Verdi, *Missa da Requiem*, Introit, begin[7]

There are, however, also important differences. Verdi's *Requiem* opens in A minor rather than major. Using a minor key is customary in requiem compositions, with a preference for D minor usual since Mozart set his *Requiem* in that key (in Baroque times, C minor had been a characteristic key of mourning). Opening a requiem in a major key is, in fact, rather unusual. Mainly due to the alla breve time signature, Stanford's tempo is also quicker than Verdi's. So while Stanford on the one hand clearly alludes to the first bars of Verdi's requiem, he also departs from it in several ways, providing an altogether more positive (or less pensive) opening. This more positive attitude is underlined further by the first vocal entry. The text 'Requiem aeternam' ('Eternal rest') opens with a rising three-note motif on the notes of the A major triad (very much the emotional opposite of Verdi's descending A minor motif), followed by another rising triad at a slightly lower pitch.

Example 6.3: Stanford, *Requiem*, Introit, opening 'Requiem aeternam' (soprano)[8]

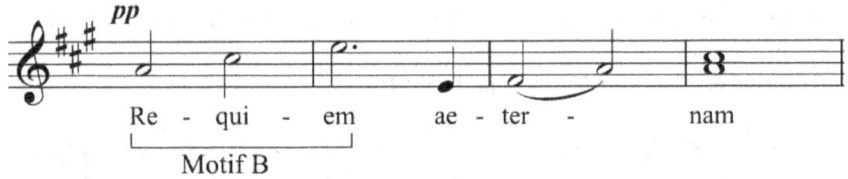

This is not only very different from Verdi's descending A minor motif but also confirms A major as the home key of this composition. Verdi's vocal entry, in turn, consists of brief, almost whispered words without any melodic movement. Stanford initially lets his choir sing unaccompanied, alternating with sparsely orchestrated orchestral interludes, thus evoking an archaic as well as a religious atmosphere.

Stanford's two three-note motifs (descending by step and rising by leap, to be called motifs A and B hereafter) are the two central thematic ideas of this movement. After appearing first in the choir, motif B is then presented by a solo horn in the orchestral interludes while the voices resort to brief, almost whispered (much more Verdian) entries in static chords and triple pianissimo. The music initially oscillates between A major and C sharp major, two harmonically very distant keys. However, with the 'et lux perpetua' ('and perpetual light') the music moves to C major – the most 'simple' key without any accidental and since Haydn's *The Creation* – where its sudden appearance musically indicates the end of darkness – a musical metaphor of light. In many requiem compositions of the long nineteenth century this moment marks the first appearance of a major key; since we have been in major all along in this setting, the moment is here highlighted by the use of a specific, symbolically charged major key and what is, so far, the largest melodic leap (a rising fifth in the soprano line).

Stanford follows generic conventions by allocating the two psalm verses 'Te decet hymnus' and 'Exaudi orationem meam' to the soloists (later joined by the chorus). Now we hear the full orchestra for the first time as it joins forces with the chorus, with motif A playing a prominent part in the orchestra. The end of this section as well as the subsequent repeat of the 'Requiem aeternam' is more subdued as it consists mainly of repeated notes with little rhythmic movement. The return of the 'Requiem aeternam' is opened with motif B in A major, yet the choir's first entry is set in the more 'traditional' requiem key D minor. Towards the end of the movement, motif A replaces motif B in the orchestra – it is as if the opening optimism has made way for a more serious and pensive attitude.

The harmonic language used in this movement is based on mediantic leaps, i.e. each new temporary home key is a third higher or lower than the previous one. Stanford's main keys in this movement (A major, C# major and C major) are not approached by the traditional way of modulation, but rather by isolating one of the notes of the previous triad and taking it as the root of the new one – a practice already used by composers such as Schubert or Cherubini at the beginning of the nineteenth century.

Kyrie

The introit determines the requiem's subject: death, afterlife and the plea for eternal rest rather than hell. The 'Kyrie' intensifies this plea, asking for mercy as we are all sinners. It begins in A minor, the key we might have expected at the very beginning. The opening block chords and timpani rolls may indicate the approaching Day of Judgement. In many ways, Stanford follows the tradition of both requiem and mass in setting this movement as a fugue and allocating the two framing 'Kyrie' sections to the choir while the central 'Christe eleison' is presented by the soloists. The tempo (Allegro tranquillo ed espressivo) is again quicker than in many other settings, and A minor soon turns into F major and later C major (again by way of mediantic leaps). The opening motif of the fugal Kyrie theme is characterized by a stepwise descend from the opening pitch, followed by a return to it. Where motifs A and B stand for movement away from a starting point (one downwards, one upwards), this new motif C (example 3) thus represents stability. In the 'Kyrie', the motif descends two quaver notes (D and C) in order to return to the opening via a crotchet D.

Example 6.4: Stanford, *Requiem*, Kyrie, begin (soprano)[9]

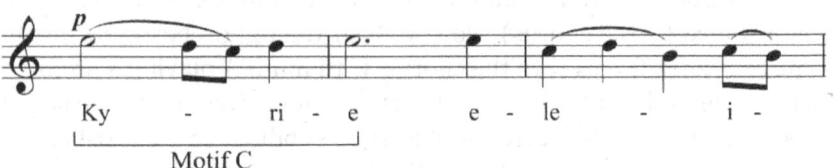

Unexpectedly, the movement ends not after the presentation of the second 'Kyrie'; it continues with another brief recapitulation of the text (now in a homophonic rather than fugal manner) over string tremolos, again in the order chorus-soloists-chorus. This time the 'Christe' occupies much more time than the two 'Kyries'. While the tremolos might indicate insecurity and fear, the final 'Christe eleison' turns to an affirmative A major which is confirmed by the choir's concluding 'Kyrie' – a strong consoling moment after the Introit's descending *pianissimo* end and the minor key that dominated the 'Kyrie' so far.

Gradual

The 'Gradual' is rarely set in nineteenth-century requiem compositions, possibly because it repeats the opening lines of the introit before continuing with a different psalm verse. Stanford may have chosen it for its first textual hint at a positive outcome, or because it also features in Dvořák's *Requiem* (more on this later). In English its psalm verse says 'Men will remember the just man for ever: no fear shall he have of evil tidings'. It is interesting that the absence of fear is here linked to commemoration on the part of the living; this is likely to appeal to a composer more interested in commemoration and praise of a great man, rather than intercession on behalf of the departed or the consolation of mourners. The music, however, offers consolation as well: again the key is A major, the tempo now a slow Larghetto. Like in the Introit the framing 'Requiem aeternam' verses are sung by an a cappella chorus with a few orchestral chords interspersed between the lines. As before, this almost automatically evokes a sense of religiosity and the sacred, although it is also repeatedly used to good effect in requiem settings for the concert hall (for example by Berlioz and Verdi). The vocal line opens with a condensed version of motif C in which the voice only descends one note (rather than originally two) before returning to its starting point:

Example 6.5: Stanford, *Requiem*, Gradual, begin (soprano)[10]

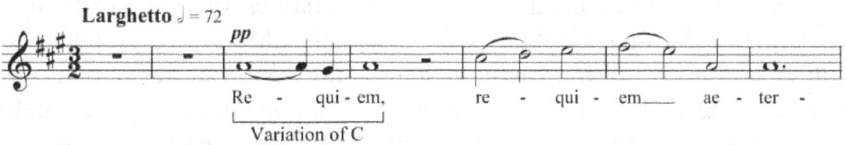

Between the 'Requiem' and 'et lux' lines we hear motif A making a brief appearance in the orchestra. As in the Introit, Stanford moves mediantically from A major to C major (via their shared note E) for the 'et lux perpetua' – the light again has to shine in C major.

The middle section is allocated to the solo soprano who is accompanied by a solo violin soaring halo-like an octave above the human voice, an effect we also know from Fauré's *Requiem*. The opening figure of its lines feature motif B so that all three basic motifs are present in this, the briefest of the work's movements.

This is followed by a repeat of the 'Requiem' lines in a different a cappella setting, finishing on another, slower return to motif A. Unlike the first movement, the 'Gradual' does not end on motif A: its descending line is balanced by an inverted line of three times three stepwise ascending notes; the absence of fear leads to a more positive finish.

Sequence

The 'Dies irae' sequence is in many ways the centrepiece of the requiem: not only is it the fifth of the nine texts that make up the liturgical ordinary (although they are rarely all set in requiem compositions), it is also by far the longest one. Unlike most other parts of the liturgy, it is a poetic text, written in rhyming, trochaic three-line stanzas. There are seventeen of them, followed by three two-line rhymes (beginning with 'Lacrimosa') which were probably added later. The main body of text is attributed to Thomas of Celano, a friend of St Francis of Assisi, and was probably written around 1250. The text is also unusual in that it starts with a third-person account of the beginning of the Last Judgement, yet in the seventh stanza suddenly switches to a poetic first person pleading for God's mercy ('Quid sum miser tunc dicturus'). This very personal, intimate prayer continues until the end of the original poem ('Gere curam mei finis!') while the final six lines return to the third-person account. The poem also contains vivid depictions of the objects of fear, from the opening reference to the day of wrath ('Dies irae, dies illa') to a general expression of fear ('Quantus tremor est futurus'), of having to face God with all his tremendous powers ('rex tremendae majestatis'), and to those condemned to the eternal flames of hell ('Confutatis maledictis, flammis acribus addictis'). This alternating of personal, intimate prayer and the frightful depiction of the Last Judgement and the furies of hell offer composers a great opportunity to use dramatic musical effects; many of them (most notably Verdi) were to face criticism for rendering their settings of the sequence in too dramatic or operatic a fashion.

Where Mozart or Verdi deployed the full forces of choir and orchestra straight away in a fortissimo blast in order to highlight the importance, power and threat of the Day of Judgement, Stanford chose a very different strategy: his choir starts in pianissimo (initially men only), declaiming rather than singing each line on the same pitch, gradually ascending line for line in semitones over foreboding rolling bass figures towards a climactic explosion that is only reached with the 'Tuba mirum'. The key is E minor, making this the first movement to decisively depart from the tonic A major and its modal shadow A minor – after a lengthy introduction of three movements we now seriously embark on the battle for salvation. For the 'Tuba mirum' (switching to a majestic E major), the full brass section underlines the 'wondrous trumpet's' call before the judge. The 'earth's sepulchres' of the next line force an immediate return to lower registers and E minor, causing another build-up for a new (albeit less powerful) climax at 'Mors stupebit' in D minor (the 'standard' requiem key that features, however, only fleetingly in Stanford's setting). Liturgically unusual is a return of the 'Dies irae' and 'Mors stupebit' stanzas after the first 'Mors stupebit' (the 'Dies irae' with new music, the 'Mors stupebit' on a variation of its first setting). While Verdi inserted two unliturgical repeats of the 'Dies irae' stanza in his sequence, it was Dvořák who clearly served as a model here as he treated the text in exactly the same way.

The 'Juste judex' brings the first major change of character, with a far more assertive and optimistic trumpet-led tune in C major over a permanently repeated descending bass line that may depict the judge sitting down on his throne – a judge whose appearance seems to hold not too much of a threat at this point. Yet this is not to last as Stanford thickens the plot by unliturgically mixing the sixth and seventh stanzas, with a solo alto presenting the first appearance of the lyrical first person (essentially asking 'But what about me?'). These questions – alternating with the 'Juste judex' lines – affect the confidence of the former's music; its chords becoming more dissonant and the key reverting to E minor. The 'Rex tremendae' – often another opportunity for a full orchestral blast – here starts with a solo soprano, and even the later appearance of the choir does not add that much power to it. The emphasis clearly lies on the 'Salva me' (save me) that is, however, mainly allocated to all four soloists, becoming in effect a 'save us'.

Broadly following tradition, Stanford allocates the middle section's contemplations of the lyrical first person (stanzas 10-15) to the soloists. These are the most extended lyrical, aria-like passages of the entire *Requiem*, with many internal repetitions of text and sudden changes of mood, such as the wish to be sided with the herd of sheep in a peaceful, pastoral F major. Unlike many other composers, Stanford does not give the alto a prominent solo role here (which is often done, particularly in relation to the 'motherly' 'Qui Mariam absolvisti' stanza). Instead, an alto solo opens the 'Lacrimosa' (after what is maybe the most intense final plea 'voca me cum benedictis' of the lyrical first person – again presented by all soloists as a 'call us' rather than 'call me'). This final section is separated into two halves, with a more agitated, harmonically and dynamically more active opening centred on E minor and C minor and a serene, peaceful and much more stable 'Pie Jesu' in E major, finishing the movement on a positive note. In contrast to many other composers, Stanford does not set the 'Pie Jesu' or the final 'Amen' as a fugue.

Unlike the previous movements, the sequence does not feature motifs A, B or C in prominent roles. At the end of the sequence the vocal score indicates, 'In concert performance, a pause of at least two minutes should be made here'.[11] This hints not only at a preference for a non-liturgical performance but also that someone – more likely the publisher than the composer – thought a liturgical performance at least possible, although the work is unlikely to have ever been performed as part of a service or mass.

Offertorium

The offertorium can be divided into four sections: the 'Domine Jesu Christe' leads into the first 'Quam olim Abrahae', followed by the 'Hostias' section and the second 'Quam olim Abrahae'. The movement's key is C major, continuing to stay away from the main key of the work (and a mediantic third below the sequence's closing E minor, as well as a third above the work's main key A major), with the tempo now a quick Allegro. On top of a continuous accompaniment of broken chords rises a triumphant theme on the notes of the C major triad in the choir, rhythmically kick-started by a double-dotted opening gesture. The mood has clearly swung to optimism at this point. The following acclamation of 'Rex gloriae' suddenly leaps to E major as another mediantic key (a second, unliturgical rendition of this acclamation will feature in E flat major a little bit later), before the solo bass opens the pleas to liberate the souls of the departed from the clutches of hell, repeating the positive opening gesture of the choir. In many settings this section prolongs the depiction of fear, or at least insecurity dominant in the sequence, but not so here: it is as if the asked-for liberation is already certain. The movement pursues another cycle of thirds from C major via A major, F major and D flat major before settling on E major for 'Sed signifier Sanctus Michael' and returning to C major for 'in lucem sanctam' – again, the light can only shine properly in C, with no room left for any fear. There appears to be no doubt at this point that the dead will indeed see the eternal, holy light.

Following generic tradition, Stanford sets the 'Quam olim Abrahae' section as a fugue – with 76 bars, the most elaborate one in this requiem. The time signature switches to 6/4 as the main four-bar theme is sung for the first time.

Example 6.6: Stanford, *Requiem*, Offertory, 'Quam olim Abrahae' theme[12]

This fugue is possibly the weakest section of the entire *Requiem* as the theme contains some strange features: its most prominent note is the B flat at the end of the second bar, reached through a large upward leap from C. This B flat is a dissonance, namely the seventh of a secondary dominant leading to an F major chord (one would rather have expected a leap up to the octave C). As a dissonance, the B flat has to resolve downwards, but this it only does belatedly as the expected entry of F major is suspended until the second beat of the next bar. Instead the B flat is repeated as the first note of a descending quaver line. After the strong, almost emphatic presentation of the B flat in the previous bar, one would have expected its resolution straight away, or after a tied-over suspension, but the repeat of the note appears unexpected and odd. The theme then ends with a hemiola on 'eius' – a rhythmic figure which does not emphasize two times three crotchets as normal in a 6/4 context but instead three times two. A hemiola is usually deployed in Renaissance and Baroque music to prepare the end of a melodic line by shortening the distances between emphasized beats, its effect being similar to the relatively sudden braking of a car. This is fine if the music is indeed coming to a (temporary or permanent) halt, but in the polyphonic texture of a fugue this is not the case – while the fugal theme comes to an end in one voice, the remaining parts are involved in other sections of the theme or contrapuntal material that keeps moving on. This means that we hear hemiolas all the time without the music as a whole ever slowing down or stopping until the very end of the fugue; a strange and very unusual effect. That Stanford was less dedicated to this fugue than to other sections could also be indicated by the fact that he repeats it literally after the 'Hostias' section (indicating a *da capo*); in other cases of textual repetition (such as the second 'Hosanna' in the 'Sanctus') he avoided a literal repetition, instead composing related yet not identical new material.

The 'Hostias' is a very slow, intimate movement presented by the quartet of soloists, beginning in A flat major yet moving quickly through a broad range of keys. Its emotional centre is the unaccompanied 'de morte transire ad vitam' – the wish for the deceased ones to experience death only as a transition to eternal life 'as promised to Abraham and his seed', as the repeat of the fugue underlines at the end of the movement. As with the sequence, the offertorium does not display motifs A, B or C prominently.

Sanctus et Benedictus

The 'Sanctus' often features the most optimistic music of a requiem setting. Its text, the praise of God by the cherubim and seraphim, does not mention death or judgement at all, and – after the positive turn over the course of the offertory – offers an opportunity to consolidate the more upbeat mood at this point.

Unlike Verdi, Stanford does not start with triumphant fanfares announcing the praise of God (maybe in part to balance the unusually triumphant nature of the 'Offertorium'); after the emotional turmoil of the previous two movements his 'Sanctus' rather depicts a vision of celestial peace and rest. It is set almost as a lullaby, in the compound triple time (here 9/8) typical for this genre and an ethereal harp and high string sound throughout. For the first time since the 'Gradual' we return to the home key of A major, which is rather stable in this movement (with brief, by now almost expected mediantic sojourns to the keys of C sharp major and F major).

The most dominant feature of this movement is a rising three-note motif that is permanently present in the 'Sanctus' and 'Hosanna' sections (and confined to these two words), alternating between the alto and soprano voices.[13] It is a combination of the motifs A and B (combining the former's stepwise movement pattern and the latter's upward direction):

Example 6.7: Stanford, *Requiem*, Sanctus, begin (altos)[14]

Through its omnipresence, this 'Sanctus motif' (together with the arpeggios of the strings and harp) provides a permanent background to the gradual unfolding of the main parts in the male voices. However, somehow this 'foreground' fades into the background as the Sanctus motif keeps dominating the scene, although moving to the orchestra as the voices unite on 'Pleni sunt coeli'. Usually the 'Hosanna' is set as a fugue on separate musical material, yet here Stanford keeps the Sanctus motif (now returned to the female parts) going and continues with a homophonic texture.

Set in common time and F major, the 'Benedictus' provides some contrast at the centre of the movement. Allocated to the soloists, the blessing of the one who comes in the name of the Lord rises from the bass up to the soprano. While the general quiet and peaceful atmosphere of the movement is maintained, motif A features prominently in accompaniment figures of the orchestra, hinting at the fact that a positive outcome is still not assured.

The 'Benedictus' is followed by another 'Hosanna'; not a literal repeat as in many other settings but instead an intensification of the original mood, with the formerly absent soloists now providing the icing on the choir's cake. The peaceful mood and the Sanctus motif in particular make this movement probably the most memorable one for the first-time listener.

Agnus Dei et Lux aeterna

If the presence of motif A in the 'Benedictus' did not alert us to the fact that it was too early for a happy end, the beginning of the 'Agnus Dei' certainly does. Low timpani rolls are followed by a slow orchestral march in A minor, and we don't need to be aware of the indication 'Tempo di Marcia funebre' in the score to recognize a funeral march. Forming the so far longest orchestral section of the *Requiem*, the march is based on a dotted version of motif A that appears twice at its very beginning.

Example 6.8: Stanford, *Requiem*, Agnus Dei et Lux aeterna, begin[15]

This motif – sometimes dotted, sometimes not – also persists in the orchestra as the choir comes in for its triple 'Agnus Dei' rendition. Usually the three acclamations of the lamb of God are set in an identical or very similar way, but Stanford surprises his listeners. While his second 'Agnus Dei' is indeed a repeat of the first one (moved up from A minor to C minor), the third one is different: where it is expected to start after an orchestral one-bar transition (identical to the one that prepared the second 'Agnus'), only the orchestra begins with the repeat of the melodic line, now in E flat minor (another minor third up from C after the previous move from A to C). The orchestra continues with the 'Agnus Dei' theme on its own, yet in its second bar the choir enters with a similar but not identical melodic line, turning the Eb minor chord into a much more complex and dissonant diminished seventh chord on C minor. The delayed rendition of the vocal line and the much more complex harmonic structure (the harmonies also change much faster than in the first and second 'Agnus') create a sense of unease and foreboding. There is a deviation from the liturgical requiem text here as the line 'Agnus Dei, dona eis requiem' ought to be augmented to 'dona eis requiem sempiternam' in the third rendition; however, there is no 'sempiternam' in Stanford's *Requiem*. As this omission does not change the content very much it is not clear whether the composer left it out on purpose or as a result of an oversight.

Again following generic convention, 'Agnus Dei' and 'Lux aeterna' are set in a single movement. The third 'Agnus Dei' is thus followed immediately by three renditions of 'Lux aeterna', each time first presented by one or several soloists and repeated by the choir. The harmonic fluctuations of the 'Agnus Dei' are followed by a very stable F major, with the harp providing upward arpeggios and the general mood again being one of peacefulness and content. The orchestra accompanies the three entrances of the choir with majestic (score indication: Maestoso) variations of motif B, almost turning the peacefulness into joyful expectation – yet again, this is not to last as the opening funeral march returns for a lengthy orchestral interlude (of more than two minutes while the opening introduction was *ca.* 90 seconds long; between them the two versions of the march cover about one third of the movement's duration). As before, the march is chromatically enhanced and harmonically unstable, but it eventually returns us to A major, and to another rendition of 'Lux aeterna', this time commencing straight away with the choir. This is followed by 'Quia pius es', the last line of this work. The music slows down to a 'Più lento' while the accompaniment is laced with motif A in dotted and 'straight' versions, but now sounding almost consoling rather than dark and sombre as before. Motif B also features in the accompaniment, introducing the renditions of the final line. At this point another deviation from the norm becomes obvious: liturgically, 'Requiem aeternam, dona eis Domine, et lux perpetua luceat eis' would be required to appear before a final 'Lux aeterna' rounds off the text, but the 'Requiem' line is missing here. This is all the more surprising as many composers utilize the return of the opening line of the requiem at its end to refer back to their opening music, thus highlighting an arch-like structure (Mozart/Süssmayr probably being the best-known example). That Stanford 'misses' this opportunity cannot be an oversight; he clearly wanted the 'eternal light' to outshine the 'eternal rest' and let the positive assurance of God's mercy have the very last word.

In summary, Stanford's *Requiem* can be divided into three sections: the first three movements are centred on the keys of A major and A minor and prominently feature motifs A, B, and C. Sequence and offertory depart from A as the tonal centre and also leave the three-note motifs behind. The final two movements then return to A tonalities, and also to variations of the three-note motif. As with many other settings, Stanford's sequence displays the most dramatic moments of the *Requiem*, with confidence or consolation being altogether stronger than the moments of insecurity, fear or even panic.

The Reception of Stanford's *Requiem*

Stanford's *Requiem* received a rather mixed reception. Harry Plunket Greene – who sang the bass solo at the premiere in 1897 – wrote in 1935:

> This is a sincere and deeply-felt work, worthy to take its place amongst the greatest modern settings of this impressive service, despite its undisguised indebtedness to Italian methods of Choralism.[16]

John F. Porte wrote in 1921:

> This is a fine work as *Requiems* go, being full of dignity, impressive and profound. It is not often performed, and has a certain cumbersome effect as a whole. ... Stanford's *Requiem* is not of the type of work that is likely to become popular. It is rather noble and contains certain passages of great distinction and high in musical value; but the task of preparing it for performance is not altogether unreasonably shirked in favour of the quite suitable better known works, when the occasion for the performance of a *Requiem* comes along.[17]

Most revealing is the review of the première published by an unnamed 'Special Correspondent' in *The Musical Times* on 1 November 1897:

> From the evidence of the new work he [Stanford] might have been all his life engaged in writing church music for the sensitive and passionate Latin peoples, whose half-swooning languors and impetuous outbursts he has reproduced in music with astonishing fidelity. 'Oh!' it may be said, 'then the requiem cannot be sincere.' ... Sincere the Requiem assuredly is, or it would not convince. Whether it represents the style most congenial to the composer's taste and judgement is another matter, and one that concerns him alone.
> Dr Stanford is, if anything, most successful in dealing with the tremendous and and exacting 'Dies irae'. ... Leading themes are freely employed, but in simple forms, and the power of the

music lies chiefly in its broad and suggestive – I had almost written pictorial – effects. Developed examples of counterpoint are sparingly given, ... but 'Quam olim Abrahae' is set as a really fine fugue on a strikingly diatonic subject. It is rather curious that the 'Sanctus,' upon which the composer obviously spent much pains, and from which he may have looked for corresponding results, is the least effective part of the work. ... To be sure, the performance came short of perfection; for which reason I do not yet suggest that Dr. Stanford should try his hand on the 'Sanctus' a second time.[18]

People will, of course, never agree on matters of aesthetic judgement, but it is interesting to note the special correspondent particularly praising the 'Quam olim Abrahae' fugue and being unhappy with the 'Sanctus' while I would rate the latter much higher than the former for the reasons outlined above. The first and third reviews reveal a general disdain for music that is mainly emotional, sensitive, 'Italianate' and – even though the word is not used here – operatic. Music in this style is regarded as typical for 'Latin' peoples, as well as not being sincere. What these British reviewers would rate highly instead would be Germanic music (particularly by composers like Brahms) that displays what is noted as lacking here: complex forms, more contrapuntal sections and an altogether more intellectual, 'sincere' approach. This may also explain the praise for the 'Quam olim Abrahae' fugue: it was not necessarily singled out due to its specific compositional quality, but rather for being the only extended fugue in a work otherwise 'lacking' contrapuntal sections.

Jeremy Dibble and Paul Rodmell, the two authors who have discussed the *Requiem* in recent times, both seem to also implicitly criticize Stanford's *Requiem* for its simple, Italianate rather than Germanic construction. Dibble writes of an 'emotional rather than cerebral atmosphere' in this piece that is 'more Verdi than Brahms'.[19] Rodmell goes into more detail when describing the features of Italianate style: he names a simplicity of construction at macro and micro levels, homophonic choral textures, a directness of expression, the recurrent use of antecedent and consequent phrasing, brilliant orchestration (namely the Verdian brass sections), clear definition and separation of sections, an antiphonal contrast between choir and soloists and, finally, the notable optimism expressed in all movements.[20] Much of this probably amounts to what the original reviewer of *The Musical News* called Italian choralism. Stanford's work certainly matches those by Verdi and Dvořák in terms of duration and overall complexity – these three are among the few nineteenth-century requiems that do not fit onto a single CD, all taking about 85-90 minutes to perform. But was Verdi's setting really Stanford's main model when devising his *Requiem*?

Links to Verdi and Dvořák

The following table compares the distribution of movements in the requiem settings by Verdi, Dvořák and Stanford.

Table 6.1: Text distribution in the requiem settings by Verdi, Stanford and Dvořák

Verdi, *Missa da Requiem*	Stanford, *Requiem*	Dvořák, *Requiem*
Introit & Kyrie	Introit	Introit
	Kyrie	
	Gradual	Gradual
Dies irae [=Sequence]	Sequence	Sequence
Offertory	Offertory	Offertory
Sanctus [&Benedictus]	Sanctus &Benedictus	Sanctus [&Benedictus]
		Pie Jesu
Agnus Dei	Agnus Dei & Lux aeterna	Agnus Dei & Lux aeterna
Lux aeterna		
Libera me		

This table shows that Stanford's selection of texts is not identical with either of the settings by his famous contemporaries. He is, however, much closer to Dvořák: both set a Gradual which was highly unusual in the nineteenth century. Apart from that, the only difference is the presence of the 'Pie Jesu' in the Bohemian composer's work. This is a repetition of the final lines of the sequence that can often be found in Italian or French requiem settings to accompany the liturgy of the Eucharist. Stanford did not set a 'Pie Jesu', but its absence is far less relevant than the much more unusual shared presence of the 'Gradual'. The repetition of 'Dies illa' and 'Tuba mirum' together after the first rendition of the 'Tuba mirum' can be found in Dvořák's yet not in Verdi's setting (the Italian repeats just the 'Dies irae' at two different points in the sequence). However, in my view the most important parallel is what Brown has called the 'skilful, subtle and economical use of ... thematic 'cells''. We have seen that Stanford operates with a number of different yet related three-note motifs (A-C) that can ascend or descend while moving by step or leap. This idea of connecting different movements motivically harks back to Dvořák's use of a motto in all of his movements while there is no equivalent of this practice in Verdi. Dvořák's motto is extremely dissimilar to Stanford's three-note cell in its internal structure, yet he also presents us with several new versions of it over the course of the composition before it eventually confirms its original shape and form (unlike Stanford, Dvořák returns to the music of the opening at the end). Dvořák develops his motto in a more 'structured' way; it is possible to interpret its changes as supporting the unfolding of a specific musical narrative in his *Requiem*. This is not the case with Stanford's three motifs and their derivatives – not least because they do not feature in both sequence and offertory, the two sections that are also harmonically most distant from the remaining, framing movements with their rather stable A major or minor tonalities.[21] Stanford may have been impressed by the motivic-thematic unifying musical power of Dvořák's motto without wanting to emulate the Bohemian's underlying philosophical narrative.[22]

As we have seen, there are also links to Verdi's *Requiem* (for example a certain similarity in the opening of the introit), but by and large the connections with Dvořák appear much stronger. In terms of orchestration, Stanford's piece is certainly closer to Verdi than to Dvořák, while in terms of dramatic or operatic power it is the other way round: by and large, Stanford's *Requiem* is much gentler than Verdi's; he does not present us with the big orchestral 'Dies irae' or 'Tuba mirum' clashes that we encounter in the Italian's setting. His 'Sanctus' is much more intimate and has nothing of the dramatic power and majesty of Verdi's brass fanfares which are followed by an extended fugue for double chorus. Unlike Verdi, Stanford does not use a 'Libera me' in his composition. Both Verdi and Dvořák do not separate Introit and Kyrie while Verdi separates Agnus Dei and Lux aeterna, but these are not important differences.

Stanford must have known both Verdi's and Dvořák's requiems very well (like his own setting, Dvořák's had been commissioned by the Birmingham Musical Festival, and Stanford may well have been present at its première). While it appears that Dvořák's mass of the dead has influenced him more than Verdi's there is an important difference: where Dvořák confirms death as a distant, alien and threatening power at the end of his work, Stanford presents us with a much more positive picture. He does not deny the presence of anxieties and fear (most prominently in the central section made up of sequence and offertorium, but also in the framing movements), yet neither death nor the last judgement or the judge himself appear as the powerful, majestic and threatening forces that they are in Dvořák's and even more in Verdi's compositions. Stanford's approach is a much more consoling one; despite the funeral march version of motif A accompanying the final vocal lines, his music is altogether more positive and upbeat, with fewer dramatic and threatening moments (particularly in the offertorium where few other composers can resist the temptation to dramatize the 'bottomless pit' or the 'lion's jaws').

Stanford's *Requiem* officially commemorates the painter Frederick Leighton, but it also stands for much more: it represents most likely the first setting of the requiem text by an Irish composer (and there have not been many since).[23] Furthermore, it is a good example of a requiem written not to console the people immediately affected by the loss of a close relative or friend but rather making a point about death in general. While it may be more emotional than the critics would have liked, it certainly does not lack 'cerebral' aspects which are mainly represented by the three-note 'cells', although a Brahms or a Dvořák would presumably have used them in the middle section as well. With this work displaying a generally positive and consoling attitude towards death and afterlife, Stanford has joined the ranks of the major requiem composers of the long nineteenth century, and it is a pity that his work is so rarely heard in our time.

Bibliography

Anonymous, *Musical News*, July-December 1897, 14 October 1897, 327.
Anonymous, 'Review of the Birmingham Musical Festival, By our special correspondent,' *The Musical Times*, Vol. 38, No. 657, November 1, 1897, 745-7.
Brown, David, 'Charles Villiers Stanford,' *Charles Villiers Stanford, Requiem*, Audio CD, recorded in 1997, Naxos 8.555201-02, 2004.
Chase, Gilbert, *Dies Irae. A Guide to Requiem Music* (Lanham/MD: The Scarecrow Press, 2003).
Cizmic, Maria, *Performing Pain. Music and Trauma in Eastern Europe* (Oxford, New York: Oxford University Press, 2012).
Dibble, Jeremy, *Charles Villiers Stanford: Man and Musician* (Oxford et al.: Oxford University Press, 2002).
Marx, Wolfgang, 'Domesticating Death? The Musical Other in Antonín Dvořák's *Requiem* Op. 89,' in *Musicology without Frontiers. Festschrift in Honour of Stanislav Tuksar*. Eds. Ivano Cavallini, Harry White (Zagreb: Croatian Musicological Society, 2010), 113-28.
Plunket Greene, Harry, *Charles Villiers Stanford* (London: Edward Arnold, 1935; reprint of the edition London: K. Paul, Trench, Trubner, 1921).
Porte, John F., *Sir Charles V. Stanford* (New York: Da Capo Press, 1976).
Rodmell, Paul, *Charles Villiers Stanford* (Farnham: Ashgate, 2002).

Stanford, Charles Villiers, *Requiem Op. 63*, vocal score (London, New York: Boosey & Hawkes, 1897).
Verdi, Giuseppe, *Missa da Requiem*, full score, Edition Eulenburg No. 975 (London et al.: Eulenburg, n.d.).
Voirin, Luc, *Une Histoire du Requiem* (Paris et al.: L'Harmattan, 2001).

APPENDIX: Charles Villiers Stanford, Requiem (Text)

Text

Introit

Requiem aeternam dona eis, Domine; et lux perpetua luceat eis.	Rest eternal grant them, O Lord; and let light perpetual shine upon them.
Te decet hymnus, Deus, in Sion, et tibi reddetur votum in Ierusalem.	A hymn befits Thee, O God, in Zion; and to Thee shall be paid a vow in Jerusalem.
Exaudi orationem meam; ad te omnis caro veniet.	Hear my prayer, to Thee all flesh shall come.
Requiem aeternam dona eis, Domine; et lux perpetua luceat eis.	Rest eternal grant them, O Lord; and let light perpetual shine upon them.

Kyrie

Kyrie eleison.	Lord, have mercy upon us.
Christe eleison.	Christ, have mercy upon us.
Kyrie eleison.	Lord, have mercy upon us.

Gradual

Requiem aeternam dona eis, Domine, et lux perpetua luceat eis.	Rest eternal grant them, O Lord; and let light perpetual shine upon them.
In memoria aeterna erit justus	Men will remember the just man for ever:
ab auditione mala non timebit.	no fear shall he have of evil tidings.

Sequence

1 Dies irae, dies illa
Solvet saeclum in favilla,
Teste David cum Sibylla.

Day of wrath and doom impending,
David's word with Sibyl's blending!
Heaven and earth in ashes ending!

2 Quantus tremor est futurus,

Quando iudex est venturus,

Cuncta stricte discussurus?

Oh, what fear man's bosom rendeth,
When from heaven the Judge descendeth,
On whose sentence all dependeth!

3 Tuba mirum spargens sonum,

Per sepulchra regionum,

Coget omnes ante thronum.

Wondrous sound the trumpet flingeth,
Through earth's sepulchres it ringeth,
All before the throne it bringeth.

4 Mors stupebit et natura,

Cum resurget creatura,
Iudicanti responsura.

Death is struck and nature quaking,
All creation is awaking,
To its judge an answer making.

1 Dies irae, dies illa
Solvet saeclum in favilla,
Teste David cum Sibylla.

Day of wrath and doom impending,
David's word with Sibyl's blending!
Heaven and earth in ashes ending!

3 Tuba mirum spargens sonum,

Per sepulchra regionum,

Coget omnes ante thronum.

Wondrous sound the trumpet flingeth,
Through earth's sepulchres it ringeth,
All before the throne it bringeth.

5 Liber scriptus proferetur

Lo! The book exactly worded,

In quo totum continetur,	Wherein all hath been recorded;
Unde mundus iudicetur.	Thence shall judgement be awarded.
6 Iudex ergo cum sedebit,	When the judge his seat attaineth,
Quidquid latet apparebit;	And each hidden deed arraigneth,
Nil inultum remanebit.	Nothing unavenged remaineth.
7 Quid sum miser tunc dicturus?	What shall I, frail man, be pleading?
Quem patronum rogaturus,	Who for me be interceding?
Dum vix iustus sit securus?	When the just are mercy needing?
8 Rex tremendae maiestatis,	King of majesty tremendous,
Qui salvandos salvas gratis,	Who dost free salvation send us.
Salva me, fons pietatis.	Fount of pity, then befriend us.
9 Recordare, Iesu pie,	Think, kind Jesus, my salvation
Quod sum causa tuae viae:	Caused Thy wondrous Incarnation;
Ne me perdas illa die.	Leave me not to reprobation.
10 Quarens me, sedisti lassus:	Faint and weary Thou has sought me,
Redemisti crucem passus:	On the Cross of suffering bought me,
Tantus labor non sit cassus	Shall such grace be vainly brought me?
11 Iuste iudex ultionis,	Righteous Judge, for sin's pollution,
Donum fac remissionis	Grant Thy gift of absolution,
Ante diem rationis.	Ere that day of retribution.
12 Ingemisco tamquam reus:	Guilty now I pour my moaning,
Culpa rubet vultus meus:	All my shame with anguish owning;

Supplicanti parce, Deus.	Spare, o God, Thy suppliant groaning.
13 Qui Mariam absolvisti,	Through the sinful woman shriven,
Et latronem exaudisti,	Through the dying thief forgiven,
Mihi quoque spem dedisti.	Thou to me a hope hast given.
14 Preces meae non sunt dignae:	Worthless are my prayers and sighing,
Sed tu bonus fac benigne,	Yet, good Lord, in grace complying,
Ne perenni cremer igne.	Rescue me from fires undying.
15 Inter oves locum praesta,	With Thy favoured sheep o place me,
Et ab hoedis me sequestra,	Nor among the goats abase me,
Statuens in parte dextra.	But to Thy right hand upraise me.
16 Confutatis maledictis, Flammis acribus addictis,	When the wicked are confounded doomed to flames of woe unbounded,
Voca me cum benedictis.	call me, with Thy Saints surrounded!
17 Oro supplex et acclinis,	Low I kneel, with heart submission!
Cor contritum quasi cinis	See, like ashes my contrition!
Gere curam mei finis.	Help me in my last condition!
18 Lacrymosa dies illa	Ah! That day of tears and mourning!
Qua resurget ex favilla	From the dust of earth returning,
19 Iudicantus homo reus.	Man for judgement must prepare him;
Huic ergo parce, Deus:	Spare, o God, in mercy spare him!

20 Pie Iesu Domine,	Lord, all pitying, Jesu blest,
Dona eis requiem.	Grant them Thine eternal rest.
Amen.	Amen.

Offertorium

Domine Iesu Christe, Rex gloriae,	O Lord Jesus Christ, King of Glory,
libera animas omnium fidelium defunctorum	deliver the souls of all the faithful departed
de poenis infernis et de profundu lacu:	from the pains of hell and from the bottomless pit:
libera eas de ore leonis;	save them from the lion's jaws,
ne absorbeat eas tartarus,	that hell may not engulf them,
ne cadant in obscurum.	that they may not fall into darkness,
Sed signifer sanctus Michael	but let Saint Michael the standard-bearer
repraesentet eas in lucem sanctam.	lead them into the holy light
Quam olim Abrahae promisisti	which Thou of old didst promise
Abrahae et semini eius.	Abraham and to his seed.
Hostias et preces tibi, Domine, laudis offerimus:	Sacrifices and prayers of praise to Thee, O Lord, we offer:
tu suscipe pro animabus illis,	do Thou receive them on behalf of those souls
quarum hodie memoriam facimus.	whom this day we commemorate.
Fac eas, Domine, de morte transire ad vitam.	Allow them, O Lord, to pass from death into life.
Quam olim Abrahae promisisti	Which Thou of old didst promise
Abrahae et semini eius.	Abraham and to his seed.

Sanctus

Sanctus, sanctus, sanctus,	Holy, holy, holy,
Domine Deus Sabaoth,	Lord God of Sabaoth,
pleni sunt caeli et terra gloria tua.	heaven and earth are full of Thy glory.
Hosanna in excelsis.	Hosanna in the highest.

Benedictus qui venit in nomine Domini.	Blessed is he who cometh in the name of the Lord.
Hosanna in excelsis.	Hosanna in the highest.

Agnus Dei & Lux aeterna

Agnus Dei, qui tollis peccata mundi:	Lamb of God, who takest away the sins of the world:
dona eis requiem.	grant them rest.
Agnus Dei, qui tollis peccata mundi:	Lamb of God, who takest away the sins of the world:
dona eis requiem.	grant them rest.
Agnus Dei, qui tollis peccata mundi:	Lamb of God, who takest away the sins of the world:
dona eis requiem.	grant them rest.
Lux aeterna luceat eis, Domine,	Let eternal light shine upon them, O Lord,
cum sanctis tuis in aeternam:	with Thy saints forever,
quia pius es.	for Thou are merciful.
Et lux perpetua luceat eis.	And let light perpetual shine upon them.

---

[1] *Musical News*, July-December 1897, 14 October 1897, 327.

[2] Luc Voirin, *Une Histoire du Requiem* (Paris et al.: L'Harmattan, 2001); Gilbert Chase, *Dies Irae. A Guide to Requiem Music* (Lanham/MD: The Scarecrow Press, 2003).

[3] See http://www.requiemsurvey.org/composers.php?id=1518, http://www.requiemsurvey.org/composers.php?id=1636, http://www.requiemsurvey.org/composers.php?id=2516 and http://www.requiemsurvey.org/composers.php?id=1991; all accessed on 30 October 2013.

[4] For a discussion of the role art and music can play in expressing grief, mourning and lament see Maria Cizmic, *Performing Pain. Music and Trauma in Eastern Europe* (Oxford, New York: Oxford University Press, 2012), particularly 20-22.

[5] David Brown, 'Charles Villiers Stanford,' in *Charles Villiers Stanford, Requiem*, Audio CD, recorded in 1997, Naxos 8.555201-02, 2004, 2-4: 4.

[6] Charles Villiers Stanford, *Requiem Op. 63*, vocal score (London, New York: Boosey & Hawkes, 1897), 3.
[7] Giuseppe Verdi, *Missa da Requiem*, full score, Edition Eulenburg No. 975 (London et al.: Eulenburg, n.d.), 1.
[8] Stanford, *Requiem*, 3.
[9] *Ibid.*, 15.
[10] *Ibid.*, 22.
[11] *Ibid.*, 76.
[12] *Ibid.*, 88-9.
[13] The alto and soprano parts are divided in this movement, resulting in a six-part choir.
[14] Stanford, *Requiem*, 100.
[15] *Ibid.*, 127.
[16] Harry Plunket Greene, *Charles Villiers Stanford* (London: Edward Arnold, 1935; reprint of the edition London: K. Paul, Trench, Trubner, 1921), 223.
[17] John F. Porte, *Sir Charles V. Stanford* (New York: Da Capo Press, 1976), 62-3.
[18] 'Review of the Birmingham Musical Festival, By our special correspondent,' *The Musical Times*, Vol. 38, No. 657, November 1, 1897, 745-7: 746.
[19] Jeremy Dibble, *Charles Villiers Stanford: Man and Musician* (Oxford et al.: Oxford University Press, 2002), 295.
[20] Paul Rodmell, *Charles Villiers Stanford* (Farnham: Ashgate, 2002), 195.
[21] Neither Verdi nor Dvořák share Stanford's preference for mediantic harmonic relationships.
[22] For details of the use and development of Dvořák's motto see Wolfgang Marx, 'Domesticating Death? The Musical Other in Antonín Dvořák's *Requiem* Op. 89,' in *Musicology without Frontiers. Festschrift in Honour of Stanislav Tuksar*. Eds. Ivano Cavallini, Harry White (Zagreb: Croatian Musicological Society, 2010), 113-28.
[23] Gerard Victory's *Ultima Rerum* (written 1975-81) is the most important Irish requiem composition after Stanford.

7 | Arrigo Boito and Giovanni Verga: the Body, Illness and Death in *Mastro-don Gesualdo*

Deirdre O'Grady

This short study takes as its point of departure the association between two Italian writers: the Paduan Arrigo Boito (1842-1918) (fig. 7.1)[1] and Giovanni Verga (1840-1922) (fig. 7.2)[2] who was from Vizzini in the Sicilian province of Catania. The latter's absorption into the iconoclastic movement known as the Milanese 'Scapigliatura' that followed the author's transference to Milan in 1872 [3] marks his turning towards realistic expression conveyed in economic terms. Later in his career, in the novel *Mastro-don Gesualdo,* Verga employs body imagery and utilizes it as a metaphor for economic hardship and the socio-political change (1821-1848) that culminated in Italian Unification (1861). Verga's treatment of the themes of illness, death, burial and afterlife contrasts with Boito's symbolic poetic presentations that are for the most part conveyed by means of images of works of art. Yet it may be argued that Verga's symbolic imagery takes its prime influence from the morbid preoccupation with death and decomposition found in the writers of 'Scapigliatura', and in the confrontation of art and science found in Boito's work. The term 'Scapigliatura' in Italian means 'dishevelled'. It alludes to the anti-conformist nature of the artistic and social vision of its members.

A study of the symbolic body as found in the poetry of Arrigo Boito, and a comparison with Giovanni Verga's treatment of the same in *Mastro-don Gesualdo* highlights the transition from Romanticism to Realism, the conflict, yet coexistence of art and science within the literary form, and the cultivation of symbolic imagery related to illness, death and burial. In his novel the Sicilian author employs images of decline, decay and rebirth in order to symbolically illustrate the demise of the Kingdom of the Two Sicilies in Southern Italy, and the slow but progressive movement that led to the birth of a 'New Italy'. The result is a historical and symbolic vision of the first stage of the Italian 'Risorgimento', while in literary terms one witnesses the realistic presentation of themes associated with the Romantic period by means of the portrayal of two families and the unhappy union forged between them. However, from a purely literary viewpoint the novel may be described as a discourse on death, illustrated with life-sized and disturbing images. The inherited consumption, slow decline, the death agony and burial are all afforded much space and detail. In spite of its portrayal of social diversity, contrasting settings, and a variety of human reactions, the text provides a lesson on the final stages of human life. These portraits of death are afforded such detail and clarity that one may be convinced that they are the fruit of the author's personal experiences.

The Scapigliatura and the Literary Scene in Nineteenth-Century Milan

The work of Arrigo Boito demands consideration in this context. Boito was the leading exponent of the Milanese Scapigliatura movement. His *Libro dei versi* or *Book of Verses* consists of a series of poems that symbolically focuses on a corpse, a mummy and a torso. These indicate an 'afterlife' separated from the traditional religious perceptions, focusing instead on science, history and art. In anticipation of its present status, Milan emerges as a business capital and as the centre of renewal and innovation. Verga transferred there in 1872 and remained, with the exception of some short absences, until he returned to Catania for good in 1893. In Milan he frequented the fashionable salons favored by the leading 'scapigliati' (including those of the Countess Claretta Maffei – a friend of Giuseppe Verdi, Vittoria Cima and Teresa Mannati). In addition to Arrigo Boito, Giovanni Verga counted among his close acquaintances Giuseppe Giacosa, Salvatore Farina, and Torelli-Viollier (founder of the newspaper *Il Corriere della Sera*). Verga's creative gifts flourished, and although separated geographically from the world of the Sicilian peasant, it was in Milan that his realistic depiction of low and rustic life was born. Verga's progression is marked by a breaking away from the style of his early novels: *Amore e patria* (1858), *I Carbonari della montagna* (1863), *Una peccatrice* (1866) and *Storia di una capinera* (1871). With *Eva* (1873) new ground is broken. It projects an objective assessment of passion and experience in the world of the artist, and tells the story of the relationship between a painter and a singer/entertainer of the variety theatre. Pictorial creativity and creative performance are linked in an artistic vision fuelled by the author's association with the artists of the Scapigliatura.4 The short story *Nedda* (1874) marks the birth of 'Verga verista' – the realistic Verga. The impression of the hardship and hopelessness of those trapped in a vicious circle of peasant Sicilian society is achieved with the use of technical devices gleaned from Verga's Milanese experience. Rather than the use of legalistic terminology defining individual rights in an urban setting favoured by Giacosa in his bourgeois dramas written during the last two decades of the nineteenth century (*Diritti dell'anima, Tristi amori, Come le foglie*),5 one witnesses 'economic realism' communicated through images verging on brutality. These depict the plight of the peasants as little better than that of animals, and their life stories are told in a fashion that embraces scenes of illness, death, and symbolic live burial. Verga's *Vita dei campi* [*Life in the Fields*, 1880] is a selection of short stories set in a society which, alienated from culture and civilization, allows instinct and passion to explode in violent communications and exchanges. Animal imagery pervades the stories as the individual resorts to brute force. The use of Italian syntax and Sicilian vocabulary further adds to the authenticity of the effect.

Boito and Verga: from Milan to Sicily

Mastro-don Gesualdo (1889) was intended as the second of a series of novels (*I Malavoglia* being the first), relating to the trials of families in the manner of Honoré de Balzac's *Human Comedy*. *I Malavoglia* is the story of a family of fisherfolk of that name, and it demonstrates how nature in the form of the sea destroys all their family assets. The series was originally planned to appear with the title of *La marea* [*The Tide*], but this was later changed to *I vinti* [*The Defeated/Vanquished*]. However, in following the lives of the Motta/Trao families Verga provided only *Mastro-don Gesualdo* in a completed form. Only one chapter of its sequel *La Duchessa di Leyra* [*The Duchess of Leyra*] appeared posthumously in 1922. The projected *L'Onorevole Scipione* [*The Deputy Scipione*] and *L'uomo di lusso* [*The Man of Luxury*] never materialized. *Mastro-don Gesualdo* is an extremely complex work in that it answers to the descriptions 'realistic' and 'historical' in a decadent and anachronistic treatment of the 'romantic' period. It indeed looks to a historical period in an original realistic style, and its focus on identity, origin, being and becoming also anticipates and lays the foundations for the modern novel.

A reading of three early poems of Arrigo Boito, later part of the collection *Il Libro dei versi* [*The Book of Verse*] of 1877 demonstrates the symbolic function of the 'literature of the body' as perceived by the 'scapigliati', where emphasis is placed on the corpse, its dissection, preservation and artistic representation. Central to these poems are the themes of illness, death, dissection, preservation and restoration. Later, through the image of the human body Verga carries Boito's symbolic representation of literary criticism and artistic decadence to a further dimension: in place of Boito's corpse as a metaphor for 'art', Verga's projection of the body before and after death acts as a prelude to socio-political change. The Sicilian author intended to thematically illustrate the crisis of the aristocracy, its need of the support of the new middle class and the birth of a new social order.

Arrigo Boito and the 'Literature of the Body' – Three Poems from *Il Libro dei versi*

Imagery in Boito's poetry does not merely cultivate a morbid or pessimistic vision of life. This is apparent in three poems from his *Libro dei versi:* 'Il torso' ['The Torso', 1862], 'A una mummia' ['To a Mummy', 1862] and 'Lezione di anatomia' ['Anatomy Lesson', 1865]. The metaphorical image extends its purpose in order to symbolize the mummification of thought (as represented by the embalmed human forming 'A una mummia'), the critical dissection of a work of art (symbolized by the images of the anatomy lesson in 'Lezione di anatomia'), the ravages of time as perceived through an artistic creation (as presented in 'Il torso'), and the refusal on the part of traditionalists to 'bury' the artistic habits of the older generation and relegate them to history. There are images of the body decapitated by time, and the body preserved with the aid of science which results in a figurative work of art (a mummy) as the subject of a poetic work of art. Finally, pure poetry is dissected, analyzed and identified in a search for an inherent literary form.[6] One may therefore argue that Boito provides poetic discourses on death, non-burial and immortality of the human form as a metaphor for art and its manipulation by critics.

Boito's artistic doctrine is contained in each of the three poems previously mentioned. Each contains images of the body after death. Restoration, preservation, and dissection are at the core of the artistic exercise. Each is rejected in order to express the belief that art is the spontaneous expression of an age or of an individual at a given time. Any forced continuity, any attempt to restore an object to its former glory after its natural demise, results in the falsification of the form. Thus any extension of a style or movement in order that it might outlive the circumstances that gave it life results in the mummification of the form. As the Torso stands decapitated by time the poet symbolically places his own head on its marble shoulders to exclaim:

> Oggi forse minaccia
> Quelle tue monche braccia
> Di più fiero dolore
> Il restaüratore.
>
> [Perhaps today
> The restorer
> Threatens your incomplete arms
> With much greater pain.]

'Il torso' l. 109-112[7]

'A una mummia' provides a poetic image of a former human being scientifically preserved to the level of a work of art. The embalmed body proved a popular poetic topic during the later nineteenth century: one recalls Carlo Dossi's homage in *Note azzurre*. Although devoid of life Boito's Mummy bears the signs of a life lived in a different civilization. Although an eternal observer of social change, *it* shall never change. Ironically it must continue to live an eternal death. This reflects the essence of the Scapigliatura movement: it contrasts and associates the opposing forces of life and death:

> Qui per andar di secoli
> Non muterà tua sorte
> Vedrai novella popoli
> Con le occhïaia morte,
>
> [Here with the passing of centuries
> Your destiny shall not change.
> Through dead sockets
> You shall see new races,]

'A una mummia' l. 80 – 84.[8]

Boito's 'Anatomy lesson' carries the date 1865. Both the Scapigliatura poets Praga[9] and Dossi[10] have provided written accounts of anatomy lessons. In 1870 Boito's brother Camillo wrote a poem entitled 'Un corpo' ['A Body'], evoking the world of the hospital and morgue. Further significant predecessors include Baudelaire and Boulilhet. In Boito's poem the subject for dissection is a young consumptive girl whose unclaimed body was handed over to medical science. Without a funeral service or religious oration her sole achievement is seen to exist in her unwitting service to science. Boito casts her as symbolic of poetry. As an art form torn apart by a literary critic, she is laid bare in a search for scientific knowledge. The body image thus contains in itself the confrontation of science and art:

> Scïenza vattane
> Co' tuoi conforti!
> Ridammi i mondi
> Del sogno e l'anima
> Perdona o pallida
> Adolescente!
> Fanciulla pia,
> Dolce purissima
> Fiore languente
> Di poësia!
>
> [Be gone Science
> With Your words of comfort
> Restore the worlds
> Of dreams and of the spirit
> Pardon oh pale
> Adolescent
> Pious maiden
> Sweet and most pure
> Languishing flower
> Of poetry]

'Lezione d'anatomia' l. 67-76.[11]

Following the association of opposites, a shock conclusion to the poem – typical of the 'scapigliati' writers – reveals a fetus of thirty days: new life is extinguished with that of its source. The 'pious maiden' assumes new characteristics at odds with her former poetic identity. Literary criticism has stunted spontaneous appreciation. The purity of poetic intent in the artistic original has been transformed. A variety of critical interpretations are possible. However, the poetic symbol shall not prove a creative source since its power of reproduction has been destroyed.

Towards Decadence: Romantic Realism and Social Decay

In Verga's *Mastro don-Gesualdo* the two principal images adopted in a vision of decline are those of the house / palazzo and the human form. Boito's 'duality',[12] which is expressed in his poetry in metaphysical terms, is replaced by the image of two families in opposition: the 'nouveau riche' Motta family and the House of Trao – the local minor nobility in decline. The third chapter of each of the four parts of the novel contains a symbolic death (that of Part I being the death of Hope), while the final part presents the demise of both a husband and a wife in the form of Gesualdo Motta and Bianca Trao. Thus concludes their unsuccessful social partnership. The passing of Bianca, the last member of the Trao family, coincides with the introduction of a tricolour hoisted by local revolutionaries demanding political change. In this context it symbolizes victorious revolt by the lower classes. As a group of revolutionaries is set to confiscate the property of the apparently well-to-do landowners, a new ruling class is set to occupy the estates of the impoverished nobility. The concept of a political and social afterlife was intended to evolve in Verga's (unwritten) sequels to *Mastro-don Gesualdo* in key social settings: a palace in Palermo in *La Duchessa di Leyra* [*The Duchess of Leyra*], the Chamber of Deputies in Rome in *L'Onorevole Scipione* [*The Deputy Scipione*], and the boardrooms of the industrial city in *L'uomo di lusso* [*The Man of Luxury*]. It can also be argued that in *Mastro-don Gesualdo* Verga has arrived at a degree of technical prowess that allows him to convincingly depict the scenes of low and rustic life associated with *La vita dei campi* (1880) and the *Novelle rusticane* (1883), and also the pretentiousness associated with the local nobility. Each social group is represented by a female figure: Diodata, the peasant mother of Gesualdo's sons, and his wife, the consumptive aristocrat Bianca. Just as Diodata is rejected by Gesualdo for Bianca, so also is the world of the fields (to which Diodata belongs both literally and stylistically). The local and humble environment is rejected in favour of that of business, and the construction of a society literally made of stone. As one who emerges as a master builder, Gesualdo is seen to construct his future out of stone. In the process his heart is hardened to the simple spontaneous emotions until, at the end of his life, he finally becomes aware of the value of loyalty and devotion (as expressed/symbolized in the person of Diodata).

As has already been pointed out, when he came to write *Mastro-don Gesualdo,* Verga had resolved to present economic hardship by means of logical progression, objective assessment and realistic effect. He then introduced his technique to his friend Salvatore Farina as part of a preface to his short story 'L'amante di Gramigna' ['Gramigna's Lover']. The latter first appeared in the Journal *Rivista minima* 1880 and was later included in Verga's collection *La vita dei campi* of 1880. In this short preface, Verga highlights the art and science of storytelling; it is one of the many devices adopted by the author in order to project a vicious circle which traps the Sicilian rustic in a life of hardship and hopelessness governed by outmoded codes of behaviour and local customs. It advocates the abdication of the teller in favour of the tale, resulting in the hand of the artist remaining invisible, with the impression that the work appears to have written itself. Thus it marks an important stage in the history of Italian storytelling:

> l'armonia delle sue forme sarà così perfetta, la sincerità della sua realtà così evidente, il suo modo e la sua ragione di essere così necessarie, che la mano dell'artista rimarrà assolutamente invisibile, allora avrà l'impronta dell'avvenimento reale, l'opera d'arte sembrerà *essersi fatta da sé* ...
>
> [The harmony of its parts shall be so perfect, the sincerity of its reality so evident, its reason for and mode of being so necessary, that the hand of the artist shall remain completely invisible. It shall thus have the stamp of an actual event. The work of art shall appear to have *created itself*...] [13]

Thus when he came to write *Mastro-don Gesualdo,* Verga's realistic technique had already been successfully established in his collections of short stories and in the full length novel *I Malavoglia*. However, it needs to be stressed that the method indicated in the prelude to 'L'amante di Gramigna' is better suited to the short story form with its immediacy of effect and potential for rapid absorption rather than to the full-length novel. In *Mastro-don Gesualdo* Verga addresses a variety of techniques. The style adopted in the short story *Nedda* and in *La vita dei campi* is employed in some, but not all sections of the work. The novel spans the period 1820-1848 and in doing so it covers the years that are seen to constitute the first stage of the 'Risorgimento' movement. This is the first concentrated effort towards independent unification. These years find Italy overrun with secret societies plotting upheaval as insinuated in the novel. Among the secret societies are the 'Carbonari' [Coal burners] with which the character Gesualdo identifies. These three decades also mark the appearance of patriotic literature with the presence of such towering figures as Mazzini and Gioberti. It is also the era of Leopardi and Manzoni. One could be pardoned for suspecting that the historical dimension was added to *Mastro-don Gesualdo* as an afterthought. The timelessness of the social environment which the peasants and nobility in decline inhabit prompts the reader to access the actual time frame of the work. It may be noted that the *actual* timeframe and the style employed to reproduce it are at odds. Neither is there a clear explanation of the political climate of the time. Verga provides a technique of visual effects through the projection of action. Need for change, social decay and the ineffectiveness of the local aristocracy appears as justification of revolt leading to a 'new' state. The world of Gesualdo is that of a terminally ill social order calling out for burial. Verga's socialist vision allows the 'people' to be seen as the creators of the new regime.

The initial quest for freedom ended in disaster. The 1848-1849 War of Independence was lost. Mazzini summed up the situation as follows: 'The war of the Kings is over; the war of the people begins'. Thus a key moment of Italian history is at the heart of a novel that was not intended as primarily historical, but designed as the announcement of socio-economic progress coinciding with a foreseeable change in political structures. Breaking out from the vicious social circle into which he was born, the craftsman / builder Gesualdo becomes the architect of a business world no longer confined to Sicily, but which also flourishes in the financial centres of the peninsula.

Set in the period of Romanticism, situations found in the work of Italy's leading Romantic poet Giacomo Leopardi[14] are both presented and reinvented in Part I, Chapter 3 and Part III, Chapter 2.[15] The resulting effect is that of a decadent intrusion into the realistically charged projection of events, emphasized by the poetic fusion of the mother and daughter figures of Bianca Trao and Isabella Motta/Trao. The marriage of reparation of the daughter echoes that of her mother, but with an essential difference: Bianca Trao was obliged to accept any suitor on account of her lack of dowry (one remembers that the Sicilian social codes of the time viewed 'dishonour' seriously; something only to be resolved by immediate marriage). Bianca does not succeed in marrying her lover. She is accepted by Mastro-don Gesualdo on account of her minor nobility status. Gesualdo shall remain unaware throughout their life together that their 'daughter' is in reality the child of Bianca's cousin the Baron Ninì Rubiera. Bianca's disillusionment on the evening of a local feast day heralds the symbolic death of her romantic hopes, echoing the mood of Leopardi's idyll 'La sera del dì di festa' ['The Evening of the Holiday'].[16] The evening marks the burial of romantic illusions in that Bianca's bridegroom is the newly rich Mastro-don Gesualdo ('Mastro' being the term given to a manual worker). Many years later, Isabella, Bianca's daughter, in possession of a considerable dowry provided by her presumed father, Mastro-don Gesualdo, is betrothed to a Duke from Palermo. Her parting letter to her cousin echoes the 'Addio' of Lucia – the character's farewell to her home and all that was dear in Manzoni's historical novel *I promessi sposi* [*The Betrothed*].[17] Thus Verga confers historical authenticity on the work by means of recreating the literary climate of the period in which the novel is set. However, the effect is one of an anachronism, with the age of Romanticism recreated in a realistic framework. This pushes sections of *Mastro-don Gesualdo* towards decadence and allows for comparison with the master of Italian decadence Gabriele D'Annunzio.[18]

The symbolic presence of decay, decline and disease is illustrated at the opening of the novel with reference to the Palazzo Trao, the family home of the Trao.

> Una vera bicocca quella casa: I muri rotti, scalcinati, corrosi ... le finestre sgangarate e senza vetri; lo stemma logoro ... appeso ad un uncino arruginito; al di sopra della porta.

> [A true wreck was that house: the walls broken down and corroded, the plaster crumbling and corroded ... the windows rotten and devoid of glass; the crest battered and hanging from a rusted nail above the door.][19]

The house of the Baroness Rubiera although indicative of wealth also shows a premonition of the illness already present in the Palazzo Trao:

> Fin dall'androne immense e buio, fiancheggiato di porticine basse, ferrate a uso di prigione, si sentiva di essere in una casa ricca: un tanfo d'olio e di formaggio che pigliava alla gola; poi un odore di muffa e di cantina.

> [From the huge dark entrance, surrounded on either side by small low doors cast in iron, as found in prisons, one got the impression of being in a rich house: (first) a smell of oil and cheese that stuck in ones throat; followed by the odour identified with mould and cellars.][20]

Part II shows *Mastro-don Gesualdo* develop as a historical novel with the protagonist as a 'Carbonaro'. Although the political dimension does not at first reading appear to occupy a significant part of the events, it is important to note that the Carbonari insurrection of 1821 in the Kingdom of the two Sicilies marks the year of the protagonist's marriage. Gesualdo's social introduction into the house of the nobility is seen as social revolution in action:

> Mastro-don Gesualdo fece così il suo ingresso fra i pezzi grossi del paese, raso di fresco, vestito di panno fine, con un cappello nuovo fiammante fra le mani mangiate dalla calcina.
>
> [Mastro-don Gesualdo thus made his entrance in the presence of the big shots of the locality, freshly shaven, finely attired, with a new hat prominently displayed between his hands, consumed by limestone.] [21]

The hands – symbolic of both industry and identity – shall be the final image presented by Verga in his presentation of the corpse of his protagonist.

Images of illness, death and afterlife

As has been seen in the poems under consideration, Boito takes his point of departure from the body artistically reproduced (represented as the torso), dissected (similarly, the subject of the anatomy lesson), embalmed (the mummy). However, Verga proceeds from the living form.[22] Illness and decline in anticipation of death are substituted for restoration, embalming and dissection. While Boito's poems are populated by former human beings, transformed and bordering on the grotesque, Verga's characters, as a result of illness and hardship, are often transformed into caricatures. Achieving his effects through clarity of descriptive images, Verga adopts both an active and passive technique. In some cases figures are observed, in others they themselves appear to keep watch on their observers. A living death (experienced by the Baroness Rubiera as the result of apoplexy) signifies a mummification of all types of advancement. The human form appears grotesque in its inability to function although it is nonetheless present. From the Baroness no inheritance may be claimed as she lives on as a guardian of her assets, and her authority is maintained. In Part II, Chapter V her form is presented as subhuman in that she resembles an animal carcass struck by a superior power: 'la baronessa stava lunga distesa sul letto, simile a un bue colpito dal macellaio ...' ['the Baroness was placed length-wise on the bed, as an ox struck by the butcher ...'].[23] The effective and expressive animal imagery of *I Malavoglia* and the earlier works finds its climax in a portrait of impotent body mass.

Verga adopts a diversity of scale in order to present death and the rites following it. It varies from the diminutive (Bianca) to the grand ceremonial manner identified with Monarchy (Diego), and from the larger-than-life effects employed in the description of the corpse (Nunzio), to the conventional laying out of the corpse (Gesualdo himself). One might here also reflect on the 'images of death' as illustrations of social customs in differing economic frameworks. Consumption depicted as a progressive illness engulfing the human form is present in all members of the Trao family. Diego, Ferdinando, and Bianca are seen to be in decline from their first appearance. Isabella has inherited her mother's poor health and Don Ferdinando is first presented 'come un fanciullo' ['like a young boy'] – a mental invalid.[24] Diego Trao's coughing is presented in both a distasteful and disturbing manner and the imagery associated with him in Part II, Chapter 3 resembles that of a corpse: 'un corpo lungo e stecchito ... con mento aguzzo ... rivolto in su, e due occhi glauchi spalancati' ['a long and wasted body ... with a pointed chin ... raised upwards, and two dark green eyes wide open'].[25] The death agony and impression of snoring can be heard from the next room. His final passing coincides with the birth of Bianca's child (the new social snob), while his funeral is the last cry of a dying class. Draped in the flag of the Two Sicilies (this contrasts with the tricolour seen at the moment of Bianca's death), the coffin bears the inscription *unum cum regibus* – illustrating his link to the monarchy. The image of Gesualdo's father, Mastro Nunzio, at the moment of death is drawn on an enormous scale. His gleaming eyes still appear to observe his family. His outline is a solid wooden mass – 'un pezzo di legno' ['a piece of wood'], and his cap casts an enormous shadow on the wall: 'Mastro Nunzio nell'ombra stava zitto e immobile, come un pezzo di legno' ['Mastro Nunzio remained quiet and motionless in the shade, like a piece of wood'].[26] He remains an example of both the immensity and isolation of the figure of the dead before burial, and his humble funeral is marked by bickering over the inheritance of his property.

Physical presence and eternal separation coexist in the contradictory associations that have become identified with the writers of the Scapigliatura. Terminal illness, a living death, final agony, and death itself become active themes in this novel that shall subtly point towards rebirth through the birth of Isabella, the newfound wealth of Gesualdo, and the final passing of Bianca Trao. The descriptions of the illness and death of Bianca Trao/Motta provides a thematic link with Part I of the novel. Bianca's dying attempt to confide in her husband is thwarted by him. Illusions may be preserved as long as truth is not formally stated and poetic refinement alternates with realistic effect. In the figure of the dying Bianca are combined the contradictory and anachronistic aspects of the novel: romantic pathos and realistic effect:

> Faceva come quegli uccelletti in gabbia i quali provano il canto della primavera che non vedranno ... Adesso quando era presa dalla tosse, si metteva ad ansare, sfinita con la bocca aperta ... branicando colle povere braccia stecchite quasi volesse afferrarsi alla vita.

> ['She did as those small birds in cages that attempt to sing of the spring that they will never see ... Then when she had an attack of coughing she began to pant, worn out, her mouth open ... stretching out with her poor withered arms, as though she wished to grasp at life'].[27]

As the last member of the Trao family, her death marks the end of that aristocratic line, pointing towards change, revolt, and the establishment of a new order. The appearance of a tricolour on a stake carried by a band of revolutionaries marks the end of the Trao dynasty and the imminent death of the Kingdom of the Two Sicilies. Ironically, the flag (in reality the group carrying it) seemed to wish to enter the house and take possession of Mastro-don Gesualdo's land, which was acquired from the local impoverished nobility. As history is written it is clear that its subjects understand little of the world around them and are merely crying out for change.

The description of the protagonist's death and the presentation of his corpse further communicate the entire irony of his situation. From the humblest of origins he ends his life in a palace in Palermo. Yet it is his hard-earned money which maintains the aristocratic household and, as already noted, his hands – the symbol of industry – carry the signs of his identity. They remain the final statement of his achievement. His death remains an ironic comment on life, and on the success and tragedy of Mastro-don Gesualdo. A final comment is expressed by the chief coachman in his son-in-law's employment: 'Guardate le mani ... vedete cos'è nascer fortunati' ['Look at his hands ... you see what it is to be born lucky'].[28] With the contrasting images of death created with reference to the father – Mastro Nunzio – and the son – Mastro-don Gesualdo – the progression from a labourer's cottage to a palace is noted without regard to the sacrifices and steadfastness entailed in effecting the transition. This is Verga's final statement illustrating, ironically, the protagonist's achievement and how the wheel of fortune – or rather of industry – has come full circle.

Descriptions of death at a time of social change and upheaval form the main sections of Verga's novel. The author's realistic technique, which gained him the title of the founder of Italian realism, takes its cue from literary activity in Milan after the middle of the nineteenth century. While Boito's symbolic and static poetic images of death and afterlife convey universality and an association of the various art forms, Verga's images of illness, death and burial point to a new social epoch. Death, representing the end of an era, provides new beginnings. Verga's involvement with the Milanese Scapigliatura carried his literary vision from that of the Romantic to the Realistic. His portraits of death point to the death of a dynasty and to the rebirth of a new socio-political structure expressed through a new literature designed to speak to society as a whole on behalf of the socially deprived.

Bibliography

Alexander, Alfred, *Giovanni Verga* (London: Grant and Cutler, 1972).
Borsellino, Nino, *Storia di Verga* (Bari: Laterza, 1992).
Campailla, Sergio, *Anatomie verghiane* (Bologna: Patron, 1978).
Farinelli, Giuseppe, *Dal Manzoni alla Scapigliatura* (Milano: Istituto Propaganda Libraia, 1991).
Farinelli, Giuseppe, *La Scapigliatura: Profilo storico, protagonisti, documenti* (Rome: Carocci, 2003).
Finocchiaro Chirmirri, Giovanna, *Postille a Verga* (Roma: Bulzoni, 1977).
Giachery, Emerico, *Verga e D'Annunzio* (Roma: Edizioni Studium, 1991).
Guzzetta, Lia Fava, *Verga fra Manzoni e Flaubert* (Roma: Edizioni Studium, 1997).
Isella, Dante, *La lingua e lo stile di Carlo Dossi* (Milano/Napoli: Ricciardi, 1958).
Mauro, Tulio De, *Storia linguistica dell'Italian unita* (Bari: Laterza, 1953).
O'Grady, Deirdre, 'The Vicious Circle,' in *Italian Storytellers Essays on Italian Narrative Literature*, eds. Eric Haywood and Cormac O'Cuilleanain (Dublin: Irish Academic Press, 1989), 204-28.
O'Grady, Deirdre, *The Last Troubadours: Poetic Drama in Italian Opera* (London: Routledge, 1990), 180-201.
O'Grady, Deirdre, 'La dissoluzione del mondo idillico leopardiano nel *Mastro-don Gesualdo* di Verga,' in *Leopardi et l'Europe: Approches Comparatistes* (Actes du Colloque International d'Avignon, 1990), ed. Georges Barthouil (Avignon: Annales Universitaire, 1994), 95-99.
O'Grady, Deirdre, 'Parola e immagine, luce ed ombra nella poesia leopardiana,' in *Giacomo Leopardi nel mondo*, ed. Franco Foschi, (Recanati: Centro nazionale di studi leopardiani, 1995), 103 – 110.
O'Grady, Deirdre, *Piave, Boito, Pirandello: From Romantic Realism to Modernism* (Lampeter / New York: Edwin Mellen Press, 2000).
O'Grady, Deirdre, 'The Shattered Self,' *Pirandello Studies*, 22 (2002), 56-75.
Origo, Iris, *Leopardi: a Study in Solitude* (London: Hamish Hamilton, 1953).

Principe, Davide Del, *Rebellion, Death and Aesthetics in Italy: The Demons of Scapigliatura* (New York: Associated University Presses, 1996).
Tellini, Gino, *Leopardi* (Roma: Salerno Editrice), 2001.
Verga, Giovanni, *Tutte le novelle*, vol. I (Milano: Oscar Mondadori, 1883), 192.
Verga, Giovanni, *Mastro-don Gesualdo* (Milan: Mondadori Oscar Classici, 1984).
Villa, Angela Ida, ed., *A. Boito, Opere letterarie* (Milan: Istituto propaganda libraria, 1996 [Milan: Otto/Novocento, 3rd ed. 2010]).
Woolf, David, *The Art of Verga: A Study in Objectivity* (Sydney: Sydney University Press, 1977).

---

[1] For an analysis of Boito's work and a critical approach to his sources and influences see: Angela Ida Villa, ed., *A. Boito, Opere letterarie* (Milan: Istituto propaganda libraria, 1996 [Milan: Otto/Novocento, 3rd ed. 2010]); Deirdre O'Grady, *The Last Troubadours: Poetic Drama in Italian Opera* (London: Routledge, 1990), 180-2001; Deirdre O'Grady, *Piave, Boito, Pirandello: From Romantic Realism to Modernism* (Lampeter / New York: Edwin Mellen Press, 2000), 27-89.

[2] See Tulio De Mauro, *Storia linguistica dell'Italian unita* (Bari: Laterza, 1953); Alfred Alexander, *Giovanni Verga* (London: Grant and Cutler, 1972); David Woolf, *The Art of Verga: A Study in Objectivity* (Sydney: Sydney University Press, 1977); Nino Borsellino, *Storia di Verga* (Bari: Laterza, 1992).

[3] See Giuseppe Farinelli, *Dal Manzoni alla Scapigliatura* (Milano: Istituto Propaganda Libraia, 1991); Giuseppe Farinelli, *La Scapigliatura: Profilo storico, protagonisti, documenti* (Rome: Carocci, 2003); Davide Del Principe, *Rebellion, Death and Aesthetics in Italy: The Demons of Scapigliatura* (New York: Associated University Presses, 1996).

[4] Verga's letters testify to an association with Arrigo Boito. While not being intimate with the writer it is clear that he was part of the poet / librettist's group. See Giovanna Finocchiaro Chirmirri, *Postille a Verga* (Roma: Bulzoni, 1977), 116, 120, 122, 129, 130, 132, 189, and 219.

[5] The playwright Giuseppe Giacosa (*Come le foglie, Tristi amori, Diritti dell'anima*) was internationally famous as a librettist for the operatic composer Giacomo Puccini. His most famous operatic texts written in collaboration with Luigi Illica are *Manon Lescaut* (1893), *La Bohème* (1896), *Tosca* (1900) and *Madama Butterfly* (1904). Although Giacosa graduated in Law from the University of Turin he did not pursue a legal career.

[6] For a more detailed analysis see *From Romantic Realism to Modernism. Piave, Boito, Pirandello* previously cited at note 1 above, and the chapter 'Decapitation, Dissection and Symbolic Deformity: the Crisis of Romanticism,' in *Textual Intersections: Literature, History and the Arts in Nineteenth-Century Europe*, ed. Rachel Langford (Amsterdam / New York: Rodopi, 2009), 165-174.

[7] Villa, ed., *Arrigo Boito*, 64.

[8] *Ibid.*, 61.

[9] For an account of Praga's literary status see Farinelli, *La Scapigliatura*, 121-128.

[10] See Dante Isella, *La lingua e lo stile di Carlo Dossi* (Milano/Napoli: Ricciardi), 1958. Dossi is also an important influence on Luigi Pirandello. See my article 'The Shattered Self,' *Pirandello Studies*, 22 (2002), 56-75, for a consideration of the influence of *Le due morali* on Pirandello's theory of the three strings in *Il berretto a sonagli*.

11 Villa, ed., *Arrigo Boito*, 76.
12 The poem entitled 'Dualismo' ('Duality') is regarded as the 'manifesto' of the 'Scapigliatura'. Boito's vision of 'duality' does not merely indicate two opposing aspects of an entity, but also an association of opposites that leads to further unresolved contrasts.
13 Giovanni Verga, *Tutte le novelle*, vol. I (Milano: Oscar Mondadori, 1883), 192. This is the germ of an idea rather than a fully exposed theory, since there is no clear-cut attempt in these words to demonstrate how his later writing shall differ from the earlier. Nonetheless, one notes a scientific approach rather than a purely individualistic creativity on the part of the author. For a detailed account of Verga's implementation of this new technique into his Sicilian *novelle* and later novels see my article 'The Vicious Circle' in *Italian Storytellers Essays on Italian Narrative Literature*, eds. Eric Haywood and Cormac O'Cuilleanain (Dublin: Irish Academic Press, 1989), 204-28.
14 See Iris Origo, *Leopardi: a Study in Solitude* (London: Hamish Hamilton, 1953); Gino Tellini, *Leopardi* (Roma: Salerno Editrice), 2001.
15 See Deirdre O'Grady, 'La dissoluzione del mondo idillico leopardiano nel *Mastro-don Gesualdo* di Verga,' in *Leopardi et l'Europe: Approches Comparatistes* (Actes du Colloque International d'Avignon, 1990), ed. Georges Barthouil (Avignon: Annales Universitaire, 1994), 95-99.
16 See Deirdre O'Grady, 'Parola e immagine, luce ed ombra nella poesia leopardiana,' in *Giacomo Leopardi nel mondo*, ed. Franco Foschi, (Recanati: Centro nazionale di studi leopardiani, 1995), 103-110.
17 For a consideration of Verga's position between Italian Romanticism and French Realism see: Lia Fava Guzzetta, *Verga fra Manzoni e Flaubert* (Roma: Edizioni Studium, 1997).
18 Emerico Giachery's study *Verga e D'Annunzio* (Roma: Edizioni Studium, 1991) provides a critical overview of realistic tendencies in Goldoni, Belli, Pirandello and D'Annunzio.
19 G. Verga, *Mastro-don Gesualdo* (Milan: Mondadori Oscar Classici, 1984), 7.
20 Verga, Mastro-don Gesualdo, 22.
21 *Ibid.*, 31.
22 Verga's use of body imagery in order to communicate hunger, decline and ambition (the large fish gobbles up the small one) is brilliantly revealed in Sergio Campailla, *Anatomie verghiane* (Bologna: Patron, 1978). However, he does not carry the argument beyond the physical dimension, ignoring the socio-political question.
23 Verga, Mastro–don Gesualdo, 211.
24 *Ibid.*, 165.
25 *Ibid.*, 173.
26 *Ibid.*, 247.
27 *Ibid.*, 281.
28 *Ibid.*, 355.

Fig. 7.1) Arrigo Boito, photographed in 1885.
Universal Images Group / Getty Images.

Fig. 7.2) Giovanni Verga, photographed in 1900.
Mondadori / Getty Images.

8 | Death, Medicine, Literature: Foucault in 1963

Douglas Smith

In *The Order of Things* (*Les Mots et les choses*, 1966), Michel Foucault notoriously announced the imminent death of Man: 'As the archaeology of our thought easily shows, man is an invention of recent date. And one perhaps nearing its end.' ['L'homme est une invention dont l'archéologie de notre pensée montre aisément la date récente. Et peut-être la fin prochaine.'][1] This effective assassination of the consensual humanism of the post-war period took place in the full public view that necessarily accompanies a best-selling book. However, it was preceded by two less spectacular but arguably more significant metaphorical deaths three years earlier, namely those of phenomenology and semiology, dispatched in the more discreet double publication of Foucault's *Birth of the Clinic* (*Naissance de la clinique*) and *Death and the Labyrinth* (*Raymond Roussel*). This double fatality, and its relation to the history of pathology and autopsy practices, might have justified entitling this chapter 'The Murders in the Rue Morgue', after Edgar Allan Poe. However, under the circumstances, a literary allusion seems out of place, and the present clinical title more appropriate. This is because, in conjunction, the liquidation of phenomenology (with its model of a full self-determining human consciousness) and the discrediting of semiology (with its model of an empty network of signs) effectively represent the beginning of the end of literature as a central presence in Foucault's work. This lessening interest in literature coincides with a gradual shift from a thematics of death and transgression towards a concern with biopolitics, understood as the management of life through the discourses and practices of health and welfare.

At first sight, the two monographs of 1963 seem very different undertakings. *Birth of the Clinic* is an enquiry into the origins of modern Western medical clinical practice at the end of the eighteenth century. *Death and the Labyrinth* is a study of the eccentric early-twentieth-century French novelist Raymond Roussel (1877–1933), whose work was dismissed during his lifetime as the product of a disturbed mind only to achieve widespread recognition after his death. However, if the books initially appear the result of two completely separate projects — one in the history of medicine and the other in literary criticism — they nonetheless share a number of common features. Both are derived from the literary and medical preoccupations of Foucault's previous book and first major publication, *The History of Madness* (*Folie et déraison: histoire de la folie à l'âge classique*, 1961). Both explicitly share four key themes: vision, language, space and, of course, death. Furthermore, and less explicitly, they both participate in a common intellectual project: that of dislodging what was still, in the early 1960s, a dominant view of death — that is, the phenomenological-existentialist view of human mortality, associated with thinkers and writers such as Jean-Paul Sartre and Maurice Merleau-Ponty. Notwithstanding this convergence, the two books also pull in different directions. The *Birth of the Clinic* is preoccupied with the role of vision in the redefinition of clinical practice, while the Roussel monograph privileges the theme of language. This may appear a simple difference in emphasis, but it leads to a more serious problem belied by the role that the theme of space is made to play in both studies. Across the two books, Foucault effectively seeks to reconcile two different interpretations of death, based on vision and language respectively, through the mediating category of space. But the spaces of vision and language are not isomorphic, so the division persists beneath a superficial harmonization. Ultimately, in *Birth of the Clinic*, language is pulled into the orbit of vision, and semiology is subordinated to discourse. This anticipates Foucault's later shift away from literature towards biopolitics — a move that itself indicates a diminishing interest in death as a focus of research.

Birth of the Clinic and Death and the Labyrinth: The Arguments

Birth of the Clinic is a contribution to the history of medicine centred on the development of the institution of the clinic and its accompanying professional discourses, anatomy and pathology. Foucault's essential argument is that modern Western clinical practice emerges in the late eighteenth century alongside a new configuration of vision and language.[2] The boundaries between the visible and the invisible and between the sayable and the unsayable are redrawn. The body ceases to be perceived as a fantasmatic surface inscribed with the physician's flights of imagination and leaps of analogy, and is reconceptualized as an objective exterior and interior to be rationally investigated and scientifically described by the clinician. This new configuration transforms medical practice and reconstructs the hospital as a clinic devoted to observation and research as well as the care of the sick.

Death and the Labyrinth takes as its subject the writer Raymond Roussel. As a patient of the psychiatrist Pierre Janet and a probable suicide, Roussel was regarded as a pathological case by most of his contemporaries and his apparently incoherent and delirious writings were dismissed as the product of mental illness. However, upon the posthumous publication of the theoretical manifesto text *How I Wrote Some of My Books* (*Comment j'ai écrit certains de mes livres*, 1935), it became clear that the superficial confusion of Roussel's work was underlain by rigorous structuring devices. Thus a key early short story 'Among the Blacks' ('Parmi les Noirs', 1900) is structured around the minimal difference between its first and last sentences. The story begins with the words: 'Les lettres du blanc sur les bandes du vieux billard' ['the white characters written on the cushions of the old billiard table'] — and concludes with the following variant on its opening: 'LES... LETTRES... DU... BLANC... SUR... LES... BANDES... DU... VIEUX... PILLARD' ['THE... LETTERS... OF... THE... WHITE... MAN... ON... THE... HORDES... OF... THE ... OLD... PILLAGER'].[3] In a sense, the entire narrative, recounting a disastrous trip to sub-Saharan Africa, is contained in the minimal difference between 'billard' (billiard table) and 'pillard' (pillager), where the harmless furniture and games of a gentleman's club and the catastrophes of imperial adventurism are separated by nothing more than the difference between a voiced and unvoiced phoneme ([b] versus [p]). For Foucault, far from being insane, Roussel possesses an extraordinarily lucid insight into the systematic yet arbitrary nature of language and the way in which a network of minimal differences can produce unexpected meanings.[4] The madness that Roussel's writing appears to manifest is then generated from within language itself and not from a disturbed mind.[5]

Redefining Death: Against Phenomenology and Existentialism

In *Birth of the Clinic* and *Death and the Labyrinth*, Foucault takes up a critical position with respect to phenomenology and existentialism. The implicit targets of *Birth of the Clinic* are Merleau-Ponty and Sartre. From his *Phenomenology of Perception* (*Phénoménologie de la perception*, 1945) onwards, Merleau-Ponty began to develop a model of embodied consciousness as the ambiguous in-between space of human interaction with the physical world.[6] For Foucault, this leads to a view of the doctor-patient relationship as one of common embodiment in a shared world, a notion he dismisses as a sentimental cover for the contractual basis of private medicine and the analytic-discursive basis of clinical practice.[7] Foucault also sets out to challenge Sartre's notion that the realization of mortality is the decisive moment in any human life. For Sartre, the inevitability of death is a personal event, confronting each individual with the anguished choice between bad faith and freedom, between acquiescence in the world as it is and active commitment to changing it.[8] Human finitude is thus an ethical demand, a call to responsibility. Foucault removes both the pathos and the ethical moment that Sartre associates with death in two ways. First, in *Birth of the Clinic*, he both depersonalizes the experience of mortality and makes death into a kind of non-event through an emphasis on its clinical study and pathological definition. Second, in *Death and the Labyrinth*, he emphasizes the ways in which, to quote Paul de Man, 'death is a displaced name for a linguistic predicament.'[9]

In *Birth of the Clinic*, Foucault draws primarily on two disciplines in order to mount his critique of phenomenology and existentialism: the history of science and linguistics. His account of the history of medicine is indebted to the work of Gaston Bachelard and Georges Canguilhem in the history of science, and in particular to the notion of that same history as punctuated by radical breaks in the fundamental presuppositions that underlie and animate scientific research.[10] For Foucault, the development of modern clinical practice at the end of the eighteenth century represents one such break, and the key to this break lies in a new interpretation of death. According to Foucault, at the end of the eighteenth century, the body acquires depth as it is reconceived as a complex layering of tissues. Through the development of clinical observation followed up by new autopsy techniques, death ceases to be understood as an isolated moment, the extinction of consciousness. It is redefined rather as a process, the result of a given pathology advancing gradually through the tissues and the organs of the body both prior to and even beyond the moment of individual death:

> La mort est donc multiple et dispersée dans le temps: elle n'est pas ce point absolu et privilégié, à partir duquel les temps s'arrêtent pour se renverser, elle a comme la maladie elle-même une présence fourmillante que l'analyse peut répartir dans le temps et dans l'espace; peu à peu, ici ou là, chacun des nœuds vient à se rompre, jusqu'à ce que cesse la vie organique, au moins dans ses formes majeures, puisque longtemps encore après la mort de l'individu, des morts minuscules et partielles viendront à leur tour dissocier les îlots de vie qui s'obstinent.[11]

> [Death is therefore multiple, and dispersed in time: it is not that absolute, privileged point at which time stops and moves back; like disease itself, it has a teeming presence that analysis may divide into time and space; gradually, here and there, each of the knots breaks, until organic life ceases, at least in its major forms, since long after the death of the individual, minuscule, partial deaths continue to dissociate the islets of life that still subsist.][12]

Jean Starobinski has pointed out how Foucault's choice of subject, the history of pathology, matches his method; for Starobinski, Foucault's emphasis on decisive breaks means that he approaches the history of medicine as a series of complete and isolated periods, each of which resembles a dead body requiring an autopsy.[13] If, however, this suggests a neat correspondence, and perhaps even a suspicious circularity, between Foucault's method and his findings, the relationship between his approach and his conclusions also constitutes a paradox; for the new pathology that Foucault installs as an epistemological break in the history of medicine actually calls into question the status of death as a moment of rupture, and so by extension the definitive 'death' of a particular set of epistemological assumptions. Far from endorsing the idea of epistemological rupture, the redefinition of death in the late eighteenth century suggests that there is no such thing as a clean break.

The epistemological break of the history of science is not, however, the only model upon which Foucault draws in his critique of phenomenology and existentialism; the structuralist account of language derived from the linguistics of Ferdinand de Saussure also plays a significant role in both *Death and the Labyrinth* and *Birth of the Clinic*. Saussure pioneered the idea that meaning is not intrinsic to individual words but generated rather by the play of phonemic differences across an entire language system or network, a network of which individual words are merely contrastive elements.[14] This shift from a substantive to a relational model of meaning severs any direct link between language and reality — between sign and referent, in Saussure's terminology — and refocuses attention on the conventional relationship between sound (signifier) and sense (signified) as regulated by the differential network of the language system. In terms of the Saussurean model, meaning is the product of language as a system of relations, where each individual element in isolation is strictly meaningless and only makes sense in relation to the other elements. Furthermore, the language system is necessarily forever out of balance. As Claude Lévi-Strauss has pointed out, no given language system is coterminous with the world its users may encounter, so all languages contain a number of catch-all phrases or 'floating signifiers' ['signifiants flottants'] to fill in for words that do not exist (words such as 'truc' or 'machin' in French and 'thingummy' or 'whatsit' in English).[15] Aside from their enormous practical value, what these floating signifiers reveal is that any given language remains of necessity an incomplete and imbalanced system, since it possesses both too few and too many words at the same time; too few because the floating signifier points to a lack of adequate words to describe the as yet unknown or undiscovered world, and too many because the same floating signifier exists in excess of the words normally required to describe the already known world. According to Foucault, Roussel's work is based on this insight; his fiction explores

> ...la carence des mots qui sont moins nombreux que les choses qu'ils désignent et doivent à cette économie de vouloir dire quelque chose. Si le langage était aussi riche que l'être, il serait le double inutile et muet des choses; il n'existerait pas. Et pourtant sans nom pour les nommer, les choses resteraient dans la nuit. Cette lacune illuminante du langage, Roussel l'a éprouvée jusqu'à l'angoisse, jusqu'à l'obsession, si l'on veut ... Misère et fête du Signifiant, angoisse devant trop et trop peu de signes.[16]

> [... the scarcity of words that are fewer than the things they designate and that owe their capacity to mean anything at all to this economy. If language were as rich as being, it would be the useless and mute double of things; it would not exist. And yet without a name to name them, things would remain in darkness. Roussel experienced this illuminating lacuna of language to the point of anguish, to the point of obsession, if

you like ... Misery and celebration of the Signifier, anguish in the face of too many and too few signs.]¹⁷

Consequently, Foucault argues that the sense of anguish and absurdity foregrounded by existentialist thinkers and writers such as Sartre and Camus is ultimately not the result of a philosophical crisis; it derives rather from the priority of the language system over the isolated word and the disequilibrium of the floating signifier:

> Peut-être un jour s'apercevra-t-on d'une chose importante: la littérature de l'absurde, dont nous voici enfin et depuis peu libérés, on a cru à tort qu'elle était la prise de conscience, lucide et mythologique à la fois, de notre condition; elle n'était que le versant aveugle et négatif d'une expérience qui affleure de nous jours, nous apprenant que ce n'est pas le 'sens' qui manque, mais les signes, qui ne signifient pourtant que par ce manque.¹⁸

> [Perhaps one day something important will be noticed: that it was a mistake on our part to believe that the literature of the absurd, from which we have recently broken free at long last, represented a true realization, both lucid and mythological, of our condition; it was nothing more than the blind and negative side of an experience that is now coming to the surface, teaching us that it isn't 'meaning' that is lacking, but rather signs, which at the same time only signify by virtue of this very lack.]¹⁹

In Foucault's view, it is language rather than mortality that constitutes the human condition, or perhaps it would be more accurate to say that what is at issue is language *as* mortality, that is, an autonomous language system that represents the death of intrinsic meaning in words and things. It is in this sense that death can be understood as, in de Man's words, a 'displaced name for a linguistic predicament' and the pathos of existential *Angst* revealed as a misrecognized 'anguish of the signifier' ['angoisse du signifiant'].²⁰

The Space of Language versus the Space of Vision: from Semiology to Discourse

So, in his double publication of 1963, Foucault redefines death through a combination of the history of science and linguistics. In clinical terms, death becomes an impersonal process of progressive organ failure rather than a decisive moment of individual choice. In linguistic terms, the anguish supposedly caused by human finitude is relocated in the emptiness of a language system conceived as a differential network rather than a full reservoir of substantive meaning.

However, while the clinical and the linguistic arguments in conjunction discredit the existentialist notion of death, in other respects they actually work at cross-purposes. For Foucault, the clinical understanding of death is grounded in observation and vision, however important the linguistic articulation of that vision may be. Conversely, no matter how central the theme of vision is to Roussel, the presence of death in his work is ultimately a linguistic one, represented by the empty echo of the differential network of language and the floating signifier.

Foucault addresses this problem in two ways. First, he attempts to resolve the dilemma by exploiting space as a mediating category. But this simply reproduces the problem at another level, since the space of vision and the space of language do not coincide. On the one hand, the space of vision in *Birth of the Clinic* is, for the most part, modelled on the body during autopsy, where layers of tissue are stripped back to create a surface of serial extension. The space of language in *Death and the Labyrinth* is, on the other hand, defined as a semiological space, where signifier and signified always run the risk of becoming identified with the conventional notions of surface expression and concealed meaning respectively, whatever efforts Roussel might undertake to subvert this distinction. Ultimately, these opposed conceptions of space as visible surface (*Birth of the Clinic*) and space as hidden depth (*Death and the Labyrinth*) cannot be satisfactorily reconciled.

Foucault's second way of dealing with the problem is more drastic. In effect, he simply abandons one space for the other. In the preface to *Birth of the Clinic*, Foucault argues that semiology should be replaced by what he calls discourse. At stake here is the status of Saussurean linguistics as an interpretative model. Foucault expresses exasperation at the play of excess and lack built into the Saussurean model of language with its floating signifier. For Foucault, it is this play that creates the space for an authoritative tradition of explanatory commentary that seeks to interpret the understatements and overstatements implicit in any linguistic proposition:

> ... commenter, c'est admettre par définition un excès du signifié sur le signifiant, un reste nécessairement non formulé de la pensée que le langage a laissé dans l'ombre, résidu qui en est l'essence elle-même, poussée hors de son secret; mais commenter suppose aussi que ce non-parlé dort dans la parole, et que, par une surabondance propre au signifiant, on peut en l'interrogeant faire parler un contenu qui n'était pas

explicitement signifié. Cette double pléthore, en ouvrant la possibilité du commentaire nous voue à une tâche infinie que rien ne peut limiter ...[21]

[... to comment is to admit by definition an excess of the signified over the signifier; a necessary, unformulated remainder of thought that language has left in the shade — a remainder that is the very essence of that thought, driven outside its secret — but to comment also presupposes that this unspoken element slumbers within speech (*parole*), and that, by a super-abundance proper to the signifier, one may, through questioning it, give voice to a content that was not explicitly signified. By opening up the possibility of commentary, this double plethora dooms us to an infinite task that nothing can limit ...][22]

According to Foucault, this tradition of commentary is ultimately founded in Biblical exegesis:

[le commentaire] repose sur une interprétation du langage qui porte assez clairement la marque de son origine historique; L'Exégèse, qui écoute, à travers les interdits, les symboles, les images sensibles, à travers tout l'appareil de la Révélation, le Verbe de Dieu, toujours secret, toujours au-delà de lui-même.[23]

[[commentary] rests on an interpretation of language that shows the stigmatas of its historical origin. This is an exegesis, which listens, through the prohibitions, the symbols, the concrete images, through the whole apparatus of Revelation, to the Word of God, ever secret, ever beyond itself.][24]

For Foucault, then, semiology is a kind of theology, invested ultimately in transcendental notions of authority and truth. What he proposes as an alternative to this theological model of language is the notion of language as discourse, whose meaning is co-terminous with itself and does not so much require interpretation as articulation within or insertion into a historical context of other discourses:

N'est-il pas possible de faire une analyse des discours qui échapperait à la fatalité du commentaire en ne supposant nul reste, nul excès en ce qui a été dit, mais le seul fait de son apparition historique? Il faudrait alors traiter les faits de discours, non pas comme des noyaux autonomes de significations, mais comme des événements et des segments fonctionnels, formant système de proche en proche. Le sens d'un énoncé ne serait pas défini par le trésor d'intentions qu'il contiendrait, le révélant et le réservant à la fois, mais par la différence qui l'articule sur les autres énoncés réels et possibles, qui lui sont contemporains ou auxquels il s'oppose dans la série linéaire du temps. Alors apparaîtrait l'histoire systématique des discours.[25]

[Is it not possible to make a structural analysis of discourses that would evade the fate of commentary by supposing no remainder, nothing in excess of what has been said, but only the fact of its historical appearance? The facts of discourse would then have to be treated not as autonomous nuclei of multiple significations, but as events and functional segments, gradually coming together to form a system. The meaning of a statement would be defined not by the treasure of intentions that it might contain, revealing and concealing it at the same time, but by the difference that articulates it upon the other real or possible statements, which are contemporary to it or to which it is opposed in the linear series of time. A systematic history of discourses would then become possible.][26]

In shifting from semiology to discourse, Foucault moves language away from the model of signifer and signified, with its implications of surface sound or script and deep meaning, into a flattened space of vision understood as serial extension. In this respect, the relationship between *Death and the Labyrinth* and *Birth of the Clinic* illustrates Foucault's tendency to use vision as a strategic tool against language-based models of understanding (in this instance, disrupting traditional exegetic commentary with its trust in the relationship between word and meaning by stressing the opacity of the body on the pathologist's dissecting table and the need to trace the cause of death through a patient investigation of juxtaposed tissues).[27] The move to discourse announces, then, a new methodology quite distinct from Saussurean notions of language and opens up fresh fields of research that Foucault would explore through the late 1960s into the 1970s. The casualties of this process are literature, which progressively becomes less of a pressing concern, and the theme of death itself, which is displaced by the technocratic management of population and public health known as biopolitics.

For and Against Literature

The shifting status of literature in Foucault's work has been remarked on by numerous critics and commentators. Some have suggested that literature simply became an object of lesser interest to Foucault as his career progressed. Thus Simon During has argued that Foucault's thinking about literature effectively divides his career in two. For During, Foucault's early work accorded a privileged place to avant-garde writing as a transgressive exploration of the limits exceeded by madness, death and sexuality, while his later work simply relegated literature to the status of one form of discourse among the many that are produced and circulated within a given society.[28] Denis Hollier has noted how Foucault's style shifts from a lyrical to a clinical mode in the course of the 1960s as his subject matter changes, moving away from a literature of death to the discursive management of life.[29] Unlike During and Hollier, other commentators have maintained that literature remains centrally important to Foucault but in less immediately obvious ways. Thus Raymond Bellour has argued that Foucault's later work leaves literary criticism behind only to become more 'literary' in its own right, not in terms of style and tone but in terms of integrating elements of fiction and abstraction into his models of discourse.[30] Judith Revel contends for her part that the apparent 'disappearance' of literature from Foucault's later work simply conceals how it transposes many of the key problematics of his early literary-critical work such as transgression and resistance onto more social domains.[31] While there are undoubtedly subtle elements of continuity in Foucault's treatment of literature across his career, it nonetheless seems clear that 1963 represents the beginning of a move away from an explicit engagement with literary texts as a privileged form of discourse or evidence.

As already mentioned, in his early work Foucault frequently draws on literary sources to support his investigation of the extreme experiences of madness, sex and death — hence the recurring references to Artaud, Hölderlin, Sade, Bataille and Blanchot, to name only a few of his preferred writers. For all their many nuances, these early studies are often characterized by a fairly clear-cut binary model of limit and transgression, and the assumption of an 'outside' beyond the remit of the law. A similar assumption of a clear break between periods of intellectual and cultural history would underpin much of Foucault's work of the 1960s, often referred to as 'archaeological' in method, since it divided its object into isolated temporal layers or strata assumed to have distinct identities. However, as we have seen, in spite of its apparent commitment to a history of medicine premised on decisive breaks and displacements, *Birth of the Clinic*'s redefinition of death as a graduated process rather than an isolated moment or event arguably began to undermine the notion of an epistemological break and so in turn the archaeological method associated with it. In the process, *Birth of the Clinic* opened the way towards the genealogical model that was to dominate Foucault's later work — a much more open-ended tracing of the complex 'family trees' of social institutions and identities that eschewed clear-cut binary oppositions. If the Foucault of *History of Madness* (1961) insisted on the impermeability of the walls that divided the traditional asylum from society, the Foucault of *Discipline and Punish* (*Surveiller et punir*, 1975) sought to demonstrate instead how the nineteenth-century prison regime was continuous with wider society rather than separate from it.[32] So, as Raymond Bellour suggests, the change in the status of literature in Foucault's work is in part related to the methodological shift from archaeology to genealogy.[33] But it is also related to a shift in Foucault's attitude to language and literature, a shift that is particularly visible in 1963. In his early work, Foucault tends to invoke literature as an authority to reinforce his arguments, even if this is often done in an ambiguous or even subversive way. The authors cited often lack the authority that should be theirs by right because of their designation as mad or criminal by the civil authorities of their day (the clearest examples being Sade and Artaud); they then function as paradoxically anti-authoritarian authorities, but authorities nonetheless. This paradox of literature as anti-authoritarian authority emerges implicitly from the double publication of 1963. In *Death and the Labyrinth*, Foucault emphasizes the dazzling creative potential of a literature premised on a language that has too many and too few words at once. In *Birth of the Clinic*, however, the same structural feature of language forms the basis of authoritative theological commentary. The semiological model of language focused on the mismatch between signs and meanings allows for both dissident creativity (Roussel) and authoritarian interpretation (Bible commentary). In 1963, as Foucault begins to develop his model of discourse as an alternative to semiology, it seems, however, as if literature and its interpretation are associated more strongly with authority than with its contestation. In progressively abandoning literary criticism and references to literature, Foucault leaves behind the authority of literature and the authority of critical commentary in the interests of a more neutral articulation of discursive elements as they intersect with power relations. Thus a certain impatience with literature is very clear by the mid-1970s, when Foucault dismisses as an anachronism the recourse to literature and the theme of death in the analysis of sexuality:

Et rien ne saurait empêcher que penser l'ordre du sexuel selon l'instance de la loi, de la mort, du sang et de la souveraineté — quelles que soient les références à Sade et à Bataille, quels que soient les gages de 'subversion' qu'on leur demande — ne soit en fin de compte une 'rétro-version' historique. Il faut penser le dispositif de sexualité à partir des techniques de pouvoir qui lui sont contemporaines.34

[And yet to conceive the category of the sexual in terms of the law, death, blood and sovereignty — whatever the references to Sade and Bataille, and however one might gauge their 'subversive' influence — is in the last analysis a historical 'retro-version.' We must conceptualize the development of sexuality on the basis of the techniques of power that are contemporary with it.]35

By the mid-1970s, Foucault is much more interested in life than death, albeit life defined in terms of biopower — the interlocking networks of power and discourse that determine individual identities within modern technocratic societies whose practice of governance is mediated largely through public health and welfare. In Foucault's view, the study of literature had little to offer the study of such networks.

1963 then constitutes a significant date in Foucault's career. His treatment of the theme of death at this time represents a double fatality, the dismissal of the existentialist-phenomenological concept of death but also the unexpected passing away of semiology. What results from this double fatality is then a third more gradual death — that of literature itself as a central preoccupation in Foucault's work, as his attention shifts towards biopolitics. Foucault's increasing concern with the political and technocratic management of life means in turn that death *per se* becomes a less compelling theme. Ultimately, behind all the other deaths, real and metaphorical, of Foucault's work in the early 1960s, what begins to die as a key feature of his work is the theme of death itself.

Bibliography

Bellour, Raymond, 'Vers la fiction,' in *Michel Foucault philosophe: rencontre internationale* (Paris, 9–11 janvier 1988) (Paris: Seuil, 1989), 172–81.
De Man, Paul, 'Autobiography as De-Facement,' in *The Rhetoric of Romanticism* (New York: Columbia University Press, 1984), 67–81.
During, Simon, *Foucault and Literature: Towards a Genealogy of Writing* (London: Routledge, 1992).
Foucault, Michel, *Discipline and Punish: The Birth of the Prison*, translated by Alan Sheridan (New York: Pantheon, 1977). Translation of *Surveiller et punir: naissance de la prison* (Paris: Gallimard, 1975).

Foucault, Michel, *The History of Sexuality I: An Introduction*, translated by Robert Hurley (New York: Pantheon, 1978). Translation of *Histoire de la sexualité I: la volonté de savoir* (Paris: Gallimard, 1976).

Foucault, Michel, *Death and the Labyrinth: The World of Raymond Roussel*, translated by Charles Ruas (London: Athlone Press, 1987). Translation of *Raymond Roussel*, edited by Pierre Macherey (Paris: Gallimard, 1992 [1963]).

Foucault Michel, 'On the Archaeology of the Sciences: Response to the Epistemology Circle,' in *Essential Works of Foucault 1954–84, Vol. II: Aesthetics, Method and Epistemology*, edited by James Faubion, translated by Robert Hurley et al. (London: Allen Lane The Penguin Press, 1998), 297–333. Translation of 'Sur l'archéologie des sciences: réponse au cercle d'épistémologie,' in *Dits et écrits (1954–1988), Tome I*, edited by Daniel Defert and François Ewald (Paris: Gallimard, 1994), 696–731.

Foucault, Michel, *The Order of Things: An Archaeology of the Human Sciences*, translated by Alan Sheridan (London: Routledge, 2002 [1970]). Translation of *Les Mots et les choses: archéologie des sciences humaines* (Paris: Gallimard, 1966).

Foucault, Michel, *Birth of the Clinic: An Archaeology of Medical Perception*, translated by A.M.S. Smith (London: Routledge, 2003 [1973]). Translation of *Naissance de la clinique: une archéologie du regard médical* (Paris: PUF, 1963).

Foucault, Michel, *The History of Madness*, translated by Jean Khalfa (London: Routledge, 2009). Translation of *Folie et déraison: histoire de la folie à l'âge classique* (Paris: Plon, 1961), republished in a revised form as *Histoire de la folie à l'âge classique* (Paris: Gallimard, 1972).

Hollier, Denis. 'Le Mot de Dieu: "Je suis mort",' in *Michel Foucault philosophe: rencontre internationale (Paris, 9–11 janvier 1988)* (Paris: Seuil, 1989), 150–63.

Jay, Martin, 'In the Empire of the Gaze: Foucault and the Denigration of Vision in Twentieth-Century Thought,' in *Foucault: A Critical Reader*, edited by David Couzens Hoy (Oxford: Blackwell, 1986), 175–204.

Lévi-Strauss, Claude, *Introduction to the Work of Marcel Mauss*, translated by Felicity Baker (London: Routledge, 1987). Translation of 'Introduction à l'œuvre de Marcel Mauss,' in Marcel Mauss, *Sociologie et anthropologie* (Paris: PUF, 1950), ix–lii.

Merleau-Ponty, Maurice, *Phenomenology of Perception*, translated by Colin Smith (London: Routledge & Kegan Paul, 1962). Translation of *Phénoménologie de la perception* (Paris: Gallimard), 1945.

Osborne, Thomas, 'Medicine and Epistemology: Michel Foucault's Archaeology of Clinical Reason,' *History of the Human Sciences* 5:2 (1992), 63–93.

Revel, Judith, 'Foucault et la littérature: histoire d'une disparition,' *Le Débat* 79 (1994), 65–73.

Roussel Raymond, *Comment j'ai écrit certains de mes livres* (Paris: Jean-Jacques Pauvert, 1963 [1935]).

Roussel, Raymond, 'Parmi les noirs,' in *Impressions d'Afrique*, edited by Tiphaine Samoyault (Paris: Flammarion, 2005), 321–26.

Sartre, Jean-Paul, *Being and Nothingness: An Essay on Phenomenological Ontology*, translated by Hazel E. Barnes (London: Methuen, 1977 [1958]). Translation of *L'Etre et le néant: essai d'ontologie phénoménologique* (Paris: Gallimard, 1943).

Saussure, Ferdinand de, *Course in General Linguistics*, translated by Roy Harris (London: Duckworth, 1983). Translation of *Cours de linguistique générale*, ed. Tullio de Mauro (Paris: Payot, 1983 [1972]).

Starobinksi, Jean, 'Gazing at Death,' *The New York Review of Books* 22:21–22 (22 January 1976): 18, 20–22.

---

[1] Michel Foucault, *The Order of Things: An Archaeology of the Human Sciences*, trans. Alan Sheridan (London: Routledge, 2002 [1970]), 422, and *Les Mots et les choses: archéologie des sciences humaines* (Paris: Gallimard, 1966), 398.

[2] Michel Foucault, *Birth of the Clinic: An Archaeology of Medical Perception*, trans. A.M.S. Smith (London: Routledge, 2003 [1973]), ix–xix, and *Naissance de la clinique: une archéologie du regard médical* (Paris: PUF, 1963), x–xv (hereafter cited as BC and NC respectively).

[3] Raymond Roussel, 'Parmi les noirs,' in *Impressions d'Afrique*, ed. Tiphaine Samoyault (Paris: Flammarion, 2005), 321 and 326 respectively.

[4] Michel Foucault, *Death and the Labyrinth: The World of Raymond Roussel*, trans. Charles Ruas (London: Athlone Press, 1987), 38, and *Raymond Roussel*, ed. Pierre Macherey (Paris: Gallimard, 1992 [1963]), 53 (hereafter cited as DL and RR respectively). The Ruas translation has been modified.

[5] DL, 164–65; RR, 207–08.

[6] Maurice Merleau-Ponty, *Phenomenology of Perception*, trans. Colin Smith (London: Routledge & Kegan Paul, 1962), 203–42 and 346–65, and *Phénoménologie de la perception* (Paris: Gallimard, 1945), 245–89 and 403–24.

[7] BC, xiv–xv; NC, x–xi.

[8] Jean-Paul Sartre, *Being and Nothingness: An Essay on Phenomenological Ontology*, trans. Hazel E. Barnes (London: Methuen, 1977 [1958]), 531–53, and *L'Etre et le néant: essai d'ontologie phénoménologique* (Paris: Gallimard, 1943), 576–98.

[9] Paul De Man, 'Autobiography as De-Facement,' in *The Rhetoric of Romanticism* (New York: Columbia University Press, 1984), 67–81: 81.

[10] For Foucault's own account of this influence, see 'On the Archaeology of the Sciences: Response to the Epistemology Circle,' *Essential Works of Foucault 1954–84, Vol. II: Aesthetics, Method and Epistemology*, ed. James Faubion, trans. Robert Hurley et al. (London: Allen Lane The Penguin Press, 1998), 297–333, and 'Sur l'archéologie des sciences: réponse au cercle d'épistémologie,' in *Dits et écrits (1954–1988), Tome I*, ed. Daniel Defert and François Ewald (Paris: Gallimard, 1994), 696–731. On the relations between the history of science and Foucault's work, see Thomas Osborne, 'Medicine and Epistemology: Michel Foucault's Archaeology of Clinical Reason,' *History of the Human Sciences* 5:2 (1992): 63–93.

[11] NC, 144.

[12] BC, 142.

[13] Jean Starobinksi, 'Gazing at Death,' *The New York Review of Books* 22:21–22 (22 January 1976): 18, 20–22: 22.

[14] Ferdinand de Saussure, *Course in General Linguistics*, trans. Roy Harris (London: Duckworth, 1983), 99–138, and *Cours de linguistique générale*, ed. Tullio de Mauro (Paris: Payot, 1983 [1972]), 141–92.

[15] Claude Lévi-Strauss, *Introduction to the Work of Marcel Mauss*, trans. Felicity Baker (London: Routledge, 1987), 62–64, and 'Introduction à

l'œuvre de Marcel Mauss,' in Marcel Mauss, *Sociologie et anthropologie* (Paris: PUF, 1950), xlviii–l.
16 RR, 207–08.
17 DL, 165, translation modified.
18 RR, 209.
19 DL, 167, translation modified.
20 DL, 167, translation modified; RR, 210.
21 NC, xii.
22 BC, xvi.
23 NC, xiii.
24 BC, xviii, translation modified.
25 NC, xiii.
26 BC, xvii.
27 On this strategic use of vision against language, see Martin Jay, 'In the Empire of the Gaze: Foucault and the Denigration of Vision in Twentieth-Century Thought,' in *Foucault: A Critical Reader*, ed. David Couzens Hoy (Oxford: Blackwell, 1986), 175–204: 194.
28 Simon During, *Foucault and Literature: Towards a Genealogy of Writing* (London: Routledge, 1992), 7–9.
29 Denis Hollier, 'Le Mot de Dieu: "Je suis mort",' in *Michel Foucault philosophe: rencontre internationale* (Paris, 9–11 janvier 1988) (Paris: Seuil, 1989), 150–63: 151.
30 Raymond Bellour, 'Vers la fiction,' in *Michel Foucault philosophe: rencontre internationale* (Paris, 9–11 janvier 1988) (Paris: Seuil, 1989), 172–81: 176.
31 Judith Revel, 'Foucault et la littérature: histoire d'une disparition,' *Le Débat* 79 (1994), 65–73.
32 Michel Foucault, *Discipline and Punish: The Birth of the Prison*, trans. Alan Sheridan (New York: Pantheon, 1977), and *Surveiller et punir: naissance de la prison* (Paris: Gallimard, 1975).
33 Bellour, 'Vers la fiction,' 176.
34 Michel Foucault, *Histoire de la sexualité I: la volonté de savoir* (Paris: Gallimard, 1976), 198.
35 Michel Foucault, *The History of Sexuality I: An Introduction*, trans. Robert Hurley (New York: Pantheon, 1978), 150.

Contributors

Pádraic Conway studied French and Philosophy at University College Cork and subsequently Biblical and Theological studies at Trinity College Dublin, being elected a Trinity Scholar in 1988. After finishing his PhD thesis on Karl Rahner he worked for Andersen Consultants, Trócaire and the Trinity Foundation before moving to University College Dublin where he became Vice President for University Relations in 2004. He was also the director of the UCD International Centre for Newman Studies, providing new impetus for research on the founding rector of the Catholic University of Ireland (UCD's predecessor). He is the editor of *Karl Rahner: Theologian for the Twenty-First Century* (2010). On 5 October 2012, Pádraic Conway passed away after fighting a three-year illness with cancer in a brave and inspirational way.

Philip Cottrell is a lecturer at the School of Art History and Cultural Policy, UCD, where he teaches the module 'Art and Death in Europe 1400-1700'. His published research, which includes several articles in *The Burlington Magazine* and *Art Bulletin*, has primarily focused on painting in Renaissance Venice. However, in addition to his research on the John Donne monument, he has also published on aspects of nineteenth-century art collecting in Britain, particularly the Manchester Art Treasures Exhibition of 1857. He is currently working on a monograph on the sixteenth-century Venetian painter Bonifacio de' Pitati in collaboration with Prof. Peter Humfrey of the University of St Andrews.

Judith Devlin is a senior lecturer in modern history in UCD. She studied in Dublin, Paris and Oxford and worked for ten years in Ireland's Department of Foreign Affairs. She was the first Irish civil servant to study at the Ecole Nationale d'Administration in Paris, and served in the Irish embassy in Moscow during the Gorbachev reforms. Among her publications are: *The Superstitious Mind: French Peasants and the Supernatural in Nineteenth Century France* (Yale University Press, New Haven and London, 1987); *The Rise of the Russian Democrats: the Causes and Consequences of the Elite Revolution* (Edward Elgar, Aldershot and Brookfield Vermont, 1995); *Slavophiles and Commissars: Enemies of Democracy in Modern Russia* (Palgrave Macmillan, London, 1999) and most recently, co-edited with Christoph Müller, *War of Words: Culture and the Mass Media in the Making of the Cold War in Europe* (UCD Press, Dublin, 2013). Her research interests concern Soviet and Russian political culture and in particular the Stalin cult.

Dan Farrelly's studies began in Melbourne with a three-year course in scholastic philosophy, followed by a four-year BA course in German and French at Melbourne University. Next he did a four-year Theology course in Frankfurt am Main and finally a Doctorate in the Philosophy Institute in Strasbourg. He lectured for twenty-five years in the German Department at University College Dublin and was head of the UCD Drama Studies Centre for four years. He has published four monographs on Goethe. Since 1998 he has also translated plays by Goethe, Büchner, and Wedekind. With St Augustine's Press he has translated the following books of the 20th century German philosopher Josef Pieper: *The Silence of Goethe, The Platonic Myths, The Christian Idea of Man, Tradition as Challenge*, and is at present working, with Una Farrelly, on a translation of volume 2 of Pieper's autobiography.

Bridget Martin's research concentrates primarily on the dead in Ancient Greek tragedy, specifically the continued conscious awareness of the dead in the Underworld and the consequential possibility of interaction between the living and the dead. Her PhD thesis (completed in University College Dublin) concentrated on the harmful interaction between the living and the dead whereby the living can avenge themselves upon the dead through the denial of burial rites and the dead may avenge themselves upon the living through the use of avenging agents. Currently, Bridget teaches Ancient Greek in University College Dublin and Trinity College Dublin.

Wolfgang Marx is senior lecturer and Head of the School of Music at University College Dublin, as well as a member of the UCD Humanities

Institute. He also chairs the research strand 'Death, Burial, and the Afterlife' at UCD's College of Arts & Celtic Studies. His research interests include the representation of death in music (with a special focus on requiem compositions), the music of György Ligeti and the theory of musical genres. Among his recent publications are *György Ligeti. Of Foreign Lands and Strange Sounds* (co-edited with Louise Duchesneau, 2011) and *Rethinking Hanslick. Music, Formalism, and Expression* (co-edited with Nicole Grimes and Siobhán Donovan, 2013), as well as essays on Ligeti's *Nonsense Madrigals* and his opera *Le Grand Macabre*, Viktor Ullmann's opera *The Emperor of Atlantis* and Antonín Dvořák's Requiem.

Deirdre O'Grady is Emeritus Professor of Italian and Comparative Studies at University College Dublin where she took the Degrees of BA, MA, and PhD. She also graduated from the Università Cattolica del Sacro Cuore, Milan with a Dott. In Lettere, with a thesis on Vittorio Alfieri, supervised by Prof. Mario Apollonio. She is the author of four books: *Alexander Pope and Eighteenth-Century Italian Poetry* (Bern/New York: Lang, 1987); *The Last Troubadours: Poetic Drama in Italian Opera 1597-1887* (London/New York: Routledge, 1990); *From Romantic Realism to Modernism: Piave, Boito, Pirandello* (Lewiston/New York: Mellen, 2000), and a critical edition of Carlo Goldoni, *La locandiera*, (Dublin: Foundation for Italian Studies University College Dublin, 1997). She has published in excess of sixty articles and is a member of the publication Board of the Journals *Théâtre, Opéra et Ballet* and *Otto/Novecento*.

Douglas Smith is a senior lecturer in French and Francophone Studies in the School of Languages and Literatures at University College Dublin, where he teaches literature, film and theory. He has published a monograph on the reception of Nietzsche in France (*Transvaluations*, Clarendon Press, 1996) and translated Nietzsche's *The Birth of Tragedy* and *On the Genealogy of Morals* for Oxford University Press. More recent publications include edited special numbers on Roland Barthes (*Nottingham French Studies*, 2008), Empire and Culture Now (*Modern and Contemporary France*, 2010, co-edited with Mary Gallagher) and André Bazin (*Paragraph*, 2013).